The Capacity to be Displaced: Resilience, Mission, and Inner Strength

Theology and Mission in World Christianity

Edited by

Kirsteen Kim (*Leeds Trinity University, UK*)
Stephen B. Bevans (*Catholic Theological Union, Chicago, USA*)
Miikka Ruokanen (*University of Helsinki, Finland/*
Nanjing Union Theological Seminary, China)

VOLUME 5

The titles published in this series are listed at *brill.com/tmwc*

The Capacity to be Displaced: Resilience, Mission, and Inner Strength

By

Clemens Sedmak

BRILL

LEIDEN | BOSTON

The Library of Congress Cataloging-in-Publication Data is available online at http://catalog.loc.gov.

Typeface for the Latin, Greek, and Cyrillic scripts: "Brill". See and download: brill.com/brill-typeface.

ISSN 2452-2953
ISBN 978-90-04-34183-8 (paperback)
ISBN 978-90-04-34245-3 (e-book)

Contents

Preface

This book is about "strength from within;" strength that can help people to flourish in adverse circumstances; strength that can help people in a situation of displacement, a situation which calls for a particular capacity, namely the capacity to be displaced. This capacity to be displaced is a necessary strength and skill for people working across boundaries and across cultures.

The capacity to be displaced is a key contributive factor to developing resilience. This book is an exploration of the inner sources of resilience. "Epistemic resilience," (as I suggest calling this inner strength) is closely connected with spiritual resources, and while thinking and remembering are invaluable assets in generating a culture of inner strength, I do believe that things spiritual play a major role in the development of epistemic resilience. Cultivating epistemic resilience draws on all the facets of a person's interior life: thoughts and memories, hopes and desires, beliefs and convictions, concerns and emotions.

The capacity to be displaced is both a universal and a collective challenge, especially now in times of globalization. Displacement is not only the cheerful choice of expatriates or foreign students to try out another culture, but is also the plight of millions of migrants forced to leave their homes in times of war and destruction. Epistemic resilience is a global phenomenon, both geographically and in the sense that it can be considered part of the human condition, no matter whether the context is African, American or Asian. Epistemic resilience is also a global phenomenon in that global challenges such as climate change and international cooperation require the tapping of such inner resources. The planet will not survive without *inward* change, without *inner* revolutions. External deserts triggered by pollution, human conflicts and short-term thinking on the one hand and the ever-growing internal human voids on the other are interlinked and cannot be tackled independently of each other.

Against this background, so the hope, it seems to make sense to set up a discussion on the capacity to be displaced and the cultivation of epistemic resilience within the framework of a series entitled: *Theology and Mission in World Christianity*. As the term underlines, *"World"* Christianity is a global religion which is at the same time locally rooted and interconnected. The term "epistemic resilience, upon which this book builds, draws on the Christian tradition, on sources from the Western and the Eastern Church and takes a deep look at individual instances of epistemic resilience in far-flung corners of the world, from Colombia, Czech Republic, France, Italy, the Netherlands, South Africa, the United States and Vietnam. Epistemic resilience is a phenomenon that can accommodate the richness and depth of religious traditions within a global context. In this book I present a primarily Christian contribution to this field. It is a contribution to Theology in World Christianity. I would like the reader to go away with the impression that the Christian tradition has a lot to offer with regard to inner richness and depth and that these epistemic qualities are of key significance for individual as well as social resilience.

I want to thank Deborah Foelsche-Forrow (Salzburg) who has given invaluable help; without her the manuscript would not have reached the publisher! I would also like to express my gratitude to Professor Steve Bevans (Chicago) who suggested I submit this manuscript for the series. I would also like to thank Professor Paul Joyce (London) who encouraged me to pursue this project. And finally a word of thanks to Brill Publishers for processing the manuscript.

I would like to dedicate this book to Deborah. She has used her life to appropriate the capacity to be displaced, she is a living example of resilience, nourished by inner wells that make it possible to see tenderness of heart and strength of spirit united. Long May You Run!

Clemens
London and South Bend/Indiana, Summer 2016

Introduction

If you are in a place that is not "yours," if you feel "out of place" in a particular context, the sense of belonging you seek must come from within, from an inner source. Drinking from an inner well in the desert of displacement can give a person the strength to endure. This is what this book is about. Experiences of displacement are challenges for migrants, voluntary as well as involuntary; development workers, missionaries, experts working in cross-cultural settings, refugees, persons in exile: they all face the pressures of displacement.

Displacement situations require special skills, essentially the skill of "being here" in a place, even if you are not from this place," in other words, the skill of being and abiding "in" a place when you feel you do not belong there. This can be identified as part of the *Conditio Christiana*, according to the Gospel of John's account of Jesus' sense of his Kingdom: "My Kingdom does not belong to this world (...) my kingdom is not here" (John 18:36). Christians as "resident aliens" (Stanley Hauerwas) may find themselves in situations of displacement as part of their "being-in-the-world." The capacity to "be" displaced and cope with the demands it makes calls for an inner center.

Yeats' poem "The Second Coming," written in 1919 in the aftermath of the brutal First World War, suggests that in the face of anarchy there is a need for a center: "Things fall apart; the centre cannot hold", yet we need a center that can hold. Displacement is that loss of external and tangible centers; the capacity to be displaced, coping with and even flourishing in a situation of displacement, then, is predicated upon the gift of a center, an inner center in the absence of external constants. From a religious perspective, this inner center is, first and foremost, the relationship with God.

Two examples of women missionaries in a centered relationship with God are Amanda Smith who sailed from Suez for Bombay in late fall 1879, arrived in an unknown city and foreign culture, and found her solace, as most missionaries would from within—on January 1st, 1880 she notes in her diary: "The Lord's Word to me this morning is, 'Lo, I am with you always.'"[1] A few decades later Amy Carmichael would observe: "Praising helps more than anything. Sometimes one wakens with the feeling of 'miss'—indescribable except

---

1 Amanda Smith, An autobiography, the story of the Lord's dealings with Mrs. Amanda Smith, the colored evangelist: containing an account of her life work of faith, and her travels in America, England, Ireland, Scotland, India, and Africa, as an independent missionary / with an introduction by Bishop Thoburn. Chicago, IL: Christian Witness Co. 1893, 300.

© KONINKLIJKE BRILL NV, LEIDEN, 2017 | DOI 10.1163/9789004342453_002

to those who know it—and the temptation is to give way and go in for a regular spell of homesickness and be no good to anybody. Then you feel the home prayers; they help you (…) and you find your cup ready to overflow after all."[2] This observation is revealing: Amy had "home prayers" at her disposal, not because she was physically or tangibly "at home," but because she carried those intangible inner home treasures around with her, she had and held on to her prayers.

In a situation of displacement an inner center can be a source of strength. Shirley Lorraine Worland has explored the experience of the Karen people from Burma in the Mae La Displaced Persons' Camp in Thailand.[3] The Karen are the most populous group in Burma, without a state of their own for which they had fought. The ruling military junta had forced the Karen people into situations of displacement, especially in camps on the Thai side of the Thai-Burma border. Worland's research, based on interviews, characterizes the displacement experience in the camp as one of fear, loss, especially the loss of being in control. Being separated from one's own land and family is hard; living in transition without a sense of durability is hard; finding oneself in roles not chosen is hard. One of Worland's students told her that he felt "like an animal in the zoo—so many 'golawahs' (literally 'white persons') coming all the time, looking and taking photographs and then leaving."[4] Worland identified the coping mechanisms of surviving in "no-man's land," sought and found in inner sources, nationalism and pride, religiosity and faith, education in values and tradition. Those she interviewed tried to explain and make sense of their experience in the light of their faith, in holding on to the belief that God was in control and had a plan for the Karen.[5] These are universal inner treasures that can serve as sources of resilience, resilience from within.

This study considers inner strengths, sources of "resilience from within," resilience not primarily based on material or social factors, but nurtured from a person's inner life and inner wealth. This type of resilience is "epistemic resilience," resilience that makes use of epistemic resources. This book sets out to explore a wide range of examples of persons who have been able to cope with

---

2 Amy Carmichael, Fragments That Remain. Compiled by Bee Trehane. Fort Washington, PA: CLC Publications 2013.

3 Shirley Lorraine Worland, Displaced and Misplaced or Just Displaced: Christian Displaced Karen Identity after Sixty Years of War in Burma. PhD Dissertation. Queensland, Australia: University of Queensland 2010.

4 Ibd., 120.

5 Ibd., 211.

difficult situations by drawing on their inner resources. Displacement comes in many forms—by way of illness, by way of imprisonment, by way of exile.

The book describes the dynamics of strength in the Italian journalist Tiziano Terzani, diagnosed with cancer, in the Vietnamese Archbishop Francis Xavier Văn Thuân who spent 13 years in prison, in the Colombian politician Ingrid Betancourt who was held hostage in the Colombian jungles for six and a half years. It talks about the story of French manager Jean Louis Cianni who found consolation in philosophy, Viktor Frankl who found an inner source of strength in imagination and hope, or Corrie ten Boom who found an inner well in her faith. These examples present us with a clearly visible thread running through diverse situations: the sources for the strength displayed in these situations come from within, they are inner resources. Religious people are generally more resilient than non-religious individuals. This book presents deep insights into the inner life by holding a conversation with the Christian tradition. It would also like to make the point that there are hidden treasures in the Christian tradition, treasures that can be retrieved and made accessible.

The capacity to be displaced cannot be separated from the capacity to cultivate inner wealth, a rich inner life. In a situation of displacement you can create a sense of belonging by furnishing your mind with belongings, with inner wealth that cannot be taken away. Max Aub (1903–1972) was born in Paris, moved to Spain in 1914, spent the first three years of the Second World War in prisons, concentration and labor camps in France and North Africa before settling in Mexico—he describes his inner strength and moral constancy in his diaries ("I am sticking to my own position," he writes in 1952, and in 1967: "I don't think that my transformations go beyond the ripeness of life and the grey hairs of experience.").[6] This inner strength in the face of exile is a matter of an inner center.

This inner center allows individual independence to be and remain divorced from actual external place. An inner center allows for an identity that does not fully depend on "belonging to one particular place." Nevertheless, being "somewhere," knowing and inhabiting a fixed place can be restrictive and the result of social constraints. In Seamus Heaney's poem *Station Island* (part IX) the poet examines himself and says: "I hate how quick I was to know my place. / I hate where I was born." He feels he has been formed and fashioned through "place," through the social class he inhabits, through a class system that teaches him where his place is, a place that imposes "the sort of circumscribed identity that

---

6   Quoted after Sebastiaan Faber, The Privilege of Pain: The Exile as Ethical Model in Max Aub, Francisco Ayala, and Edward Said. *Journal of the Interdisciplinary Crossroads* 972 (2006) 15–37, at 20.

these conditions push him toward."[7] Resilience from within is really a source and foundation for the capacity to be displaced. It allows liberation from a place, detachment.

There is a beautiful word in Welsh, *cynefyn*, which can be translated as: "fierce attachment to a patch of land;" some sheep have *cynefyn*, so much so, that they cannot be uprooted; they are so attached to the land that they cannot be herded to another place. Transplanted sheep will not find rest in a new flock, in a new pasture. Peter Ho Davies plays with this motif in this novel "The Welsh Girl," exploring the question of what it means to be from a particular place and to face challenges of conflicting identity contexts. Inner strength allows for "place within displacement," the strength to be uprooted. The capacity to be displaced overcomes *cynefyn* in a physical sense and provides a sense of *cynefyn* in a spiritual, mental sense as the attachment to values, to intangible infrastructures, to knowledge, to memories, to beliefs.

This book looks at an array of examples to do with this very idea of strength from within, resilience from within. In this way, there should be a clear *Sitz im Leben* of the discussion. The structure of the book is as follows: Chapter 1 discusses this sense of displacement and elements of the capacity to be displaced in conversation with missionary experiences of exile and imprisonment, encountered by Ella Schneider Hilton, Edward Said, Vaclav Havel, and Dietrich Bonhoeffer. Chapter 2 reconstructs the current view of and research on resilience, it develops an understanding of the idea of "resilience from within" ("epistemic resilience") and suggests a concept of "robust identity" (ability to resist external threats and to flourish in a situation of displacement). Chapter 3 deepens this understanding of inner resources by putting forward three testimonies on the capacity to be displaced, by illness (Tiziano Terzano), by kidnapping (Ingrid Betancourt), and by imprisonment (Francis Xavier Văn Thuân). Chapter 4 develops the concept of the Self as based on a sense of inwardness and interiority using the Jewish-Christian tradition (biblical background languages, Augustine and John Cassian). Chapter 5 deepens these insights from the Christian tradition still further by bringing in three interlocutors from the Eastern Orthodox tradition (Isaiah the Solitary; Mark the Ascetic; Hesychios the Priest) and their perception of epistemic resilience. Chapter 6 pools these observations in outlining a concept of cultivating interiority by developing a rich inner life—through thought and memory. Chapter 7 discusses existential

---

7 Magdalena Kay, Knowing One's Place in Contemporary Irish and Polish Poetry. London: continuum 2012, 163; cf., Patrick Rafroidi, The sense of place in Seamus Heaney's poetry. In: Jacqueline Genet, ed., Studies on Seamus Heaney. Caen: Presses universitaires de Caen 1987, 79–88.

commitments from both a moral standpoint and a faith perspective as sources of epistemic resilience, and chapter 8 explores hope and love as main sources of strength from within. A concluding epilogue shows that epistemic resilience and the capacity to be displaced have social and even political dimensions— epistemic resilience points to the kind of freedom totalitarian regimes cannot take away. Paul's Letter to the Romans says that nothing can separate us from the love of Christ (Romans 8:35–39), neither distress nor trouble and not adversity; if we have a strong sense of the point of life, if we have an inner center, we can build up the kind of strength described in this book as epistemic resilience.

This inner center can help us to see our life as a whole, to weave the different elements of that life into a coherent pattern. In his poem *The Way It is* William Stafford describes a thread we follow, a thread that is hard for other people to see, but a thread that is there nevertheless and gives us a center: "While you hold it you can't get lost."[8] The "thread" can be understood to be a coherent narrative, a consistent commitment to values, and a consequent concern with what has been identified as really *really* important. The capacity to be displaced is predicated on this sense of what really *really* matters.

---

8   William Stafford, The Way It Is. Minneapolis, Mn: Graywolf Press 1998.

CHAPTER 1

The Capacity to be Displaced

When Steve Reifenberg went to work in Chile as a young man he was enthusiastic and ready to save the world, particularly the orphanage he had come to work in—but then found himself in situations where he was challenged by his own ignorance and at the same time posed a major challenge to the people he was supposed to be supporting.[1] He struggled in helping Veronica, a girl living in the orphanage, with cleaning the living room ("she was amazed that I was so ignorant of something so simple"),[2] he struggled in playing soccer: "I had played soccer twice before in my life. These boys had been playing since they were three. Nor did it help that my running shoes were falling apart, the right sole of my shoe flapping freely every time I ran. I got the ball and immediately kicked it over the fence and into the bushes",[3] and, of course, he struggled with the language: "Each morning I'd wake up hoping that today my Spanish would be better: that I would get off this plateau where I'd been stuck for the last month—understanding just enough to get me in trouble. I tired of always stopping conversations with 'What?' or 'I don't understand,' so I'd taken to nodding and agreeing even when I had no idea what was being said."[4]

Struggling with a foreign language is like moving around in a dimly lit room, where you can only refer to bigger objects, where you can only move slowly and warily like in some obstacle course, and where you can continually crash into objects standing on your way—either hurting yourself or the object. Reifenberg's experience of displacement can be encapsulated in his first round of "Good Nights" on the first evening at the orphanage: "Following Olga's lead, I went from bed to bed giving each child a goodnight kiss on the cheek. When I bent down to kiss two-year-old Andrés, who was in the bottom bunk, he shot up his leg and caught me in the face with his foot. I jerked up my head and cracked it against the top bunk bed."[5] Here again, the experience of being unfamiliar with everyday practices in everyday places.

---

1   Steve Reifenberg, Santiago's Children. What I learned about Life at an Orphanage in Chile. Austin, Tx: University of Texas Press 2008.
2   Ibd., 14.
3   Ibd., 17.
4   Ibd., 19.
5   Ibd., 12.

Steve Reifenberg had to appropriate the place, make it his own after going through the desert of displacement, the experience of being out of place. His experience begins with challenges but does not fully follow Oberg's U-curve model of cultural adjustment with its four stages of honeymoon, crisis, recovery, and adjustment.[6] Maybe Reifenberg had his "honeymoon" during the months anticipating his adventure in Chile, but his immersion in an unknown culture, this, new place was clearly crisis and shock—to be followed by recovery and adjustment to the new place, overcoming the sense of being "out of place."

This sense of feeling out of place is quite common in cross-cultural settings. The micro-financer Vikram Akula, for instance, was asked to open a new branch of the Decan Development Society in a remote area in India in the mid-1990s: he immediately realized that he was helpless to carry out what he had been sent to do—to teach the poor. "As I quickly learned, I pretty much didn't know how to do anything I needed to do."[7] He had his share of embarrassing learning moments, e.g., how to protect his accommodation from marauding animals, how to cook rice, even how to use the bathroom village style—experiencing the humbling effects and learning needs connected with displacement.

Let us call this "the missionary experience"—there is a mission (in Reifenberg's case: helping children at an orphanage; in Akula's case: setting up a pro-poor financial infrastructure) and this mission takes a person into an unknown, unfamiliar context. A missionary experience may be voluntary or involuntary. This mission may be imposed (top-down) and may involve forcing people or groups of people against their will into exile. Unwanted exile under the exertion of undue force will intensify the sense of displacement being experienced. Violent measures may be implemented e.g., when someone is imprisoned or held captive and the sense of displacement will be the same for the innocent or the guilty person. Voluntary and involuntary displacement share certain challenges and effects, such as "loss" and "transition", and the "struggle for orientation."

1.1   The Missionary Experience as Exodus into Displacement

The missionary experience, of a development worker, of a religious missionary, or of a migrant in more general terms is necessarily an experience of displacement—missionaries have to leave "home" and find themselves in unfamiliar

---

6 K. Oberg, Culture shock: adjustment to new cultural environments. *Practical Anthropologist* 7 (1960) 177–182.

7 Vikram Akula, A Fistful of Rice. Boston, Mass: Harvard Business Review Press 2011, 37.

territory with the challenges of cultural and perhaps moral displacement which has to be tackled together with the phenomenon of frustration and disorientation.

John G. Paton (1824–1907), a Scottish missionary to the New Hebrides, describes his first encounter with natives in his new mission territory in emotional terms: "My first impressions drove me to the verge of utter dismay. On beholding these Natives in their paint and nakedness and misery, my heart was as full of horror as of pity. Had I given up my much-beloved work and my dear people in Glasgow, with so many delightful associations, to consecrate my life to these degraded creatures?"[8] The language ("dismay," horror" and "pity") betrays a sense of frustration; there is no sense of "kinship" enabling "home-building" by recognizing oneself in the other. There is only a sense of difference and distance ("nakedness," "misery," "degraded") as well as a sense of loss and sacrifice ("given up my much beloved work").

Paton's remarks reveal a certain sense of homelessness, defined as "the commonly experienced state of distress among those who have left their house and home and find themselves in a new and unfamiliar environment."[9] Homesickness may lead to a tendency to idealize what has been left behind and a lack of attentiveness to the new context. Homesickness is a kind of separation anxiety combined with a longing for the familiar; it is an experience of being "dis-attracted" to a place and of being drawn *back-wards*. Homesickness may be nurtured by the experience of loss of attachment, interruption and discontinuity, reduced personal control, transition and liminality, and inner conflicts between accepting the new and rejecting the old.[10] Displacement is an experience of opportunity costs in the light of possible worlds, of "what could be" and "what could have been." The deep sense of opportunity costs may lead to decisions and choices, crossroads and junctures being questioned. There may be the painful questions: "Is this my place?," "Is this the right place?"

---

8   John G. Paton, Missionary to the New Hebrides. An autobiography edited by his brother. New York: Fleming H. Revell 1889, 108.

9   M.A. Van Tilburg, A.J. Vingerhoets, G.L. Van Heck, Homesickness: a review of the literature. *Psychological Medicine* 26 (1996) 899–912, 899; homesickness can also be characterized as "a psychological state created by the prospect or the reality of social isolation" and summarized as the state "when home isn't home": Dieu Hack-Polay, When Home Isn't Home. A Study of Homesickness and Coping Strategies among Migrant Workers and Expatriates. *International Journal of Psychological Studies* 4,3 (2012) 62–72, 62.

10   These are basically the five models suggested by Shirley Fisher—Shirley Fisher, Homesickness, cognition and health. London: Erlbaum 1989.

Johann Heinrich Friedrich Wohlers (1811–1885), a German missionary, was confronted with these questions at the outset of his missionary adventure in New Zealand in the 19th century:

> After we had landed and made the acquaintance of a few English settlers, we at once made inquiry about the natives, and then learned that in the neighborhood of Nelson there were none. We thought they might live further inland, but soon learnt that was not the case, that in this great southern island there were but few natives, and that these few lived in widely scattered places on the sea coast. For our intended farm buildings no suitable mission station could, therefore, be found. When we applied to the two English missionaries already stationed here, one of whom belonged to the Episcopalian and the other to the Wesleyan Church, we learnt that all the natives of the whole of New Zealand were already under spiritual guidance. It is true many were still heathens, but almost all had already adopted Christian customs and had native Christian teachers amongst them. Our prospects were therefore gloomy.[11]

Questions of "place" and "mission" became vexing and burdensome. Wohlers and his companions were not able to travel for logistical reasons, so they decided to appropriate "the place", to build a residence, to get used to the country—and trust in God to show them the missionary work to be done. But at the beginning of this commitment to the place they found themselves in, they experienced disappointment at not having "proper appointments," in other words, they experienced a new place which did not at first sight have an obvious or glaring need for the skills they had brought with them. Rather like the Karen, they had not planned to come to this place and it had not been on their mission agenda. To make matters worse, there was no one to greet them with open arms, the people in this place were not in dire need of the newcomers or their missionary services. A similar experience was recounted by Father Frumentius Renner about the beginnings of the Benedictine mission to the Zulu lands, a mission forced to struggle with the material poverty of the missionaries, open opposition to the Catholic Church, the division of Christianity

---

11   Johann Friedrich Heinrich Wohlers, Memories of the life of J.F.H. Wohlers, missionary at Ruapuke, New Zealand: an autobiography / translated from the German by John Houghton. Dunedin: Otago Daily Times & Witness Newspapers Co. 1895, 66.

into many different groups, a deeply rooted traditional belief system; King Dingane rejected the missionaries who felt a deep sense of displacement.[12]

However, it is also part and parcel of the missionary experience to disrupt home-thinking and to shake mental, spiritual and moral landscapes which will ultimately induce an experience of displacement in the people they work with and live with. It can lead and has led to substantial levels of frustration: "Christ entered the African scene as a forceful, impatient and unfriendly tyrant. He was presented as invalidating the history and institutions of a people in order to impose his rule upon them."[13] While Christ challenges established categories and belief systems, e.g., in his conversation with Nicodemus in John 3 or in his encounter with the woman at the well in John 4 he did not overrule, disrespect or "abolish the law" (Mt 5:17). In missionary contexts things have indeed often "fallen apart" as Chinua Achebe famously pointed out in his novel *Things Fall Apart*. Overly zealous missionary activities often made local inhabitants in missionary countries feel out of place in their own cultures. Some theologians have used the term "faith schizophrenia" to describe this phenomenon.[14]

The challenge of this alleged schizophrenia could perhaps be compared to the challenge of a visitor becoming a family member. Hospitality can be described as the art of making a person feel at home away from home, which paradoxically implies that hospitality tries to take away the visitor's status as guest in order to make her feel at home. This paradoxality is predicated upon two elements of hospitality: an element of displacement, the guest is not "in her own home" which underpins the role of the host as host and the role of the guest as guest and an element of integration and thus home-building; however, the fact that the guest is treated with special consideration, not the same as family members, means that she remains a stranger and an outsider. A Christian missionary will find herself in a similar though more ambiguous role with regard to hospitality: on the one hand, she is a guest in another culture; on the other hand, she is a host in that same culture, involved in evangelization efforts and inviting people as guests to the house of the Lord and the table of the Word and Bread. These dynamics lead to a process of mutual transformation: "The one

12   Frumentius Renner, Der fünfarmige Leuchter. Beiträge zum Werden und Wirken der Benediktinerkongregation von St. Ottilien. Volume IV. St. Ottilien: EOS 1993, 79–80.

13   Enyi Ben Udoh, Guest Christology: An Interpretative View of the Christological Problem in Africa. Frankfurt/Main: Peter Lang 1988, 64.

14   Michael L. Cook, The African Experience of Jesus. *Theological Studies* 70 (2009) 668–692, esp. at 668, 669, 682—Cook refers to John V. Taylor, Christian Presence amid African Religion. Nairobi: Acton 2001, 7.

who comes to us as a guest in search of a home amongst us, gradually comes to be kin, and in the case of Christ, our Lord."[15]

There is a journey, a process, a development, a gradual transformation at work here: the missionary experience is based on stages of "being at home", "undergoing exodus", "appropriating a new place." Without the first stage ("being at home") it is difficult to envisage a person with a mission and a message, however, (and this will be one of the key concerns of this book) if one has a stable "inner home", external circumstances will not have the same destabilizing power or potential to leave someone displaced long-term. Undergoing exodus is an experience of moving on, of leaving behind the familiar and setting off into the unknown; it is "being in the desert," "being on a pilgrimage." It is a liminal, "in between" state, between a "not anymore" and a "not yet." Thirdly, there is the dynamics of appropriating a new place; this act of making something one's own ("making" oneself "feel" at home even if one isn't) can be compared to the act of appropriating knowledge since it is only when knowledge is processed and properly becomes one's own, does it become—absorbed and integrated into the body of knowledge one already has and employed with authority. The process of appropriating and amalgamating place is the process of assimilating it into one's inner "home" landscape, connecting it to one's doings and being, by "cultivating" it. The American Homestead Act of 1862, for example, gave 160 acres of land to settlers who were willing to cultivate the land for at least five years, it gave American settlers the opportunity to appropriate land and make it their own; they would put in labor, adjust their life style to the requirements of the soil, and shape the land and in turn according to their own requirements and possibilities within the given (physical, financial) constraints. Land can only be appropriated by putting in a lot of time, effort and hard labor and by putting your whole self into that labor. Then you "settle"— Robert Goodin has reflected on the art of settling; settling entails not being on the lookout for something else, even though settling is compatible with an openness to new possibilities.[16]

In the process of transitioning from exodus to appropriation a missionary, a development worker, or a refugee will invariably undergo the experience of displacement. They amass and accrue, to differing extents, knowledge by acquaintance of what it means to be a displaced person. The term "displaced person" emerged at the end of the Second World War; at that time it primarily denoted people who were dispossessed of their homeland, had no home to go back to because it had been 'appropriated' by a foreign force, destroyed, or no

---

15   Udoh, Guest Christology, 243.

16   Robert Goodin, On Settling. Princeton: Princeton University Press 2012.

longer had the means or wherewithal to return. Thousands of such displaced persons were now seeking refuge elsewhere. In her short story "The Displaced Person" Flannery O'Connor describes the arrival of Polish immigrants to the US; in a dialogue between two protagonists we find a personal take on "displaced person" ("It means they ain't where they were born at and there's nowhere for them to go") as well as an astute observation: "It seem like they here, though (…). If they here, they somewhere."[17] Displacement is that state of "being" neither nowhere nor somewhere at the same time and in the same place, displacement is also the "irretrievable loss of home," "displacement" does *not* mean "no place," but a shift in being, an imbalance of here and there, a "different place."

O'Connor manages to express many aspects of the displacement experience such as strange pre-notions (conceptions before actual encounter),[18] the gratitude of strangers empowered to start a new life on the basis of donations from generous people; the new skills strangers brought to the new place ("Mr. Guizac could driver a tractor, use the rotary hay-baler, the silage cutter, the combine, the letz mill (…) He was an expert mechanic, a carpenter, and a mason.");[19] the new social order was fuelled and driven by such skills and all the concomitant phenomena including the moral challenges involved in negotiating status and power, negotiations of changes and jealousy. Such elements of bias, dependence, innovative skills, and a new social order can also be identified in the missionary experience; both Steve Reifenberg and Vikram Akula, above, were confronted with prejudices against "gringos" and "intellectuals," they depended on local knowledge and local generosity, they brought new skills to an existing context and place, and changed the social order in that place. In this sense, the arrival of displaced people displaces not only the place and the parties on both sides but puts the place in a new context as well.

If we look at the person herself, however, the missionary experience is one of exposure to displacement, of being "out of place." This sense of displacement clearly has the potential of widening horizons, of challenging the established status quo, and of both firing and undergoing mental transformation.

---

17   Flannery O'Connor, The Displaced Person. In: Flannery O'Connor, The Complete Stories. New York: Farrar, Straus and Giroux 1971, 194–235, at 199.

18   Mrs. Shortley, one key figure, was surprised when confronted with the strangers from Poland: "The first thing that struck her as very peculiar was that they looked like other people. Every time she had seen them in her imagination, the image she had got was of the three bears, walking single file, with wooden shoes on like Dutchmen and sailor hats bright coats with a lot of buttons" (ibd., 195).

19   Ibd., 201.

Ways of perceiving, thinking and judging (on both sides of bias) are challenged in going through and enduring the "out of place experience." Displacement thus becomes an encounter with the unexpected, the unforeseen, the unclean. "Uncleanness is matter out of place,"[20] Mary Douglas famously stated. What is "out of place" is "a threat to good order,"[21] it is an experience challenging the boundary between "in-place" and "out-of-place," it makes people realize that there are boundaries, which are, not infrequently, hidden. Dirt, understood as "matter out of place," says a lot about the boundaries as well as the existing frameworks of power within a culture. Invisible structures are translated into material and tangible matter. There are clearly material aspects of *dirt* as a phenomenon of displacement as Mary Douglas herself wrote in her field notes during her second trip to study the Lele people in the Belgian Congo in 1953: "'dirt is any matter displaced' e.g., hair, crowning glory etc. and hair in the soup (...)."[22] These features underline the fact that dirt can be "seen" and "touched," "felt", "smelt" and "tasted" even though it is not really visible and even though one is not supposed to touch it. There is an ambiguity associated with "out of place" or "dirty" matter as per Douglas' reading; dirt is not "purely dirt," it may be something "clean" but alien and unknown in the context it finds itself displaced into, as such "dirt" becomes a comparative compass point referring to what is and what is not normal.

Douglas' findings can therefore be translated into spatial language: "The spatialised discussion of prohibition, transgression, and punishment provides a platform for exploring the role of the built fabric as a reflection of, or an instrument on the production of, individual, social, or cultural ordering systems."[23] Certain spaces should not be accessed by certain people. William Vollman has described "unwantedness" as a characteristic feature of poverty—poor people are not welcomed, they are not wanted in a particular place.[24] The experience of "unwantedness" or "unneededness" is a constitutive element of not finding one's place; Ben Rawlence studied the lives of nine inhabitants of one of the

---

20   Mary Douglas, Purity and Danger. New York: Routledge ARK Edition 1984, 41.

21   Ibd., 161.

22   Richard Fardon, Margaret Mary Dougles 1921–2007. *Proceedings from the British Academy* 166 (2010) 135–158, at 154. A test case for Mary Douglas' relativistic thesis of dirt may be faeces, but even here one can easily introduce social readings: Sjaak Van der geest, The social life of faeces: System in the dirt. In: R. van Ginkel & A. Strating (eds) Wildness and sensation: An anthropology of sinister and sensuous realms. Amsterdam: Het Spinhuis 2007, 381–397.

23   Ben Campkin, Placing 'Matter Out of Place': Purity and Danger as Evidence for Architecture and Urbanism. *Architectural Theory Review* 18,1 (2013) 46–61, at 51.

24   William Vollmann, Poor People.

largest refugee camps in the world in North Kenya, a city in itself filled with
Somali refugees.[25] The camp is a "limbo" that has basically become permanent,
a limbo without privacy, and yet a world with its own rules and its own boundaries "in place." Rawlence describes displacement in this context as the result
of the act of fleeing that is predicated upon key factors:

> To flee one needed three things: money, courage and imagination.
> Money, because nothing in Somalia was free and transport was espe-
> cially expensive when in demand. Courage, because the route south
> was booby-trapped with checkpoints, lawless militias and bandits that
> attacked one in three vehicles heading for the border. And imagination
> because, for a mind shaped by the confusion of war, the ability to imagine
> that life might be different or better elsewhere is an uncommon leap.[26]

The very act of taking flight requires imagination, demands a sense of possibilities, elements that are important for the capacity to be displaced. One former
inhabitant of the camp, "had achieved the ultimate refugee dream: citizenship.
He had followed the path of the wealthy and bought himself a Kenyan ID card—
everything is for sale in Kenya."[27] He had bought himself a *place*, he had bought
himself out of displacement. Isha had fought displacement as long as she could:

> When, twenty years before, the first of her neighbors had left for Dadaab,
> Isha had stayed. She was a young, unmarried woman committed to her
> people. Since then, she had given birth six times in the place they lived
> called Rebay, between Baidoa and another town called Dinsoor. *Rebay*
> meant 'stay' in the Somali language and Isha had taken it as an invoca-
> tion. She had a connection, she said, with the red soil of that land.[28]

Isha had tried to settle and stay knowing that "to leave means to lose everything."[29]
Leaving her own land behind meant abandoning it, and in turn making space for
new settlers, new appropriation, new claimants. Displacement is an experience
that can make people feel "out of place," at the same time others find and acquire
"a place of their own" benefiting from access to the competitive good of place,
the good of that particular place.

---

25   Ben Rawlence, City of Thorns. Nine Lives in the World's Largest Refugee Camp. New York:
      Picador 2015.
26   Ibd., 19.
27   Ibd., 54.
28   Ibd., 58.
29   Ibd., 61.

1.2   Searching for "My Place"

The refugees in Dadaab are searching for a place; "their place." We all long to find a place—the "perfect place"; we need to be "somewhere" a place where we can stay and grow, a place we can properly call "home." A place is not only and not even primarily a geographical location, but rather "a unique web of social and material spatiotemporal life connections and associated meanings emerging on the basis of the life world."[30] Historical and social dimensions of place prevail, place refers to personal experience and subjective meanings contained in biographies. Finding a place means building a life world, a world of the everyday, the familiar, and the habitual. "The familiar environment, in part because it can be taken for granted, is a source of ease and comfort. The unfamiliar environment evokes 'fight or flight' responses, especially a heightened awareness of danger and attention to detail in the surroundings."[31] Being somewhere and not "out of place" and not "nowhere" is an identity-forming factor. Intimate knowledge of one's environment is a source of trust; it is a source of comfort to be familiar with one's surroundings. Displacement happens in many different ways. The missionary frequently finds herself displaced in that she is suddenly "in between," in a liminal state, exodus without arrival; a sense of displacement is what anybody crossing boundaries is bound to experience, development workers, refugees, or writers in exile all have to go through it at some time.

Sally Morgan describes this search for a place in her well-known autobiography *My Place*.[32] She did not find her childhood home a safe place because of the Posttraumatic Stress Disorder her father was suffering from after returning from the War: "When Dad was happy, I wished he'd never change. I wanted him to be like that for ever, but there was always the war" (MMP 20); there were scars in the soul, in the mental landscape of her father's mind that took away his freedom, "there were things in his head that wouldn't go away" (MMP 21);

---

30   A. Paasi, Deconstructing Regions: Notes on the Scales of Spatial Life. *Environment and Planning* 23,2 (1991) 239–256, at 248.

31   Mindy Thompson Fullilove, Psychiatric Implications of Displacement: Contributions From the Psychology of Place. *Annual Journal of Psychiatry* 153,12 (1996) 1516–1523, at 1518.

32   S. Morgan, My Place. London: Virago Press 2012 (reprint). In the following I will be using the abbreviation "MMP"; cf., H. Sonoda, A Preliminary Study of Sally Morgan's *My Place*. *The Otemon Journal of Australian Studies* 35 (2009) 157–170; a different and more extensive account of these reflections can be found in my article: Clemens Sedmak, "My Place"? Catholic Social Teaching and the Politics of *Geborgenheit*. In: Johannes Drerup, Gunter Graf, Christoph Schickhardt, Gottfried Schweiger, eds., Justice, Education and the Politics of Childhood. Dordrecht: Springer 2016, 235–250.

Sally's father turned to drinking with his mates, most of whom were returned soldiers as well, and behaved irresponsibly: "He was just like a child, sometimes, he never mended anything around the house, or took any responsibility. I felt very disappointed in him" (MMP 46). There was no sense of the family home being an inviting place to stay and a place to grow. After her father's death Sally embarked more deeply on the journey of finding her place. She remembers moments of "home," that sense of a secure family life on evenings in front of the fire: "I'll never forget those evenings, the open fire, Mum and Nan, all of us laughing and joking. I felt secure, then. I knew it was us against the world, but I also knew that as long as I had my family, I'd make it" (MMP 53). She develops a clear sense of home-making through memory and in using inner resources to cultivate her imagination. Fairy tales and the discovery of Winnie the Pooh were key factors in Sally's sense of safety; she writes that Winnie the Pooh: "made me feel more normal. I suppose I saw something of myself in him (...) Pooh lived in a world of his own and he believed in magic, the same as me" (MMP 45). But disruption is also waiting for her.

Sally gradually begins to find out—against the resolute resistance of both her grandmother and her mother—that her family roots mean she belongs to the Aboriginals.[33] In her first attempt to ask the question: "Where do we come from" she is fobbed off with the reply: "Tell them, you're Indian" (MMP 38), her attempts to understand her history are met with the reply: "There's no point in digging up the past, some things are better left buried" (MMP 99). Her search for identity and place becomes a burden; after an encounter with her cousins, a "small group of dark children", her sense of identity is more confused than it was before. One day after school she finds her grandmother weeping about the fact that she is not white. "For the first time in my fifteen years, I was conscious of Nan's coloring. She was right, she wasn't white. Well, I thought logically, if she wasn't white, then neither were we. What did that make us, what did that make me? I had never thought of myself as being black before" (MMP 97). The abrupt realization that she is Aboriginal is a heavy burden with the social stigma it has attached to it. She has lost that place she thought was her own, she thought she lived in to find out that all the time she has been an outsider, has not belonged, she finds herself caught "in between," a mental state of exodus and a physical state of staying. She begins to see the fragmented nature of her childhood, given the fact that she was denied access to her roots; she begins to understand that she cannot excel at school because of certain factors within her self: "The sum total of all the things I didn't understand

33   M. Renes, Sally Morgan: Aboriginal Identity Retrieved and Performed within and without. *My Place. Estudios Ingleses de la Universidad Complutense* 18 (2010) 77–90.

about them or myself. The feeling that a very vital part of me was missing and that I'd never belong anywhere" (MMP 106).

Sally Morgan was looking for a place: "her place". This longing for a place could be described in different terms, as seeking "rescue, relief and recovery," "sanctuary, security and safety," a "sense of belonging," and a "safe haven", a "longing to feel safe and protected," a "deep desire to feel protected against injury," and "experiencing the warmth, and the bliss of being loved, wanted and cared for." All these nuances of expression provide variations on a philosophically neglected term, the German word *Geborgenheit*. This noun has an etymological connection with the German verb *bergen* (rescue, save, conceal, hide) providing subtle nuances of "safety" as well as "privacy." The term "is commonly translated as 'security' but actually evokes an immediately positive sense of sheltered-ness, nested-ness, and well-being."[34] In other words: "The notion of Geborgenheit first and foremost conjures up a sense of being nested within a sheltering space to which one can open up. While the notion of 'safety' tends to be defined in terms of a negation of fears and dangers, 'Geborgenheit' retains a moment of 'security' in a directly positive sense."[35] "Nestedness" and "safety", "being nested" and "being safe" emerge in a first analysis as two key features of the term.

While there is little philosophical material available on the term. Hans Mogel, a psychologist, has described *Geborgenheit* as an existential driver that makes us search for a certain condition, it is an existential feeling, a sentiment fundamental to life, a certain disposition vis-a-vis the world, a fundamental attitude.[36] One of the few philosophers who have hitherto considered this concept is the German philosopher Otto Friedrich Bollnow (1903–1991) who characterized *Geborgenheit* as the "givenness of a Thou," "robust being," "integrity of things and the world," and who reflected on the importance of "home" and "place".[37] According to Bollnow "space" and "place" constitute frameworks and foundations for *Geborgenheit*.[38] That is why the question of "where to live" and "how to furnish the home" are existential questions and not just middle-class luxury problems. A "home" is a protected space that is constituted by a

---

34   J. S. Hutta, Geographies of Geborgenheit: beyond feelings of safety and the fear of crime. *Environment and Planning D: Society and Space* 27 (2009) 251–273, at 252.

35   Ibd., 256.

36   H. Mogel. Geborgenheit. Psychologie eines Lebensgefühls. Heidelberg: Springer 1995.

37   O.F. Bollnow, Neue Geborgenheit. Das Problem einer Überwindung des Existentialismus. Stuttgart: Kohlhammer ²1960, part II. Close to Bollnow's phenomenological analysis is Gerhard Kaminski's approach: G. Kaminski, Geborgenheit und Selbstwertgefühl. Frankfurt/Main: Haag and Herchen 2003.

38   O.F. Bollnow, Die erzieherische Bedeutung der Geborgenheit im Hause. *Vierteljahresschrift für Heilpädagogik und ihre Nachbargebiete* 45,2 (1976) 149–158.

difference between "inside" and "outside." Doors are key elements for the cultivation of *Geborgenheit*. The home is a non-agonal sphere of familiarity and peacefulness. "Being at home" means "inhabiting a living space," a space that speaks a familiar language.

Politically speaking, *Geborgenheit* can be understood to mean "not feeling out of place in public." Adam Smith famously characterized the non-poor person as the one who "can walk about without shame;"[39] by way of analogy we could suggest that the person living in *Geborgenheit*, "can abide (physically and mentally) without fear." *Geborgenheit* is construed as a term which comprises a private and personal relationship between subjective attitudes and feelings and a (social) situation including a dimension of spatiality.

It is against this background that I would like to put forward a strong case for a deep understanding of *Geborgenheit* particularly in the context and framework of displacement based on space and relationships. A person feels *Geborgenheit* in a space if she inhabits the space and experiences it as safe, stable, and welcoming especially because of the caring relationships within this space. The latter may not even be necessary if a person can experience *Geborgenheit* on the basis of inner wealth, of her sense of inner home, and inner resources, rather than social relationships. John Paton, for instance, mentioned above, suffered a terrible loss in the Hebrides, when his wife and baby boy both died. He found refuge, a sense of *Geborgenheit*, in God ("I was never altogether forsaken. The ever-merciful Lord sustained me") and in the fact that he built a place for his deceased loves ones, laying

> the precious dust of my beloved Ones in the same quiet grave, dug for them close by at the end of the house; in all of which last offices my own hands, despite breaking heart, had to take the principal share! I built the grave round and round with coral blocks, and covered the top with beautiful white coral, broken small as gravel; and that spot became my sacred and much-frequented shrine, during all the following months and years.[40]

Paton manages to connect his own inner space and intangible center with this external tangible place by creating a shrine in memory of those who have now been dis-placed from this world. This creative and crafting process binds inner and outer space both visibly and invisibly. *Geborgenheit* means "being somewhere."

---

39   Cf., D. Zavaleta Reyles, The ability to go about without shame. A proposal for internationally comparable indicators of shame and humiliation. OPHI Working Paper Series. Oxford: OPHI 2007. Reyles makes the important point that "humiliation" is a conceptual device to obtain a deeper understanding of the dynamics of being poor.

40   Paton, Missionary to the New Hebrides, 130.

1.3   Exile and Displacement

Exile is the experience of being uprooted and the loss of home, of having the emotional attachment to that home cut, and maybe having a nostalgic image of the lost place, and the experience of two fold exclusion (being expelled from one place and being an outsider in another). Exile is "a way of dwelling in space with a constant awareness that one is not at home (…). Exile is also an orientation to time, a plotting of one's life story around a pivotal event of departure and a present condition of absence from one's native land."[41] Exile is painful, especially with constant reminders of the fact that one is in exile. Exile is displacement and quite literally cries out for specific skills, such as remaining faithful to self and at the same time being prepared to open up to growth. Exile is an "in between" state of not fully settled in the present and of not fully disencumbered of the past. The challenge is to be "present" and "distant" at the same time without foregoing the capacity to flourish. Let us look at two examples exploring the experience of displacement and being out of place.

In her moving autobiography[42] Ella Schneider Hilton recounts the events of her life shaped by the experience of displacement; she was born in Russia and lived with her family in Kiev, they were Volga Deutsche and spoke German at home; in 1943 they fled to Germany after Ella's father had been taken by the Soviet Authorities, never to be heard from again. They arrived with illusions about "home," about a "Fatherland," described by Ella's grandmother as an orderly society, full of cleanliness and orderliness (HDP 45).[43] Later, Ella would find out, that many had left their home country to come to Germany, "the land of their forefathers, the land of promise" (HDP 113)—they expected to be welcomed and embraced and treated like citizens, however, when they arrived in Germany they were taken to a camp and carefully questioned about their family history and potential Jewish connections, the experience of being examined and disinfected was humiliation of the highest degree, and then they had to stay in Quarantine; but most importantly, they had to carefully

---

41   John D. Barbour, Edward Said and the Space of Exile. *Literature & Theology* 12,3 (2007) 293–301, 293.

42   Ella E. Schneider Hilton, assisted by Angela K. Hilton, Displaced Person. A Girl's Life in Russia, Germany, and America. Baton Rouge: Louisiana State University 2004; I will use the abbreviation "HDP" for this book.

43   "Oma began to share her view on how our life in the 'Fatherland' would be. 'How different and good the land of our forefathers looks, and how happy we will be to be part of this cleanliness and orderliness. We have reached an orderly society. Not like the Russians, who have no breeding, who are stupid never saw soap and water and can't even farm for profit. We should always be thankful that the Germans came to Russia to liberate us from the Communists" (HDP 45).

construe their story. The camp was a "u-topia" in the sense of a "no-place," she describes this first camp as "this nameless place (…) There are no calendars, clocks, or watches to tell time. Time for meals is announced from loudspeakers. Other information is conveyed the same way" (HDP 42). There were no points of reference to make this place "home." It remained a transitory place without identifiable features.

From this first camp they were taken to another camp for displaced persons in Regensburg, in Southern Germany. Again, they had to go through a process of registration, and they stayed in this camp just to be transferred to yet another camp, this time in Passau, close to Austria. They remained second-class citizens; in the butcher's shop the best meat was always given to the "real Germans":

> Everyone at school treated me like a second-class citizen. It did not matter that I spoke perfect German. It was not the local Bavarian dialect. As soon as I said anything, they knew I was not one of them. Not a day passed without someone at school telling me to go back to Poland where I came from. It hurt, but it didn't matter. As long as the bombs were not falling, I could endure almost anything or any treatment by the natives (HDP 75);

Ella had to attend mandatory Catholic classes and learnt that non-Catholics could not go to heaven, another experience of displacement.

In 1945 the Americans took control of Passau and yet again Ella's family felt out of place, many people were repatriated against their will, some committed suicide. Ella's mother remarried a man she hardly knew, a widower who had also come from Russia as a Volga Deutscher; she was resilient in a certain way, had plans and hopes for the future and needed a husband with an occupation; she forged plans to have a full life, to emigrate to the United States and for that she needed a spouse—she explained her plans clearly to Ella: "We will not have much of a life here in Germany being Volga Deutsche and Refugees. If we ever get a chance to emigrate to America, Australia, or Canada, we must have a family" (HDP 92); unfortunately Theodor, Ella's stepfather, "hated everybody. He blamed the Jews for starting the war. The Russians for killing his first wife. The Germans for losing the war. The Americans for getting into the war and bombing Germany. Most of all, the Communists who would continue to pursue him to the end of the world" (HDP 101). He isolated himself, was physically violent and seems to have had an alcohol problem. After living in a monastery the family was taken to a new place, Hofstetten, a former Army Training Camp, where they remained "out of place:" "*Flüchtlinge* was stamped across our official papers. There was no running away from the label" (HDP 93), "there was no future. Once a refugee, always a Refugee. It might as well have been branded on our foreheads" (HDP 113).[44]

Ella's mother took the initiative and managed to organize the emigration to the United States making some tough moral decisions including the decision to undergo an abortion in order to be eligible for the voyage since America would not have taken pregnant women (HDP 165); they were sponsored by a family in Mississippi and, in return, had to work on their farm, hard work in an unfamiliar culture. They were shocked to see their accommodation, they were shocked to see the kind of hard manual labor they were expected to do, Ella's mother was shocked about the food, her stepfather deeply shocked to learn about the Prohibition. They encountered snakes, chiggers, bugs, and ticks and concluded: "what an exchange! German fleas, bedbugs, and lice for all kinds of new American pests" (HDP 179). The experience of displacement did end for Ella eventually, but not for her parents.

Ella's parents dealt with the experience of displacement in the United States in two ways: Firstly, they found an explanatory narrative and they took solace in nostalgia; the explanatory narrative was quite simple:

> Why had God brought us to such a land? We had been through so much. Mama concluded that the reason was to punish us. For what? Papa had the answer. The Bible said the sins of our fathers were handed down to the third and fourth generation. It must have been something our forefathers did for which we had to suffer. God said it, my parents believed it, and that settled it. It was God's plan (HDP 188).

Ella's father read the Old Testament and applied it to the family. Secondly, there was nostalgia; talking about Germany would make Ella's mother cry, she would cultivate nostalgia—"a yearning for a different time," the desire "to revisit time like space, refusing to surrender to the irreversibility of time that plagues the human condition."[45] She would spend her time in Passau talking to her friends about the good old days (HDP 76), later, she would recount her first encounter with the red earth in Mississippi with nostalgic points of reference: "Look at the red earth (...). Only the devil could create such a red earth. God only creates good and pretty things. Remember the earth in Russia and even in Germany? It was rich and dark" (HDP 172); in the United States she never

---

44   Hannah Arendt reflects on a similar experience as an immigrant: "we don't like to be called 'refugees'" (Hannah Arendt, We Refugees. In: Marc Robinson, ed., Altogether Elsewhere. Writers on Exile. Boston: Faber and Faber 1994, 110–119, at 110).

45   Svetlana Boym, Nostalgia and Its Discontents. *The Hedgehog Review* 9,2 (2007) 7–18, at 8.

felt at home, she would not be able to "settle" in the full sense, she never learnt English, she only had one friend with whom she would speak Russian.

Ella herself would get married to an American army officer and become fully Americanized; but before that, she had deep experiences of displacement: (i) she experienced displacement in a physical sense (being uprooted again and again, leaving her home to be taken to camps which would not fully be home, but also the experience of being severely beaten, by her father, her mother, her stepfather); (ii) she experienced displacement in separations when she was admitted to hospital and separated from her mother ("my imagination went rampant. Where would I go? Who would take care of me?" HDP 60); again, when her mother traveled to a nearby village to get married to Ella's stepfather she "was too worried to go to sleep, imagining all sorts of things. Someone will come and steal us before Mama gets back. Maybe she sold us to someone. What happens to us if she doesn't come back? Will we be sent back to Russia without her?" HDP 88.

(iii) Perhaps her deepest experience of displacement was being forced to fashion a broken narrative identity: She had to learn how to lie about her past and carefully construe her identity, this started in Germany: "At every opportunity Mama reminded us, 'Now we are in Germany, none of you will speak Russian again'" (HDP 45); in Regensburg they construed their story as if they had come from Poland, "old papers had been conveniently lost by Mam. She decided it would be better if we were from Poland" (HDP 47). She became used to lying:

> Lying had been an integral part of my life (…). We all lied about where we came from. We lied wherever we went. In most instances, the lies were for self-preservation (…). Our identification papers were full of lies. Every time we moved, we reinvented our family and ourselves. Whenever we registered in a new city, we Refugees invariably had lost, misplaced or thrown away our original papers and could make up any story we felt like (HDP 121).

Because most people had lost their papers in the chaos of bombings and evacuations, you could easily reinvent yourself and construct name, age, home towns, place of birth, professions. When she was questioned by US authorities in the immigration process "it became very hard for me to sort out the truth" (HDP 158), having told all these different lies. Lies construe possible worlds. They distort a person's contact points with reality and the life stories of others.

Connected to this challenge of loss of narrative identity was Ella's experience of displaced history, the experience of having to come to terms with a different reading of her past and her identity when she learned about the atrocities the Germans had committed during the war. "It was the first time I had ever heard such things" (HDP 211)—her stepfather, adding to the weight of the displacement experience, refused to believe and then refused to discuss the matter leaving her without a coherent narrative yet again.

(iv) An important nuance to Ella's experience of displacement was her sense of being "between social worlds," i.e. the social world of her family and the social world of her sponsor family, the Deans, in whose air-conditioned house Ella spent a few weeks after she had suffered a sun stroke; Ella would do domestic chores and "had inadvertently found a career" (HDP 196); it was on the basis of this newly appropriated point of reference and possibility for making comparisons that she was now ashamed of her family, noticing her parents body odor. "I didn't have the heart to tell Mama to shave under her arms or take a bath in the pond every day (...). Up until then, I had never noticed the foul body odor of my family. Now I could hardly stand it" (HDP 198). This is an experience of displacement within a displacement situation. Ella feels disconnected from her family because of new connections in the new place and this experience thus reduces and increases the sense of displacement at the same time. While she is gaining a deeper understanding and acceptance of the new place she becomes aware of existing aspects of her life and her family life which are no longer tenable in her eyes, she feels shame and an increasing sense of the displacement from her loved ones.

Ella Hilton experienced displacement on different levels and in various ways, but she also developed life-saving coping mechanisms, i.e. she worked on her capacity to be displaced—by building social networks, in the camp ("The people at Camp Hofstetten had become extended family, not by blood, but by a shared history;" HDP 162–163), on board of the ship to New York ("I was busy with my friends (...) I found a group of boys and girls our age who talked together in the library;" HDP 166), and, as mentioned above, in her dealings with the Dean family. She tried to cope with her experience by cultivating and treasuring inner resources, such as dreams ("How good it was to dream;" HDP 166) and a transcendent horizon in her faith (God "realized our wish and brought us to America (...). I prayed faithfully that He would watch over us and bless us;" HDP 177); she also found inner strength in (nostalgic) memories ("The only way I could go to sleep was to think about the beautiful German countryside, the Danube River, and my precious years of growing up in our last camp;" HDP 177), she would "get lost in the few photos Mama had brought out of Russia, and the pictures my friends had given me of themselves before I left Germany (...) they filled my heart with warm memories;" HDP 205).

Here again, we see that both social and inner skills, social bonds and epistemic sources aid in the state of displacement; Ella's story also illustrates the ambivalent nature of nostalgia which can be a source of strength in coping and finding focus in a transition period (as in her case), or a quagmire, a trap with no escape, in which one's sense of displacement is heightened even more, suffocating any possibilities to adjust (in the case of Ella's mother). The external situation makes demands on the existing inner situation, and the coping strategies developed (or not) from inner sources are the watershed between surviving and going under.

A second example I would like to explore is Edward Said's memoir; a deep sense of displacement was a defining feature of his life—so much so that he entitled his memoir *Out of Place*.[46] "To me," he writes, "nothing more painful and paradoxically sought after characterizes my life than the many displacements from countries, cities, abodes, languages, environments that have kept me in motion all these years" (SOP 217). Born in Jerusalem in 1935 into a family of Arab Christians, he had to leave different childhood homes and moved to Egypt with his family at the time of partition in 1947, to then attend secondary school and College in the United States since his father held American citizenship. He moved between Arabic, English, and French as well as between "the West," and the Arabic world. There are also elements of hybridity in his religion; Said, a defender of Islam, "was raised a Christian by parents who were married in a Baptist church in Nazareth where his mother's father was the minister (after holding a ministry in Texas, of all places)."[47]

Said's autobiography contains vivid descriptions of his experience of being out of place, in at least four different ways:

(i) He felt out of place in the family system with a mother who sent out ambivalent messages about warmth and disapproval, saw all her children as a disappointment (SOP 56), and ruled the family on the basis of bilateral relationships with her husband and her children without a "common emotional space" (SOP 60).[48] He suffered from his mother's withdrawal (SOP 156) and her physical distance that deepened over the years (SOP 59). He felt out of place in the family because of his father who "came to represent a devastating combination of power and authority, rationalistic discipline, and repressed emotions" (SOP 12); a father who—a model of manliness and virile bullying—instilled a sense of

---

46   Edward Said, Out of Place. A Memoir. New York: Alfred Knopf 1999; I will use "SOP" as the abbreviation for this book.

47   Paul Armstrong, Being 'Out of Place': Edward W. Said and the Contradictions of Cultural Differences. *Modern Language Quarterly* 64,1 (2003) 97–121, at 100. Armstrong describes how Said dramatizes the tensions and contradictions in his identity-conferring commitments.

48   "Unlike my father, whose general solidity and lapidary pronouncements were a known and stable quantity, my mother was energy itself, in everything, all over the house and our lives, ceaselessly probing, judging, sweeping all of us, plus our clothes, rooms, hidden vices, achievements, and problems into her always expanding orbit. But there was no common emotional space. Instead there were bilateral relationships with my mother, as colony to metropole, a constellation only she could see as a whole" (SOP 60).

insufficient accomplishment in his son. Edward was plagued by the fear of being deformed, of becoming a "hunchback" as he described it, inculcated by his father admonishing him at every opportunity "to stand up straight." His father would still physically abuse him even when he was a Harvard graduate student in his early twenties (SOP 65). His parents made it difficult for him to grow up and would constantly confront him with a purer version of himself when he was smaller—he was told that he now lacked character, that he was naughty, lazy, and he "was also made aware of an earlier Edward, sometimes referred to as 'Eduardo Bianco,' whose exploits, gifts, and accomplishments were recounted to me as signs of pre-1942 early promise betrayed" (SOP 27). "So I became delinquent, the 'Edward' of punishable offenses, laziness, loitering, who was regularly expected to be caught in some specific unlicensed act" (SOP 42).

(ii) He felt out of place because of his body which he learnt to eye with suspicion and shame (he was taught to recognize "the body's peculiar, and problematic status;" SOP 59), which made him become "awkward about and uncertain of my physical identity" (SOP 67); he was brought up to think that there was something wrong with his body, the constant criticism of his physical appearance of specific body parts had "the net effect (...) to make me deeply self-conscious and ashamed" (SOP 63). Said recalls "staring at myself disgustedly in the mirror well past my twentieth birthday" (SOP 66); it goes almost without saying that sexuality was a key challenge and that he found himself thinking that he was sexually ill.

(iii) Edward Said felt out of place linguistically. With an Arab family name like "Saïd", connected to a British first name (Edward Said's mother much admired Edward VIII) there was "the basic split" in his life, "the one between Arabic, my native language, and English, the language of my education and subsequent expression as a scholar and teacher" (SOP xiii). Languages were a major factor in Edward Said's experience of displacement—in Victoria College he was exposed to three languages and could not find a primary or neutral place to inhabit: "Arabic was forbidden and 'wog'; French was always 'theirs,' not mine; English was authorized, but unacceptable as the language of the hated British" (SOP 198); he would negotiate the three languages without being able to separate them clearly: "While speaking English, I hear and often articulate the Arabic or French Equivalent, and while speaking Arabic I reach out for French and English analogues" (SOP 198). In Victoria College English was the school language, "Arabic became our haven, a criminalized discourse where we took refuge from the world of masters and complicit prefects" (SOP 184). Language was not a "safe place," but politically charged, a place of partiality and group pressure.

(iv) Fourthly, Said felt culturally and geographically out of place, and this dimension became a core facet of his memories, "especially in the displaced

form of departures, arrivals, farewells, exile, nostalgia, homesickness, belonging, and travel itself" (SOP xiv). He found himself a foreigner in Cairo, "a city
I always liked yet in which I never felt I belonged. I discovered that our apart-
ment was rented, and that although some (…) thought we were Egyptian, there
was something 'off' and out of place about us (me in particular), but I didn't yet
quite know why" (SOP 43); he would not overcome this feeling of not-belonging;
towards the end of the 1940s he observed: "Despite the fact that I spoke—and
I thought looked—like a native Egyptian, something seemed to give me away.
I resented the implication that I was somehow a foreigner, even though deep
down I knew that to them I was, despite being an Arab" (SOP 195). In other
words, even in Egypt and Lebanon [where the family spent every summer for
27 years] "he had felt out of place, because his family lived in an enclave created
by his father's wealth and, as Protestant Christians, were isolated from the larger population."[49] His sense of displacement was heightened since he could not
get hold of "his people" with relatives disappearing in the Palestinian struggle:
"My mother never mentioned what had happened to all of them. I did not ask
my father. I had no available vocabulary for the question, although I was able
to sense that something was radically wrong" (SOP 115).[50] In the United States
he had to negotiate belonging as well: "The first was to adopt my father's brash-
ly assertive tone and say to myself, 'I am an American citizen,' and that's it"
(SOP 6)—at the same time, he tried to be "as anonymous as possible" (SOP 137),
only sparingly talking about his family; he would develop by his own account a
split between a public, outer self and his private, inner life.

   This sense of displacement, fed by so many sources on so many levels, translated itself into a struggle for identity; he felt himself defined by his school
teacher, Miss Clark, who saw him as morally inferior thus imposing her constructed identity on him ("I came to detest this identity, but as yet I had no
alternative for it;" SOP 87), he was unsure about his name,[51] reduced to "Said"
when he entered Victoria College at the age of fourteen (SOP 179); he made the

---

49   John D. Barbour, Edward Said and the Space of Exile, 294.
50   He remarks critically: "It seems inexplicable to me now that having dominated our lives
      for generations, the problem of Palestine and its tragic loss, which affected virtually ev-
      eryone we knew, deeply changing our world, should have been so relatively repressed,
      undiscussed, or even remarked on by my parents" (SOP 117). Fatin Abuhilal has argued
      that Said's "'growing sense of Palestinian identity' comes together with his consciousness
      of his marginality, seclusion and isolation" (Fatin Abuhilal, The Discourse of Palestinian
      Diaspora in Edward Said's Out of Place: A Memoir: A Post-orientalism Analysis. Journal of
      Postcolonial Cultures and Societies 4,3 [2013] 30–50, at 42).
51   "For years, and depending on the exact circumstances, I would rush past 'Edward' and
      emphasize 'Said'; at other times I would do the reverse, or connect these two to each other
      so quickly that neither would be clear" (SOP 3).

painful experience again and again of not fitting in,[52] for example in a vivid description of his first school day: "As I threaded my way hesitantly through a football game, several wrestling matches, an intense game of marbles, and a small crowd of guffawing older boys, I felt myself assaulted and dislocated by the uninhibited strangeness of the place in which I alone seemed to be new and different" (SOP 180).

Said's account of his life is a testimony to the inner resources necessary to cope with displacement, especially the rich inner world built up by his memory: "My memory provided crucial to my being able to function at all during periods of debilitating sickness, treatment, and anxiety" (SOP xi). Writing his autobiography was an act of resilience from within, of fighting leukaemia which would be the cause of his death in 2003. He fostered and nurtured an inner life retreat and as a teenager began "to notice the almost absolute separation that existed between my surface life at school and the complicated but mostly inarticulate inner life I cherished and lived through the emotions and sensations I derived from music, books, and memories intertwined with fantasies" (SOP 202); his imagination was vivid and helpful in finding orientation when among others, in appropriating a sense of place, even as a child: "One of my earliest and most long-lasting passions therefore has been an almost overpowering desire to imagine what other people's houses were like. Did their rooms resemble ours? Did their kitchens work the way ours did? What did their cupboards contain, and how were these contents organized?" (SOP 38); he developed a deep sense of inner resources in his capacity to distance self from the actual place he may have been in. This capacity to distance self, combined with an inner cornucopia of notions and ideas became a defining feature of Said's work.

In his *Reith Lectures* Said would underline the existential importance of the intellectual being able to distance self from the external here and now; in this regard, exile can productively shape a person's thinking, displacement can be a source of creativity.[53] An intellectual is a person, always on the move; she can transport self beyond her immediate experience. An intellectual is a

---

52   An observation from his school years: "I had no sustained contact with the English children outside the school; an invisible cordon kept them hidden in another world that was closed to me. I was perfectly aware of how their names were just *right*, and their clothes and accents and associations were totally different from my own. I cannot recall ever hearing any of them refer to 'home,' but I associated the idea of it with them, and in the deepest sense 'home' was something I was excluded from" (SOP 42).

53   Edward Said, Representations of the Intellectual: The 1993 Reith Lectures. New York: Vintage 1996; see also: Mark Muhannad Ayyash, Edward Said: Writing in Exile. *Comparative Studies of South Asia, Africa and the Middle East* 30,1 (2010) 107–118.

representative figure, someone who represents a position "unbound" to a particular space; at the same time, the intellectual will not be able—nor want—to fully adjust to a place. She may face the challenge of being in universal "space" and at the same time have a particular standpoint. Displacement can also mean a moment of freedom, "displacement can and often does represent the essence of modern liberation from the tyranny of contingency, the accident of place and culture."[54]

In his *Reflections on Exile* Said lists (epistemic) advantages of exile such as acquiring a more truthful vision of inner self, by the sheer fact that exile breaks through habits of thought and perception, and a deeper sense of the contingent nature of the world, including religious questions.[55] Exile makes people turn to and depend on inner space in an environment where identity is wounded and broken. In a lecture in the Freud museum Said reflected on Moses through the lens of Freud's *Moses and Monotheism*, and emphasized the outsider role of Moses, the Egyptian. He explored the possibility that "identity cannot be thought of or worked through itself alone; it cannot constitute or even imagine itself without that radical originary break or flaw which will not be repressed."[56] In other words, the capacity to be displaced is predicated on embracing breaks in identity, wounds to identity. Identity needs displacement to "come out;" this gives us a sense of the link between the capacity to be displaced and the capacity to recognize one's own vulnerability. Resilience, as we shall see in the next chapter, is not the art of being unscathed, but the art of living with one's wounds.

1.4   Cases of Displacement: Prison Experience

Displacement wounds a person's sense of her identity. Displacement transforms (sometimes threatens) a person's identity, her search for a "place in life," a "life place." One of the most fundamental experiences of displacement is experiencing imprisonment. Prison confinement imposes pressures on individuals that can be dealt with only if the person has the capacity to be displaced. The humiliating emptiness of the prison cell calls for an inner center; German

---

54   Stan Smith, Poetry and Displacement. Liverpool: Liverpool University Press 2007, 2. On the benefits of DPPD, see Y.T. Seih et al., The benefits of psychological displacement in diary writing when using different pronouns. *British Journal of Health Psychology* 13 (2008) 39–41.

55   Edward Said, Reflections on Exile. In: Marc Robinson, ed., Altogether Elsewhere. Writers on Exile. Boston: Faber and Faber 1994, 137–149.

56   Edward Said, Freud and the Non-European. London: Verso 2003, 54.

missionaries from the Benedictine abbey of St. Ottilien were imprisoned in North Korea in the late 1940s and early 1950; they found themselves in utter displacement in a foreign country; they drew from their inner center: they experienced the celebration of the Eucharist as their source of inner strength and social cohesion; they also found biblical sources as points of reference in interpreting their situation (climbing Mount Tabor through suffering and exile).[57] The fact that they knew songs and prayers by heart helped to maintain the contact with the inner center. A sister wrote prayers in the form of poems.[58] These are signposts of the capacity to be displaced in a prison situation. The prison experience, one could even say, works as the litmus test of resilience from within. Prison is a context of severe displacement.

Pope Francis' visit to Curran-Fromhold Correctional Facility in September 2015 topped the agenda of the Pontiff's first visit to the US. On his flight from Cuba Pope Francis expressed distress at long prison sentences, saying: "Life imprisonment is almost a hidden death penalty. You are there and you are dying every day without any hope of freedom." He shares views held by a world renowned expert on the subject who in 1842 (also on his first visit to the US) wrote: "(*A prisoner*) is a man buried alive; to be dug out in the slow round of years (...). And though he lives to be in the same cell ten weary years, he has no means of knowing, down to the very last hour, in what part of the building it is situated; what kind of men there are about him; whether (...) he is in some lonely corner of the great jail, with walls, and passages, and iron doors between him and the nearest sharer in its solitary horrors."[59]

This man was Charles Dickens who was very clear in expressing his moral disgust:

> I (...) am only the more convinced that there is a depth of terrible endurance in which none but the sufferers themselves can fathom, and which no man has a right to inflict upon his fellow creature. I hold this slow and daily tampering with the mysteries of the brain to be immeasurably worse than any torture of the body; and because its ghastly signs and tokens are not so palpable to the eye and sense of touch as scars upon the flesh; because its wounds are not upon the surface, and it extorts few cries that human ears can hear; therefore the more I denounce it, as a secret punishment which slumbering humanity is not roused up to stay.[60]

---

57   Renner, Der fünfarmige Leuchter IV, 172.

58   Ibd., 176.

59   Charles Dickens American Notes for General Circulation. New York: Charles Scribner's Son 1910, 119f.

60   Ibd., 118.

Prisons provide miserable external conditions; they create adverse settings and a context of life filled with inflictions of pain and suffering.

On another continent some 100 years later a man was sentenced to 27 years of imprisonment (many in solitary confinement), allowed to write only one letter and receive one visitor from outside of the prison every six months. Such was the predicament in which Nelson Mandela found himself at age 46. In his autobiography Nelson Mandela talks about a lesson learnt: "I learned that courage was not the absence of fear, but the triumph over it. The brave man is not he who does not feel afraid, but he who conquers that fear."[61] In this passage he talks about the inner situation of a person and the challenge of having to drink form the well within you; on another occasion he describes the learning curve of his prison years in the following words: "It is never my custom to use words lightly, if 27 years in prison have done anything to us, it was to use the silence of solitude to make us understand how precious words are and how real speech is in its impact on the way people live and die."[62] Nelson Mandela had his words, his thoughts, his inner conversations in prison. He left prison as a man who was neither broken nor embittered.

Pope Francis, Charles Dickens, Nelson Mandela and many, many more besides share the same deep sensibility to the human capacity—or lack of capacity to survive or succumb to confinement, but also a sense of one's "strength from within," a sense of resistance to being broken, a sense of being able to grow as a human person even in the face of adverse circumstances, to flourish in a situation of displacement. This book is about these inner sources of strength. It is about a particular form of resilience. The Oxford & Merriam Webster Dictionary defines resilience as "the capacity to recover quickly from difficulties" and further "the ability to become strong, healthy, or successful again after something bad happens i.e. misfortune of change." These are all pillars of our enquiry here. Ecological systems can regain their balance and societies can show political stability under uncertainty if they are resilient. There are social and political sources of resilience, material and infrastructural ways of enhancing the capacity to cope with challenges.

If a person is in prison, she will not have access to enriching external resources, she will have to rely on "sources from within." As we have already noted, it is not external place, but inner space that can provide stability. Some people, like Nelson Mandela, are remarkably strong in this venture. This observation is part of the fascination with the phenomenon of resilience. Let us look at another example: In 1979, Vaclav Havel, then a Czech dissident, was

61   N. Mandela, Long Walk to Freedom. London: Little, Brown and Company 1994, 748.
62   N. Mandela, In His Own Words. New York: Little, Brown and Company 2003, 402.

sentenced to four and a half years imprisonment—not a rosy prospect—for his political zeal and activity. Nevertheless, he was determined not to let his imprisonment break him: he vowed not to leave prison feeling embittered. So, he put together a strict day-to-day agenda: a resilience plan. Havel used the time he was allocated to write one four-page letter a week to his wife, Olga. In these '*letters to Olga*', Havel set down his ideas and views about everything under the sun, so much so, that his wife complained that instead of writing her tender love letters, her husband was expounding in detail on Martin Heidegger's Philosophy of Existentialism—such were the letters she was receiving, and as we all know, Heidegger's work is not exactly full of terms of endearment.

Similarly, Havel decided to make use of the time in gaol to learn German and English, to read and study the Bible and to write two plays.[63] In line with this, his rigid daily agenda included doing regular workouts to keep physically fit, refraining from moaning and whingeing, and to be under no illusions that he might be released early did not expect miracles. He saw his 'stay' in prison as a quasi 'trip'. In one letter, he told his wife: "You should lead a completely normal life, as though I were off on a trip somewhere. This is how you can help me the most, if I know you're well and taken care of. I don't know, of course, how long this trip will last: I'm not harboring any illusions, and in fact I hardly think about it at all."[64] He sought meaning and even joy in the little things in life, he set about re-structuring his life, finding new interests, new goals and concentrating on a project which he called: self-consolidation, aiming to reinforce his own inner strengths and keep himself in check: "After all those earlier experiences, I can experience everything in a reflective manner and I keep a watchful eye on myself, so that I am in no danger, I think, of succumbing to the various forms of prison psychosis. I try to respond to many subtle warning signs—which is why I am writing to you in my normal hand and not in that neat little chicken-scratch; even such details, it seems to me, are important."[65] Havel described his 'stay' in prison as the ultimate test in self-control. He also took an active interest in his fellow inmates, and realized that wallowing in self-pity was not an option to be considered. He meticulously prepared—and afterwards went over—every minute detail of the one monthly visit he was entitled to. Vaclav Havel was not released from prison until 1983: he came out not on a low but on a high, not broken but almost refreshed from his experience,

---

63   V. Havel, Letters to Olga. Transl. P. Wilson. New York: Alfred Knopf 1988.

64   Ibd., 23.

65   Ibd., 32.

and it was not long before he was back taking active part in politics, later to become Head of State.

A prison cell does not provide much visible space; a prison as 'a total institution,' to use Erving Goffman's words, will have its own rhythm, its own routine, uneventful, more often than not. There is not much happening here "inside" and so life must be brought into prison through inner resources. Especially under circumstances where the outer world is empty or threatening, an inner life will have to be carefully cultivated, a life rooted in thoughts and emotions, memories and hopes, desires and beliefs.

This was Havel's experience. If one compared Havel's attitude, approach and experience with insights of resilience research one could see a pattern. Resilience is not about leaving things to chance, it is about cultivating, nurturing and encouraging something to grow "inside": something to be consciously pursued, involving effort, to be achieved. Some people are indeed remarkably strong—they can flourish in spite or because of difficult situations. This strength, called "resilience," is the ability to thrive in the face of adversity, the ability to cope well with a crisis. Resilient people are strong, but where does this strength come from? Some of its sources can be found in structural support systems and environmental aspects, others in deep relationships and social contacts. This book explores yet different sources of resilience—namely sources rooted in the person herself. We have seen some of these sources at work in Havel's and in Edward Said's coping strategies; they are inner sources of resilience and in times of adversity, they can be the lifeline between sanity and insanity.

German theologian Dietrich Bonhoeffer experienced displacement when he was imprisoned in April 1943. A member of the resistance movement against the Nazi regime (with Wilhelm Franz Canaris), Dietrich Bonhoeffer was forbidden to publish and speak publicly and in April 1943 he was imprisoned. Just a few weeks before his imprisonment he got engaged to Maria von Wedemeyer, a nineteen year old woman who was eager to learn from Bonhoeffer's religious maturity.[66] Bonhoeffer entered prison with the idea that his stay would not last more than a few weeks. It is impressive and moving to follow his struggle with his concern for his loved ones, for his fiancée and his old parents, with the uncertainty of his future, the painful fact that he had been robbed of his freedom, and his trust in God's providence to make all things good. As Havel and Said would do years later, Bonhoeffer put his intellectual and spiritual resources to good use, he wrote letters, poems, theological

---

66   Cf., E. Bethge, Costly Grace. An Illustrated Biography of Dietrich Bonhoeffer. San
       Francisco: Harper and Row 1979.

texts while confined to prison.[67] He maintained a clear sense of identity and maturity which for him meant that the "center of gravity is always where he actually is, and that the longing for the fulfilment of his wishes cannot prevent him from being his whole self, wherever he happens to be" (LP 233): "There is a wholeness about the fully grown man which enables him to face an existing situation squarely." (LP 233f)[68] It takes matured inner resources to face the world as it is. Bonhoeffer talks about the temptation to remain a child in the world, a child that leaves everything up to the heavenly father without accepting responsibility.[69] Bonhoeffer stressed 'responsibility' and assuming responsibility as the key to a moral life, expressing the hope that his godchild would develop a sense of responsibility.

Bonhoeffer proved himself to be resilient in the face of displacement, by placing his life in a larger framework, reconstructing life's task as a challenge to serve.[70] Turning our minds from worrying about our own safety to caring for other people changes the tone of a situation, life "is kept multi-dimensional and polyphonous" (LP 311). Bonhoeffer was prepared to see the many facets of life even "inside" a prison cell, trying to live "a full human life, gain experience, learn, create, enjoy, and suffer" (LP 3). "The great thing is to stick to what one still has and can do—there is still plenty left—and not to be dominated by the thought of what one cannot do, and by feelings of resentment and discontent" (LP 39; cf. LP 234). Bonhoeffer was confidently convinced that not one of the days spent in prison had been wasted (LP 114). We can live abundant lives even with many wishes remaining unfulfilled. It is matter of properly framing one's experience.

---

67   D. Bonhoeffer, Letters and Papers from Prison. London: SCM 1971 (LP). I will use the abbreviation "LP" for this book.

68   In his own testimony, Bonhoeffer showed that even in prison, a mature person does not drown in self pity (LP 168), that she does not cease to have and show concern for others (LP 233f).

69   Some of these concerns can be found in Rollo May's instructive book *Power and Innocence* where he utters the warning not to mistake "ignorance and naiveté" with "innocence" as religious values (R. May, Power and Innocence. A Search for the Sources of Violence. New York, NY: Norton 1998). Bonhoeffer stressed "being in the world" again and again to avoid these traps (cf., LP 369: "I discovered later, and I'm still discovering right up to this moment, that it is only by living completely in this world that one learns to have faith").

70   Cf., LP 381f.

Unlike Havel, Bonhoeffer drew on an explicit spiritual *weltanschauung* which we would not find in Havel's writings, and decided to accept his prison sentence as a learning experience. "It's a strange feeling to be so complete-ly dependent on other people," he could write, "but at least it teaches one to be grateful, and I hope I shall never forget that. In ordinary life we hardly re-alize that we receive a great deal more than we give, and that it is only with gratitude that life becomes rich" (LP 109).

Interestingly and perhaps even surprisingly, one important inner resource that Bonhoeffer relied on while in prison was an attitude of gratitude. Dietrich Bonhoeffer ended every prison letter to his parents with the words "Your grate-ful Dietrich." Gratefulness is an important resource for resilience, it is an inner attitude and connected to a worldview which does not measure one's relation-ship with the world in terms of entitlements. Ultimately, Bonhoeffer's struggle for strength was a question of trust, trust in God (LP 29).[71] As Bonhoeffer was a deeply religious person, he was able to cope with obstacles and challenges others may have fallen foul of. The source of his life and the source of his mo-tivation did not lie in himself: "Who stands fast? Only the man whose final standard is not his reason, his principles, his conscience, his freedom, his vir-tue, but who is ready to sacrifice all this when he is called to obedient and re-sponsible action in faith and exclusive allegiance to God" (LP 5). The religious person may be ready to sacrifice everything for a yet higher good and this is one of the reasons why people of strong faith can have surprising reserves to resist and endure. But by doing so they manage to stay in this world, remain part of a community.

Bonhoeffer was cautious in perceiving religious life in private terms (such as "private religious virtues").[72] In other words, he did not support the notion that a religious person has to withdraw from the world in order to live what she believes, in fact, pursuing a religious life is about accepting the responsibilities

---

71   Trust in God for Bonhoeffer meant to believe in God's presence and in God's guiding providence: "God is in the facts themselves. If we survive during those coming weeks or months, we shall be able to see quite clearly that all has turned out for the best" (LP 191). Trust in God means, however, walking by faith and not by sight: God does not give us every-thing we are asking for, but God keeps all His promises (LP 387). Obviously, from a human perspective there is no ultimate criterion to judge—let alone in an "intersubjective" way—divine fidelity and faithfulness.

72   "The displacement of God from the world, and from the public part of human life, led to the attempt to keep his place secure at least in the sphere of the 'personal', the 'inner', and the 'private'" (LP 344). The religious person who entertains a relationship with God acknowledges the non-calculability of God who cannot be contained in the boxes of expectations and private webs of desire.

associated with the *Hic* and *Nunc*, since a religious person will associate his or her life with a profound sense of mission and task.[73] Bonhoeffer used the term "this-worldliness" to refer to "living unreservedly in life's duties, problems, successes and failures, experiences and perplexities" (LP 370). This responsiveness is not only a way of responding to the world, but also a way of responding to God, to God's being in the world.

In the extreme situations he found himself in, Bonhoeffer was forced to go back to his basic inner resources, to the essential:

> The heavy air raids, especially the last one, when the windows of the sick-bay were blown out by the land mine, and bottles and medical supplies fell down from the cupboards and shelves, and I lay on the floor in the darkness with little hope of coming through the attack safely, led me back quite simply to prayer and the Bible . . . In more than one respect my time of imprisonment is being a very wholesome though drastic cure (LP 149).

Bonhoeffer developed "resilience from within," drawing on inner resources in the midst of displacement; he saw his life in a wider context that gives meaning and significance to human existence. This may be seen as one of the major sources of strength of a religion—to have "reasons to live," to acknowledge "sources for life." When we talk in such terms, we are referring to inner resources, resources of inner strength. I will systematically explore this type of resilience, resilience based on inner sources of beliefs and memories, convictions and hopes. It is the basis for the capacity to be displaced.

---

73   Bonhoeffer is suspicious of people who do not take the human condition seriously: "There is such a thing as a false composure which is quite unchristian. As Christians, we needn't be at all ashamed of some impatience, longing, opposition to what is unnatural, and our full share of desire for freedom, earthly happiness, and opportunity for effective work" (LP 132).

CHAPTER 2

The Discourse on Resilience

The capacity to be displaced is an expression of resilience. Resilience is coping with unfavorable situations and learning from the experience. Unpleasant circumstances are those in which we feel overwhelmed, we are convinced we will not 'come out' alive and if we do, then not unscathed. Sometimes a missionary experience takes a person into the lion's den of atrocities and evil; it takes resilience to be able to survive despite one's own helplessness in the face of chaos or destruction, in the face of suffering or in the face of inhumanity. Miriam Therese Winter experienced this need for strength in her encounter with evil; as a Medical Mission Sister she joined Dee, a physician friend of hers, in Cambodia:

> Dee had accepted responsibility for meeting the basic medical needs of Khmer Rouge Soldiers, the very ones who had implemented a four-year reign of terror that culminated in the death of several million Cambodian people. Overthrown by the military of Vietnam, they were now dispersed in disillusioned groups in the jungle along the border. I will never forget the stone-cold stares, eyes boring into me from the men who were in that isolated camp in a small, sunless clearing miles from anywhere. I met the leader of the camp, a small, unassuming woman who, Dee had informed me, had been personally responsible for the deaths of approximately seventy thousand people. I had ministered to some of the survivors several years before. So that's what unadulterated evil looks like. The thought frightened me even more when I realized that it looks human, just like me.[1]

These are difficult situations—recognizing the humanness, that inner space in the other person, a shared way of being, a common ground, almost always proves helpful. However, things become difficult when you reflect on what you see and how you see. What benchmark universal codes of human understanding do you turn to? It is a situation of displacement, precisely because of the recognition of common ground. Generally speaking, discovering familiar space in a situation of (physical and moral) displacement strengthens resilience. The ability to identify this familiar space is part of the capacity to be displaced,

---

1 Miriam Therese Winter, The Singer and the Song. Maryknoll, NY: Orbis 1999, 100.

to deal with difficult situations. But there may be the issue of losing trust in familiarity in a situation like the one experienced by Miriam Therese Winter. She did not so much encounter obstacles *to* common ground, as obstacles to drawing the usual conclusions *from* recognizing common ground.

Difficult situations in general are experiences of "a good" being "out of reach." Difficult situations may be those obstacles standing in the way of our reaching a desired goal, and sending us back to square one to start all over again. Difficult situations make us struggle with "circumstances beyond our control." We feel out of place, out of control. This is very much part of the missionary experience.

If we stop a moment to think about the effects of a terminal illness, the horrors of war, the trauma of being taken hostage and break downs in personal relationships, then we might come nearer to the end of the spectrum of such situations, sensing the gravity of adversity. "Circumstances beyond our control" come in all shapes and sizes, they can all bring suffering to those wittingly or unwillingly involved. Hurricanes, earthquakes, redundancy and cancer do not choose their 'victims': life-changing crises can and do hit all of us in as many ways as there are stars in the sky. Displacement speaks many languages and comes in many forms.

If we understand resilience as the capacity to cope with such situations, we could arrange coping strategies in three main categories (i) living vigilantly and prudently and thus minimizing the risk of adverse situations; (ii) actively denying adversity and living in blissful ignorance, mentally blocking out what we convince ourselves has nothing to do us and conveniently sweeping it under the nearest carpet; (iii) facing and tackling adversity head on. Resilience in a narrower and more genuine sense is not avoiding and denying, but accepting, surviving, moving on and growing. Resilience is embracing displacement as displacement.

Experiencing adversity can provide the fertile soil on which to cultivate resilience, even exposure to traumatic events may help resilience as a sort of "inoculating effect".[2] In some cases and instances adversity can actually help to foster resilience.[3] Resilience is *not* 'not being bothered', it is *not* recklessness, it is *not* taking risks with no regard as to the consequences. Resilience is a

---

2   D.M. Khoshaba, S.R. Maddi, Early experiences in hardiness development. *Consulting Psychology Journal* 51 (1999) 106–116; Z. Berger et al., Resilience of Israeli body handlers: Implications of repressive coping style. *Traumatology* 13 (2007) 64–74.

3   See the overview article by Mark Seery: M.D. Seery, Resilience: A Silver Lining to Experiencing Adverse Life Events? *Current Directions in Psychological Science* 20,6 (2011) 390–394.

dichotomy; either the person 'hit' makes a giant leap forward in her life *despite* what has happened, or that leap is prevented *because of* the dire situation. It might be worth considering in how far these two might be forged into one; utilizing resistance with recovery. Rather like an illness, one is either weakened or strengthened, "inoculated" by adverse circumstances.

2.1   The Concept of Resilience

If we look at the actual word *resilience*, we see that it has to do with resisting—rejecting, refusing to give in, in the face of intolerable conditions, but more besides in growing and even thriving. The classic definition as coined by ecologist Crawford Stanley Holling describes resilience as: "a measure of the persistence of systems and of their ability to absorb change and disturbance and still maintain the same relationships between populations or state variables."[4] Resilience has to do with persevering whereby *learning by doing* plays an enormous role. In the field of psychology, resilience is the discovery and realization of personal and individual greatness due to exceptional situations and suffering, whereby it seems to be pliability rather than persistence, and pliancy rather than doggedness which tends to be the dominant aspect. Resilience has been characterized as "the reduced vulnerability to risk experiences, the overcoming of a stress or adversity, or a relatively good outcome despite risk experiences."[5] Hence, the concept of resilience and the concept of vulnerability are connected. Resilience is a way of dealing in a non-destructive way with vulnerability. Resilience is not so much the prudence to avoid dangerous situations, but the ability to face and cope.

The US resilience researcher Pauline Boss compares resilience to a suspension bridge which gives with the onslaught of gale-force winds, rocks and sways but remains intact and does not 'crack up'; in a crisis it is resilience which prevents the bridge from breaking apart under strain; rather like the shock absorbers in a car, it can withstand heightened tension and overload

---

4   C.S. Holling, Resilience and stability of ecological systems. *Annual Review of Ecology and Systematics* 4 (1973) 1–23, at 14; see the collection of articles by Gunderson and Holling (L.H. Gunderson, C.S. Holling, eds., Panarchy: understanding transformations in human and natural systems. Washington, DC 2002), and Gunderson and Pritchard (L.H. Gunderson, L. Pritchard, eds., Resilience and the behavior of large-scale systems. Washington, DC 2002).

5   M. Rutter, Resilience as a Dynamic Concept. *Development and Psychopathology* 24 (2012) 335–344.

without being damaged.[6] Catastrophes do not bounce off a resilient person like an arrow off a shield leaving no mark whatsoever; they hurt, injure and bruise, it is feeling the impact of the shock which builds and strengthens resilience: Thus, if we look at the image of the suspension bridge again, we see that it is not avoiding gale-force winds but the ability to deal with them which makes it resilient. This image suggests suppleness and elasticity; a liminality on the threshold of leaving the known and entering the state of the unknown in which previous stability and familiar signposts vanish, to be replaced by an unfamiliar environment.[7]

Resilience is that capacity to actually thrive in improvised contexts and as such we might ask whether a system which can brace itself against crisis, is unfazed by disaster, is resilient, or is a system one which is able to adjust, cope and move on because of crisis? In other words, is resilience the capacity to block threat or is it the capacity to absorb catastrophe in some way? More recent research tends to point towards transformation and not absorption,[8] which suggest that inner factors of attitude and frame of mind play a decisive role in whether resilience thrives or dies.

Emmy Werner, US psychologist and pioneer in resilience research, studied the development of 698 children born on the Island of Kauai in 1955. Her results showed that children from similar backgrounds developed differently with varying degrees of 'success': amazingly and intriguingly some managed to prosper and flourish while others in the same conditions did not.[9] Werner identifies protective properties which boost resilience in children;[10] these are closely linked with social attitudes and an inner frame of mind strongly influenced by temperament

---

6   P. Boss, Loss, Trauma, and Resilience. New York: W.W. Norton, 2006.

7   The term *liminality* was coined by the social anthropologists Arnold van Gennep and Victor Turner in a theory of ritual whereby ritual is part of mastering the transition phase from what is 'no longer' to the 'yet to come'; cf., A. van Gennep, The Rites of Passage New York, 1960; V. Turner, The Ritual Process. New York 1969.

8   We might consider in how far the term 'adapting' can be seen as a bridging term between absorption and transformation. Thus, we might plausibly assume that resilience (as that double capacity to absorb outside disruption and then transform it into active inner change) and in a wider context could be defined as an "adaptative capacity" (R.J.T. Kleina et al., Resilience to natural hazards: How useful is this concept? *Environmental Hazards* 5 [2003] 35–45).

9   Cf., E.E. Werner, Overcoming the odds: High risk children from birth to adulthood. Ithaca, NY 1992; E.E. Werner, Vulnerable, but invincible. New York 1998; E.E. Werner, R.S. Smith, Journeys from childhood to midlife. Risk resilience and recovery. Ithaca, NY 2001.

10   E. Werner, The children of Kauai: Resiliency and recovery in adolescence and adulthood. *Journal of Adolescent Health* 13 (1992) 262–268: E. Werner, How kids become resilient: Observations and Cautions. *Resiliency in Action* 1,1 (1996) 18–28; E. Werner, R. Smith, Vulnerable but Invincible: A Longitudinal Study of Resilient Children and Youth. New York 1989.

and disposition, (a 'cheerful soul' will manage better), good relationships, social integration, communication networks, self-esteem, and being able to think in terms of long-term goals and not immediate rewards. How we cope (or not) says a lot about our level of 'inner' vulnerability which will be heightened by neuro-psychological deficits, chronic illness, high levels of distractibility, low cognitive dexterity, weak self-regulatory capacities and the 'external' risk factors we are faced with such as being locked in a low socio-economic status, living in chronic poverty with poor housing facilities, and permanent family conflict compounded by the bad health of family members, but the main deficiency children face is having parents with addictions of one kind or the other and living in social isolation. Vulnerability and risk factors raise the probability of dysfunctional behavior patterns setting in which are simply too big to cope with.

The notion of vulnerability is closely intertwined with the notion of resilience.[11] Resilience is the recognition of vulnerability and the readiness to protect the strength of this vulnerability. To give one missionary example: William O'Leary joined a farm project in Mekong/Thailand, not knowing anything about farming or indeed the language spoken by the Thai people: "I arrived at the chosen site for the project, built a fence around it, and started to grade the land as best as I could. With that done, the hard part started. What seeds to buy? When to plant what? Which end of a seed went up and which went down? How deep to plant the silly things? And on and on."[12] Father O'Leary found himself in a situation of displacement, beyond his spectrum of competences and skills; he experienced his ignorance as a source of vulnerability, he needed support. He found this support in his neighbors who

> came to watch for a few days, and they soon realized that I knew nothing at all and they offered to help. They were afraid that I'd die of starvation right on my own farm. Each day they came to teach me … I had placed myself as a disciple to those neighbors, my farmer teachers, and they were very much at home with that. They were the ones with knowledge and skills, and they became my teachers. I was no longer the usual foreign missioner who comes with a whole agenda to teach.[13]

O'Leary was resilient for social reasons, but also because of his courage to recognize vulnerability.

---

11   This point is clearly argued in S.B. Maneyna, The concept of resilience revisited. Disasters 30,4 (2006) 434–450.
12   Joseph Heim, ed., What They Taught Us. How Maryknoll Missioners Were Evangelized by the Poor. Maryknoll, NY: Orbis 2009, 104.
13   Ibd., 106.

The resilient person disposes of existential knowledge of the susceptibility to being wounded; knowing that our own identity and integrity can be jeopardised reminds us that identity is tentative and transient.[14] It is this knowledge of vulnerability which constitutes the identity of who we are and the knowing that we are fallible and fragile.

Hence, there is a way to establish a conceptual connection between resilience and vulnerability. Vulnerability can be taken to be the condition "to be susceptible to harm, injury, failure, or misuse."[15] Vulnerability is part of who we are as human beings. It is a reminder that life risks cannot be reduced to zero—and this means that we are not in full control over our lives. Or in Robert Goodin's words: "Vulnerability amounts to one person being able to cause consequences that matter to the other."[16] Resilience is a response to vulnerability, it is holding on to life goals even in the face of adversity. Coping mechanisms of some kind or another are part of a person's character, but there are also more structural issues involved. Regardless of personal inner conditions, from a social ethics perspective, we do always have to ask how individuals in their macro social systems cope with stress.[17]

Norman Garmezy who has been working on this since the 1970s has pinpointed characteristic traits in coping competences. Garmezy anchors his study in poverty research and particularly among those individuals who are *more* vulnerable in an already vulnerable group of the population.[18] Resilience research focuses on 'the immune system' of human inner strength and it soon becomes apparent that not everyone is equally "equipped" to build or maintain a healthy (inner) immune system. A child who has been abused will be less competent to deal with stress and less proficient in acquiring skills since the child lacks role model mentors; nevertheless, there is always room and ways for skills to be cultivated and crafted. This is something which Pauline Boss

---

14   This approach is clarified in F. Delor. M. Hubert, Revisiting the concept of "vulnerability". *Social Science and Medicine* 50 (2000) 1557–1570.

15   P. Formosa, The Role of Vulnerability in Kantian Ethics. In: C. Mackenzie et al., eds., Vulnerability. Oxford: OUP 2014, 88–109, 89.

16   R. Goodin, Protecting the Vulnerable. Chicago: University of Chicago Press 1985, 114.

17   Cf., S.S. Luthar et al., Conceptual Issues in Studies of Resilience. *Annals of the New York Academy of Sciences* 1094 (2006) 105–115; C.L.M. Keyes, Risk and Resilience in Human Development: An Introduction. *Research in Human Development* 1,4 (2004) 223–227.

18   N. Garmezy, Stress-resistant children: The search for protective factors. In: J.E: Stevenson (ed.), recent research in developmental psychopathology. Oxford 1985, 213–233; Garmezy, Stress, competence, and development. *American Journal of Orthopsychiatry* 57,2 (1987) 159–174; see too N. Garmezy, A.S. Masten, Stress, competence, and resilience. *Behavior Therapy* 17 (1986) 500–521.

emphasizes: unrealistic expectations and unfounded hopes stand in the way of the growth of resilience; in fact it is the ability to live *with* uncertainty and unanswered questions which contributes most to a healthy immune system of resilience.[19] People who need answers to cling to are clearly at a disadvantage.

Seen thus, it soon becomes obvious that individuals with no deep sense of reality or self will have significant difficulties in threshold situations, crossing over from a known environment into an unknown 'land'. This is typical of the missionary experience, the experience of leaving a context with a mission in order to live out this mission in a different context. A deep sense of mission is the source of openness to displacement. To give one example: Mother Amadeus from the Montana Ursulines considered her mission in Montana as completed after having built eight schools; she approached Father Pascal Tosi, Vice Superior of the Jesuits in Alaska and wrote in a letter: "The poverty of the Alaska missions does in no way discourage us. We are ready, with the help of God, for every sacrifice (...). We can live on what the natives live on and in the same kind of houses or dwellings."[20] She was ready for anything, she was ready to move into unknown territory, given her sense of mission, and her sense of self within the mission.

Individuals with no deep sense of self or reality might have significant difficulties coping with adaptation. Such individuals depend on an experience of normality in which cause and effect can be easily worked out and relied on. Resilience requires a sense of agency, and people with a fertile and vivid imagination can create a familiar setting within an unknown environment and thus trigger their own inner resources of resilience. The more an individual can adapt and adjust behavior patterns by dipping into her own inner pool of resources, the more she will be able to conquer the unknown ahead.

Furthermore, being able to make sense of things (without finding the answer) and having a sense of what is meaningful can boost resilience tremendously. Those who have a tangible philosophy of life or who perceive self within the wider context of the cosmos will be better able to cope than those who have a narrow outlook on the world and are unsure as to how they fit in. People with a pronounced sense of insecurity will have difficulty moving on after a crisis situation, intent on looking back at what is lost and mourning what can never be retrieved. A resilient person will cross the threshold—will be able to deal with that state of liminality. Expressed somewhat poetically:

---

19   See P. Boss, Ambiguous Loss. Cambridge, MA: Harvard UP 1999.

20   Suzanne H. Schrems, Uncommon Women, Unmarked Trails. The Courageous Journey Of Catholic Missionary Sisters in Frontier Montana. Norman, Oklahoma: Horse Creek Publications 2003, 95.

Faced with a gale force wind they will not resist and snap but yield to the inevitable and use it to strike a new course.

2.2 Stages of and Distinctions between Research

Resilience research has developed over the years moving from an individual to a more political understanding. Literature in the field identifies distinct phases in resilience development:[21] a first phase can be observed in the research on childhood with the main insight that in a protected environment with favorable conditions a solid foundation stone for future resilience construction will be laid. Long-term observational studies define a second phase as concentrating on those contextual aspects which accompany biological and socio-cultural factors. In a third phase, institutional and political attitudes and aspects of intervention and prevention have been addressed.[22] A fourth phase sees resilience as a trans-boundary, multi-disciplinary venture.

Overall, these results show that resilience is: (i) a dynamic process of interaction between person and context; (ii) an unknown quantity which can vary according to unknown circumstances and can be compared to e.g., riding a bike—once you can do it, you can always do it; (iii) a kaleidoscope of facets and aspects involving biological and psychological factors as well as social and political ones.

Seen as a dynamic process, the roles of characteristic traits and capacity are not of primary concern;[23] resilience takes place within a given context involv-

---

21   C.M. Layne et al., Risk, Vulnerability, Resistance and Resilience. In: C.M. Layne, Handbook of PTSD Science and Practice. New York 2007, 497–520; M. O'Dougherty Wright, A.S. Masten, Resilience Processes in Development. In: O'Dougherty/Wright, eds., Handbook of Resilience in Childhood. New York 2006, 17–37; A.S. Masten, Resilience in developing systems: Progress and promise as the fourth wave arises. *Development and Psychopathology* 19 (2007) 921–930.

22   Cf., A.S. Masten, J. Obradovic, Competence and resilience in development. *Annals of the New York Academy of Sciences* 1094 (2006) 13–27; A.S. Masten, J.L. Powell, A Resilience Framework for Research, Policy and Practice. In: Masten, Powell, Resilience and vulnerability. Cambridge 2003, 1–28.

23   Resilience has been described as a: "process of coping with adversity, change or opportunity, in a manner that results in the identification, fortification, and enrichment of resilient qualities and protective factors" (M.K. Kitano, R.B. Lewis, Resilience and coping: Implications for gifted children and youth at risk. *Roeper Review* 27 [2005] 200–205, here 200). Hetherington and Blechman describe resilience as a process which is mobilized by high-risk circumstances and aims to achieve a state comparably equal to one in which

ing a range of systems working with and against each other; in the event of a catastrophe these systems have to work together simultaneously i.e., sense of orientation, communication skills, social systems and infrastructures, and so on to rescue and retrieve human life from prevailing inhuman conditions.[24]

The second aspect ("an unknown quantity") shows that although not exactly like learning to ride a bike, resilience is a skill that can be learnt and acquired, developed and strengthened. If crisis management skills are encountered and practiced in childhood, they can be honed and 'perfected' over time and used to safeguard one's own vulnerability.[25] In this regard an individual's sense of self-efficacy, in other words self-confidence, is vital in strengthening conviction by deeds and decisions which can impact the world.[26]

The third aspect indicates that social networks of family and friends, and psychological aspects, i.e., a positive perception of self linked with a sense of optimism and ability to be flexible, together with cultural traditions such as rituals and habits, a spiritual view of life and sense of *carpe diem* can fortify and intensify a resilient character.[27] It becomes clear, too, that complex as it is resilience needs to be handled with care.

While it might be tempting to put positive and negative attributes into neat little boxes to be ticked off as and when relevant, there is more. But attributes are definitely a good start. A well-known researcher in the field, Ann Masten, mentions the following factors as being conducive to building resilience: good relationships to not only parents but other people in *loco parentis*, developing intellectual resources; founding a healthy sense of self and self-confidence; hope and finding a meaning and purpose to life. Environment and cultural

there are no risk factors, (E.M. Hetherington, E.A. Blechman, Stress, coping and resiliency in children and families. Mahwah, NJ 1996, 14).

24   A. Ripley, The unthinkable: who survives when disaster strikes—and why. London 2008.

25   Cf., M.A. Zimmermann, R. Arunkumar, Resiliency Research: Implications for Schools and Policy. Social Policy Report. Society for Research in Child Development 8,4 (1994) 1–20.

26   Cf., Albert Bandura: Self-efficacy: Toward a Unifying Theory of Behavioral Change. *Psychological Review* 84,2 (1977) 191–215.

27   Cf., S.O. Utsey et al., Cultural, socio-familial and psychological resources that inhibit psychological distress in African Americans exposed to stressful life events and race related stress. *Journal of Counseling Psychology* 55,1 (2008) 49–62; together with a team of authors Conger discovered that marriage as 'institution' played a major supportive role in weathering financial storms—R.D. Conger et al., Couple Resilience to Economic Pressure. *Journal of Personality and Social Psychology* 76,1 (1999) 54–71.

backgrounds are equally important in furthering positive patterns of behavior, including the ability to cross-check those patterns.[28]

Frederic Flach characterizes a resilient personality as one that is creative, has staying power, a clear awareness of self and capacity to assess one's own capabilities, and the ability to learn from mistakes and make new friends.[29] A wide ranging review of the psycho-biological mechanisms of resilience has identified key attitudinal and behavioral factors such as positive attitude (optimism and sense of humor), active coping, cognitive flexibility, moral compass, physical exercise and social support and role models.[30] While these are useful lists serving as points of reference, they are at the same time dangerous for the very same reason: There is the risk of interpreting resilience as something which can be picked up in a bookstore and learnt like a foreign language if you have the patience, time and energy to do so; there is an even greater risk of it being seen as some magic potion which taken at the right time and with the right spell will work its magic in no time. These lists in all their variations tend to be used like recipes for secret potions with the perfect 'solution' to any hazard no matter how unbearable or impossible it might—you just need the right ingredients and hey presto you can fight and overcome the most threatening of adversaries. A further danger lies in the fact that such recipes imply DIY action, isolated behavior, self-sufficiency attitudes and self-contained cognitive patterns, or suggest that each item needs quarantining, to be treated in isolation, completely autonomous of each other with no links or connections relating back to self. While there may be good and valid arguments for resilience requiring an emergency to-do list,[31] at the same time, one would do well

---

28   A.S. Masten, Ordinary magic: lessons from research on resilience in human development. *Education Canada*, 49,3 (2009), 28–32.

29   F. Flach, How to Bounce Back When the Going Gets Tough! New York, NY: Hatherleigh Press 1998.

30   M.E. Haglund et al., Psychobiological mechanisms of resilience. *Development and Psychopathology* 19 (2007) 899–920.

31   A. Shaikh, C. Kauppi, Deconstructing Resilience: Myriad Conceptualizations and Interpretations. *International Journal of Arts and Sciences* 3, 15 (2010) 155–176. The authors discuss a range of definitions which can roughly be divided into two groups, psychological and socio-scientific; Carl Folke analyzes the meaning of the term resilience with focus on ecological factors which support a non-linear development C. Folke, Resilience: The Emergence of a perspective for social-ecological system analyzes. *Global Environmental Change* 16 (2006) 253–267.

to remember that such lists (as already mentioned above) are a reference guide only; even for the purpose of understanding resilience they have limited value. In addition to that there is the point of not overrating the importance of resilience: resilience is not all that matters in life, nor indeed, is it all life is about.

Primo Levi, in remembering his harrowing experience in a concentration camp during WWII, was convinced that after the War the best had perished. There is, too, a real danger of moralizing the conduct and attitudes of others; meaning there is an inherent danger of pigeon-holing someone as being morally defect if they fail to bounce back "to normal." It is when resilience is reduced to ticks in boxes as proof of passing or failing some invisible test that it can become a language game of morals, e.g., "You have to be able to do or be XYZ," or "you ought to be able to cope."

Thomas Buergenthal, a prominent judge at the International Court of Justice In The Hague, was born in Czechoslovakia in 1934, incarcerated in the Nazi ghetto of Kielce, Poland, with his parents when he was only four years old, then separated from them in Auschwitz at the age of ten. He survived to walk out of Sachsenhausen alive when it was liberated in 1945 by the Soviets having, he declares, not really learned the "tricks" needed to survive; in his memoirs, *A lucky Child*, he picks out one attribute, one ingredient not found in the usual recipes: he says that his whole survival was a matter of sheer luck, luck he had no control over whatsoever and for which he could not be held to account.[32] Buergenthal said that he was lucky to meet the right person at the right moment. Well, "luck" is not something which can be "learned" or "obtained." Survival or even coping cannot be guaranteed no matter which mix of ingredients one uses in any one particular resilience recipe. Life is infinitely richer and deeper than any list an individual or group of individuals may care to concoct regardless of circumstances and contexts.

This complexity calls for differentiations. One obvious differentiation which begs to be made within the framework of the term itself is: just who or what is resilient? And this immediately takes us on to the second question: what or who is one resilient to? If we consider the basic issues: "who is resilient against what?" this would suggest that one subject can show differing degrees of resilience in different degrees of adversity.[33]

---

32   Th. Buergenthal, A lucky Child: a memoir of surviving Auschwitz as a Young Boy. New York: Little, Brown and Company 2009.

33   Cf., S.R. Carpenter et al., From metaphor to measurement: resilience of what to what? Ecosystems 4 (2001) 765–781.

There are people who may be able to cope well enough with displacement and disruption in their lives, but are vulnerable when it comes to permanent stress and perpetual external pressures; and then there are certain phases in life with which, despite supportive, steady relationships, some of us cannot come to terms with, such as being made redundant or being diagnosed with a terminal illness. In other words, resilience is not a known measurable quantity which is there when needed—on tap 24/7, so to speak; it depends on the circumstances and it depends on the person, too. So, just who or what is resilient and perhaps, when and how?

2.3   Five Levels of Resilience

Resilience is a way of responding to stressful situations, situations of displacement that make a person leave her "safety zone". Challenges of displacement can happen to individuals, communities and systems, too. That is why it is not surprising that different types and levels of resilience can be identified. If we look first at who and what, we will find at least five levels of resilience we need to distinguish: (i) the individual, (ii) family structures, (iii) community and social environments, (iv) workplace and institution, (v) the state: realms and domains.

(i) The individual: under certain circumstances some people prove to be amazingly resilient.[34] This has to do with inner personal traits—persistence, self-directedness and cooperativeness have been found to correlate positively to resilience[35] as have self-control and goal orientation, adapting to and tolerating negative effects, trusting in one's instincts and spiritual coping. There are, however, also external forces at work so that inner traits and external conditions cannot be clearly divorced from each other. During a lifetime inner

---

34   Cf., G.O. Higgins, Resilient adults: Overcoming a cruel past. San Francisco 1994; S.S. Luthar et al., The construct of resilience: A critical evaluation and guidelines for future work. *Child Development*, 71 (2000) 543–562; A. Masten, Resilience in individual development: Successful adaptation despite risk and adversity. In: M. Wang, E. Gordon (eds.), Educational resilience in inner-city America: Challenges and prospects. Hillsdale, NJ 1996, 3–25; S. Wolin, S. Wolin, The Resilient Self: How Survivors of Troubled Families Rise Above Adversity. New York 1993; R. Lifton, The Protean Self: Human Resilience in an Age of Fragmentation. New York 1994.

35   J.W. Kim et al., Influence of temperament and character on resilience. *Comprehensive Psychiatry* 54 (2013) 1105–1110.

attitudes and external circumstances change, and that impacts our degree and depth of resilience.[36]

Gill Windle has pointed out that resilience research focuses mainly on youngsters and child development which will be biased first if extrapolated across that 'child's' whole life; if we take for example the ageing process, we soon realize that this alone is a huge challenge to come to grips with for anyone in and beyond childhood—regardless of degree of resilience.[37] An individual's aptitude for resilience cannot be reduced to a black and white category of: 'either, or'; people are not *either* resilient, *or not* resilient, as much as such a simplification would be welcome. An inner *either or* depends on an outside *either or*, too: in some situation we are, and in others we are not: resilience is not a static trait, something we are *either* born with *or* not. It is not a "fixed" personal characteristic.[38] However, our having to constantly inwardly adapt in the face of ever-changing outside factors, resilience can grow and develop, meaning it can be cultivated and acquired.

(ii) Family structures are commonly recognized as being under pressure both from within and without; the pressure of sticking together as a unit and not yielding to undercurrents tugging in multiple directions; outside pressures and expectations can break the family unit and incapacitate it. The term "exhausted family", introduced in German sociology,[39] is one most of us have direct or indirect experience of: families can no longer cope with everyday demands; they leave mail in the envelope, afraid of what might confront them if they open it, they do not pay their bills and hide them away, they fail to send the kids to school for a string of strange and not so strange reasons; they

---

36   A.J. Lamond et al., Measurement and predictors of resilience among community-dwelling older women. *Journal of Psychiatric Research* 43 (2009) 148–154; this study points to contextual factors and specific challenges given a person's particular place in her life cycle.

37   G. Windle, What is resilience? A review and concept analysis. *Reviews in Clinical Gerontology* 21 (2011) 152–169. In her book *La chaleur du coeur empêche nos corps te rouiller* (Paris 2008) Marie de Hennezel pinpointed the factors decisive in growing old happily. She put social factors at the top of the list e.g., loneliness and isolation, integration and appreciation of the elderly, which is neither obvious nor easy in a society orientated towards the young and their needs, and the notion and sense of being grateful, love-of-live, joy in seeing others blossom and flourish. But more than anything else, it is our basic inner perception of—the way we see—those around us: getting old becomes a problem if we see the struggle and interpret it as our own process of growing old.

38   Cf., C.L. Cooper et al., Building Resilience for Success. Basingstoke, UK: Palgrave Macmillan 2014.

39   Cf., R. Lutz (Hg.), Erschöpfte Familien. Wiesbaden: VS Springer 2012 (especially the introduction by Ronald Lutz, 11–70).

are exhausted by the sheer pressures of everyday life, by anxieties linked with personal relationships and quality-of-life factors. When tensions are over-stretched beyond reasonable limits there is a family systems shut-down, often leaving irreparable damage in its wake.

Family resilience is a property of families that can cope with stress and pressures on the basis of 'permeability,' a property of being open towards external systems such as neighborhood networks, welfare institutions, or professional help.[40] What is important is the *narrative coherence* of a family, its ability to tell its own story in such a way as to make sense—is coherent—and gives overall meaning to family experience regardless of time factor. A narrative reveals patterns of organizational skills, means of communication and positive problem-solving strategies. Pauline Boss underlines three decisive factors for strong family resilience: a positive outlook on life and a sense of spirituality, reliable habits such as being flexible and not rigid, connectivity, i.e., social and economic resources, sound communication links, i.e., being able to express emotions and feelings in a safe environment and find solutions together.[41] It does, of course, help if there are reliable social-security and health systems available, and no one would challenge the fact that strong political structures and institutions also strengthen resilience.[42] There are systemic factors involved in a family's not being able to stand up to undesirable pressures. Consequently, family resilience can be strengthened by appropriate systemic support, but is also related to the "inner situation" of the family with its sense of direction and its sense of values.

---

40   The last twenty years has seen a surge in the number of publications on family resil-
      ience: J.M. Patterson, Integrating Family Resilience and Family Stress Theory. *Journal of
      Marriage and the Family* 64,2 (2002) 349–360; F. Walsh, A Family Resilience Framework:
      Innovative Practice Applications. *Family Relations* 51,2 (2002) 130–137; F. Walsh, The
      Concept of family resilience. *Family Process* 35 (1996) 261–281; R.D. Conger, K.J. Conger,
      Resilience in Midwestern Families. *Journal of Marriage and Family* 64,2 (2002) 361–373;
      A.P. Greeff, B. Human, Resilience in families in which a parent has died. American Journal
      of Family Therapy 32 (2004) 27–42; D.R. Hawley, L. DeHaan, Toward a definition of family
      resilience: Integrating life-span and family perspectives. *Family Process* 35 (1996) 283–296;
      M.A. McCubbin, H.I. McCubbin, Families coping with illness. In: C.B. Danielson et al.
      (eds.), Families, Health, and Illness: Perspectives on Coping and Intervention. St. Louis,
      Mi 1993, 21–63; F. Walsh, Strengthening family resilience. New York 1998.
41   P. Boss, Trauma, Loss and Resilience, 83–87 and 103.
42   In recent years the significance of school as institution has been acknowledged as play-
      ing a major role in strengthening powers of resilience; cf., N. Henderson, M. Milstein,
      Resiliency in Schools. Making It Happen for Students and Educators. Thousand Oaks,
      Ca 2002.

(iii) A third level of resilience is the communal and structural one: community and social structures is an area of particular importance to social scientists who are interested in the common characteristics of these structures and how they stand up to outside tensions and pressures from those forces which threaten to disrupt and debilitate them.[43] A social system is said to be resilient if it can deal with disasters and devastation without going under and, more importantly, can mitigate the effects of the calamity by implementing restorative procedures effectively.[44] Those safety-net systems which work smoothly under normal circumstances, must not break down under pressure; such systems need to be robust, rich in resources with the ability to react spontaneously and effectively to new conditions. Speed also plays a key role here, in other words, how long does it take for a system to react to disruptive forces and implement suitable repair strategies? And of course, sense of community is paramount in any catastrophe, as studies of hurricane disasters show.[45] When social systems break down, rot sets it and confirms just how vital resilience is. Disaster situations and contexts of emergency aid test a system to the extreme.

In his book, *Collapse: How Societies Choose to Fail or Succeed*, Jared Diamond makes a detailed analysis of those factors which break the back of society.[46] Diamond sees the collapse of a society reflected in a drastic drop in the population and, or, in the ever-mounting complexity of politico-economic and social machinery which has to function over increasingly wider areas for longer and longer spans of time. It is vital that certain aspects are not overlooked, says Diamond, namely, the impact of damage on the environment; climate change; friendly trading and business partners; and the way a society reacts to outside influences. Damage and change are the external factors and resilience is the way a society reacts inwardly to and upon those factors. What Robert Edgerton

---

43   W. Neil Adger researches the crossover point between ecological and social systems: W.N. Adger, Social and ecological resilience: are they related? *Progress in Human Geography* 24,3 (2000) 347–364; W.N. Adger et al., Social-ecological resilience to coastal disasters. *Science* 309 (2005) 1036–1039.

44   M. Bruneau et al., A Framework to Quantitatively Assess and Enhance the Seismic Resilience of Communities. *Earthquake Spectra* 19,4 (2003) 733–753.

45   Cf., C.E. Colten et al., Community Resilience: Lessons from New Orleans and Hurricana Katrina. CARRIE Research Report 3. Oak Ridge, TN: Community and Regional Resilience Initiative 2008.

46   J. Diamond, Collapse: How Societies Choose to Fail or Survive. New York: Viking 2005; cf., Peter B. Demenocal and Edward R. Cook, Perspectives on Diamond's Collapse: How Societies Choose to Fail or Succeed. *Current Anthropology* 46 (Supplement, 2005) S91–S99.

terms *maladaptation* in a social-anthropological study is the inability or failure
to cope and adapt, and this will ultimately lead to collapse.[47]

(iv) Business structures and institutions—are resilient if they manage not
to go under, if they manage to resist or even thrive under pressure. The resiliency of businesses and institutions is shaped by social networks, cultural
climates as well as political frameworks. Social resilience must be anchored
in its institutions which need to be creative and pluralistic in their attitudes
thus nurturing a culture of co-operation rather than competition. Resilience
within and outside an institution is strengthened if private initiatives within
the framework of the institution are encouraged, if institutions are prepared
and able to absorb the shock of risks taken and gone wrong, and there is a
strong and non-diffuse sense of agency within the institution. A further key
factor is the value basis.

Swiss economists Bruno Frey and Emil Inauen carried out a study on why it
was that Benedictine monasteries in Germany and Austria were 'economically
resilient.'[48] They discovered that "good governance" was absolutely crucial, as
was an effective democratic system in electing the abbot and making major
decisions; this internal framework was regularly checked and monitored by
external supervisors, furthermore the mechanisms in place for selecting and
allocating the right 'man' for the right job were exacting, (prior, cellerar, master
of novices, etc). Alongside these mechanisms and structures were, crucially,
those common value systems shared by all members of the monastery, tried
and tested over time (centuries!) by generations of monks. Benedictine monks
do not "follow" a rule, they "live" the rule, the rule which has been fully internalized and becomes a defining factor in the way of life. In short, while a resilient
institution needs sound structures, it is its intangible infrastructures which
count in 'overcoming vulnerability' and it is shared value systems which make
or break an institution especially in times of crisis.[49] Intangible infrastructures
exist in codes of values and networks of knowledge; knowledge exists in its ability to co-ordinate and pass on its inbuilt and acquired knowledge—enabling

---

47   R. Edgerton, Sick Societies. Challenging the Myth of Primitive Harmony. New York 1992.
      Edgerton uses *maladaptation* to describe the inaptitude of a society to adapt to shifts and
      change in their environment, which is often rooted in irrational convictions or religious
      beliefs in the realms of "bounded rationality", nurtured by a psychological culture of tak-
      ing "minimal risk" and making the "least effort", but also hand in hand with social hierar-
      chies of power and status which assess and react to external threats equally as irrationally.

48   E. Inauen, B.S. Frey, Benediktinerabteien aus ökonomischer Sicht. On the extraordinary
      stability of an exceptional institution. Working Paper No. 388. Institute for Empirical
      Research in Economics. University of Zurich. Zürich 2008.

49   Cf., Y. Sheffi, The Resilient Enterprise. Cambridge, MA 2005.

tangible structures to be constructed, created and established; intangible infrastructures may be described as cultural codes, as "ideas" that serve as basis
and point of reference for constructing tangible infrastructure such as buildings. Ultimately, the resilience of a business or an institution does not primarily depend on its tangible and measurable assets (bricks and mortar), but on its
intangible values and knowledge basis.[50]

(v) The state, in realms and domains—can be resilient by reacting and acting in the right way and at the right time to internal and external circumstances. In his momentous opus on the fall of the Roman Empire (*The Decline and
Fall of the Roman Empire*), Edward Gibbon mentions the decline and deteriora-
tion of virtue as one major contributive factor together with an increasing lack
of control in co-ordination. This would suggest that there is a close connection
between "size and scale" (requiring competent co-ordination) and "capacity
to co-operate" and it is this which holds the key to maintaining the status quo
of a state system which in turn strongly suggests that it is the value system of
principles and commitments which are vital factors in resilience.

Toby Wilkinson, likewise, in his enquiry into the rise and decline of Egypt,
draws the conclusion that in the final analysis it was Egypt's sheer inability to
co-operate both within the state and beyond its borders that dealt the final
blow.[51] The death of Ramses IX in 1111 BC marked the end of dynastic rule; the
country was forced back on its forward looking ideal of national unity, achieved
under this dynasty and instead began to break up and 'fall apart', literally.
Immigration had brought significant changes to Egypt's inward looking political organization, non-native rulers without the traditional value basis took
over, transforming Pharaonic civilization. At the same time traditional forces,
especially the representatives of ancient Egyptian religion, sealed themselves
off from outside influences; a mixture of atrophic introspection and the vitality of more dynamic civilizations led to the extinction of the Egyptian regime.
In other words, refusal to move with the times, face new challenges head on
and an unwillingness to tap new resources did almost ironically finally lead
to the tombs of the kings being pillaged and their gold plundered sparking a
never-ending spiral of conflict. The resilience of a dynasty was weakened by its
own self-centeredness, inner conflict and devaluation of shared, common values. This seeming chain reaction of shut-down stems, basically, in the collapse

---

50   Cf., C. Sedmak, Intangible Infrastructures and Identity. In: E. Kapferer et al. (eds).,
      Strengthening Intangible Infrastructures. Newcastle upon Tyne: Cambridge Scholars
      Publishing 2013, 3–222.
51   T. Wilkinson, The Rise and Fall of Ancient Egypt. London: Bloomsbury 2010.

of co-ordination and co-operation. These two concepts are pivotal in our understanding the resilience enhancing profile of nations and states.

It is easy to see, then, that resilience is relevant on different levels and in different ways which makes the concept colorful and multifarious. For good reasons resilience can be said to be multidimensional in that it has (among others) social, physical and political dimensions.[52] Resilience on a personal level is strengthened or weakened by political factors and frameworks. The different levels are interconnected, there is a "permeability" between them, of mutual enforcing or antagonistic weakening because of a lack of coherence.

2.4 Pillars of Resilience

If we look at the five levels on which resilience is played out, we could attempt to identify pillars of resilience or common denominators relevant on each level, and in this regard I would suggest aspects of co-operation and co-ordination; internal coordination and external cooperation, coherence and contacts, inner cohesion and social capital as being major contributors. These factors, however, point to one unifying and fundamental component, namely identity: identity at each and every level, whether it be the personal identity of the individual, the family, communities, businesses, institutions, or state sovereignty. Resilience requires what I would describe as "robust identity," a clear sense of identity-conferring commitments, as well as an understanding of crucial alliances. The key to a flourishing and fruitful missionary experience is a robust identity. People who can cope with displacement are those who know who they are.

Resilience and identity cannot be dealt with as two separate units. Questions associated with identity issues can arise in conflict situations both in self, family relationships, civic life, workplace and also state institutions—local government. Central to the structure of identity is the fabric of relationships, scope of options and a sense of values. Resilience comes into the equation when identity is in danger and integrity is under threat. Such external circumstances can be described as *crisis*, while *trauma* is the inner psychological reaction to shock experience, irreparably damaging identity and integrity structures: resilience *in extremis*. Trying to keep identity—literally body and soul together—is hard work, involving finding (or maintaining) the equilibrium between inner needs and demands made by outer circumstances; in

---

52   Cf., G.E. Richardson, The metatheory of resilience and resiliency. *Journal of Social and Clinical Psychology* 58 (2002) 307–321, esp. 309–313.

other words, the balance between understanding inner-self and understanding the outer-cosmos. This can be seen as a negotiation process: Not surprisingly, Gina O'Connell Higgins characterizes resilience as the "active process of self-righting".[53] The person is negotiating her equilibrium using social and epistemic sources. This idea of equilibrium-building can also be seen in the works of Flach and Bonnano. Frederic Flach characterized a resilient personality as one with the capacity to restore balance.[54] George Bonanno pursues a similar idea in describing resilience as a capability to maintain and preserve physical and mental stability in the face of traumatic events.[55] He depicts resilience as being able to stay on one's feet despite major disruption thus drawing upon the image of the balancing act of desperately not allowing the scales of internal and external circumstances to tip irretrievably in one direction. This act of funambulism is not only about keeping identity intact, not allowing it to slip off the radar in times of 'war', it is about coping in a way which allows identity to survive and thrive.[56]

This balancing or tight-rope act, reminds us not to focus on self alone as core source of resilience, since that would imply that we as individuals cannot be harmed, injured or hurt, instead it tells us to focus on our *knowing* that we are vulnerable and can be 'bruised'. Identity is fragile but can become a source of resilience if we recognize the fragility of our own identity. Situations of displacement increase our sense of fragility and make us more aware of the vulnerability of identity. This fragility can be internal as well as external, consequently, protective factors can be internal or external, as well. Aid workers in their missionary experience are confronted with this phenomenon as part of their basic professional challenge—Alessandra Pigni who worked with poems by Rumi and Rilke to help aid workers build up inner space and inner strength testifies to this fragility: "I often encountered aid professionals who had come to the field hopeful and enthusiastic, with a sense of purpose and meaning, but had sooner or later found themselves exhausted, cynical about

---

53   G.O.C. Higgins, Resilient adults: overcoming a cruel past, San Francisco 1994, 1.

54   F. Flach, Resilience. How to bounce back when the going gets tough. New York 1997.

55   G.A. Bonanno, Loss, trauma, and human resilience: Have we underestimated the human capacity to thrive after extremely aversive events? *American Psychologist* 59,1 [2004] 20–28, at 20.

56   Cf., Ch.S. Carver, Resilience and Thriving: Issues, Models, and Linkages. *Journal of Social Issues* 54,2 (1998) 245–266.

the value of their work and doubtful of their capacity to perform."[57] They had lost their sense of mission, or at least, the sense of the efficacy of mission, feeling drained of their inner resources and being overwhelmed by the external pressures. In pursuing this thought further we could say that there is an inner and a social dimension to identity and, as a result, to resilience. And here too we are reminded of those inner sources of identity outlined above, commitments, a coherent narrative of life, and "robust concerns" and external sources of identity such as recognition and belonging.[58]

Robust identity will be based on these respective sources of identity and will lead to three main properties: particularity, definability, and self-efficacy. "Particularity" points to a sense of uniqueness, difference, and "being special" and therefore, most importantly, not exchangeable; "definability" expresses the fact that entities with robust identity have recognizable traits, a profile, "self-efficacy" communicates the sense of agency and the belief in the possibility to shape and change the world. An entity with robust identity, be it a person, a community, or even a state, will demonstrate those three features on the basis of two types of sources: epistemic (commitments and concerns, coherent self-narrative) and social (recognition, belonging). While the latter point to issues of place, the former refer to a sense of inner space even in the midst of displacement.

Epistemic sources of identity strengthen the inner dimension of resilience: Resilience is fortified by a self-regulatory system; terms such as mastery and agency play a major role in this regard since processes involved in identifying possibilities and choosing one course of action over another depend on them.[59] Resilience is strengthened by a sense of agency; upholding a sense of agency in situations of displacement is crucial to the capacity to be displaced. Self-regulatory mechanisms are inner processes which make up (or fail to make up) self-discipline, self-control and resistance to adversity. Resilience also benefits

---

57   Alessandra Pigni, Building resilience and preventing burnout among aid workers in Palestine: a personal account of mindfulness based staff care. *Intervention* 12,2 (2014) 231–239, at 232.

58   Cf., C. Sedmak, Innerlichkeit und Kraft. Studie in epistemischer Resilienz. Freiburg: Herder 2013, 62–63.

59   Roberta Apfel and Bennett Simon define resilience as: "the capacity to survive violence and loss, and moreover to have flexibility of response over the course of a life time. The inner experience of such behavioral flexibility includes a sense of agency and a sense of capacity to choose—among courses of action and among conflicting moral values" (R.J. Apfel, B. Simon, Bennett, Mitigating discontents with children in war: an ongoing psychoanalytic inquiry. In A.C. Robben, M.M. Suárez-Orozco [eds.], Cultures under Siege: Collective Violence and Trauma. Cambridge 2000, 102–30, here 103.

from having objectives; goals provide us with a clear sense of direction and equip us for the road ahead. Aaron Antonovsky mentions a "sense of coherence" as being vital in this regard which means having a good sense of orientation in the world; this affects the way we deal with and overcome stress in our lives.[60] Coherence is like a framework within which we can interpret our own lives and the decisions we make.

An important internal factor in resilience is perception and clarity of judgment: *Ex negativo*, when we feel completely isolated and the victim of circumstance our own passivity numbs us and deactivates the necessary choice and decision mechanisms we might have. With faculties of perception blurred, we are unable to assess the possibilities we have to hand and fail to see things as they really are. A clear sense of perception is a core component in self-control (in the widest sense) mechanisms, meaning we retain our own perception of self, i.e., we know we are not monsters with two heads even though we may be made to feel that way; we are normal human beings 'after all' with cognitive powers to think positively and find a way out of the dilemma.[61] Inner clarity is a core pillar in building a sense of resilience—but so too is social affirmation and support.

Social sources of identity nourish the social dimension of resilience: to enable the "wounded party" to survive—bounce back—after a crisis, resilience needs to be fortified at the social level—via networks of friends and like-minded fellows, by cultivating social interests and competences. People who admit to being in need of help can more readily accept help when it is offered; because of that they are able to develop resilience mechanisms, which those who unable to accept help (let alone admit that they are in dire need of it) will not. People, who retreat into their own inner 'cave', rotate in their own vicious circles of suffering and torment will find it difficult to cultivate resistance.

It takes both, the epistemic and the social, as we have seen in Ella Schneider Hilton's life story: resilient human beings have a sense of personal responsibility and growth.[62] An example, knitting those two factors together, can be found in the work of Boris Cyrulnik; Cyrulnik, a French psychiatrist and physician born to émigré Jews in 1937, lost his parents in Auschwitz and was not treated well by his foster parents. He worked (as a 7 year old boy!) with the resistance movement. This makes his existential background for talking about resilience deep and rich. Cyrulnik insists resilience is "a mesh," not "a

60   A. Antonovsky, Health, Stress and Coping: New Perspectives on mental and physical well-being. San Francisco 1979.
61   Cf., L. Valentine, L.L. Feinauer, Resilience factors associated with female survivors of childhood sexual abuse. *The American Journal of Family Therapy* 21 (1993) 216–224.
62   Higgins, Resilient Adults, 131.

substance." Resilience, he goes on to say, is a "sweater" that we are forced to knit ourselves, using the people and things we meet in our emotional and social environments. It is the "history" of our knitting capabilities—the way we combine the yarn of our experiences, "the things we've been through," and the way we set them in the context of *l'histoire*—the history and narrative of our lives and the greater picture of things.

This, then, is the 'wool' which contributes to our emotional clothing.[63] Resilience is a process, a continuous process of knitting and adding all the threads and wools we come across as we work—knit—our way through life. Cyrulnik depicts resilience as a form of anti-fatalism, as resisting quirks of fate. People who can actively contribute to their own lives and put their lives in a larger narrative, people who do not succumb to overpowering and irreversible circumstances have better chances of acting resiliently. Sensing that we are part of a bigger framework is vital when faced with life-threatening circumstances. Maryknoll's, sister Ita Ford, had lost her best friend and co-worker Sr. Carla Piette in a car accident while crossing a creek in their jeep. The jeep had been capsized by a sudden surge in water; Ita barely survived and had to come to terms with the loss of her friend; she held on to the interpretative framework of her faith; in a letter to her mother she wrote:

> This is kind of a heavy experience, but I guess it just says that God is extremely active in our lives and certainly the Lord of life, the one who's in charge, the one who decides... I'm sure that what all this means will come about and be clearer later on. Meanwhile, I must stand humbly before the wisdom and love of our God who chose to call Carla and not me. Our years together are a great gift and source of strength.[64]

This is a matter of "framing;" she holds on to the shared experience as a source of gratitude and sets the lives of herself and her friend in the wider framework of divine providence and divine mercy, by remembering she is part of a larger horizon, a wider mission. Boris Cyrulnik tells a story he attributes to Charles Péguy:

> On his way to Chartres, Péguy saw a man breaking stones with a big sledge hammer by the side of the road. His face was a picture of misery and his gestures were full of anger. Péguy stopped and asked: 'What are you doing, monsieur?' 'You can see what I'm doing,' the man replied, 'this

---

63   Boris Cyrulnik, Parler d'amour au bord du gouffre. Paris 2004; Boris Cyrulnik, Resilience. London: Penguin 2009.

64   Judith M. Noone, The Same Fate as the Poor. Maryknoll, NY: Orbis 1995, 126.

stupid, painful job is all I could find.' A little further on, Péguy saw another man. He was breaking rocks, too, but his face was calm and his gestures were harmonious. 'What are you doing, monsieur?' asked Péguy. 'Oh, I'm making a living. It's hard work, but at least I'm out of doors.' Further on, a third stonebreaker radiated happiness. He smiled as he put down his hammer and looked at the fragments of stones with pleasure. 'What are you doing?' asked Péguy. 'Building a cathedral.'[65]

Summing up, we could say that epistemic factors (such as sense of control, sense of direction, and clarity of perception and judgment) and social factors (such as openness to support systems and social correction) seem to be essential for robust resilience-building. It is about cultivating—appropriating— an inner space and this is especially important in situations of displacement. Resilience is based on robust identity expressed in particularity, definability, and self-efficacy and nourished by inner sources (commitments, concerns, a coherent narrative of self) and external sources such as recognition and belonging. Resilience is strengthened by a sense of coherence, a sense of direction, clarity of judgment, and a sense of control. If, then, we acknowledge that resilience affects and is affected by these factors, we will also recognize that epistemic resilience is closely connected to issues related to integration and coherence, control and self-discipline, questions about future prospects and perspectives, as well as to quality of judgment and perception and how they can be constructed. We now need to turn to epistemic resilience.

2.5   The Concept of Epistemic Resilience

Epistemic resilience is "resilience from within," it is the ability to withstand external harmful forces by drawing on one's own positive resources, re-charging one's batteries from an inner source. It is an indispensable coping strategy in situations of displacement; it is a constitutive element of the capacity to be displaced. The inner dimension comprises mental, cognitive and spiritual resources. One important aspect of epistemic resilience is the spiritual dimension. Craig Steven defines spiritual resilience as: "the capacity, when faced with hardship and difficulty to cope actively using religious resources, to resist the destruction of one's spiritual competencies, and to construct something

---

65   B. Cyrulnik, Talking of Love. How to Overcome Trauma and Remake Your Life Story. London: Penguin 2009, 29.

positive in line with larger theological goals."[66] The spiritual dimension makes us aware of the possible connection between a culture of resilience (even epistemic resilience) and virtues.[67]

Virtues are well grounded inner dispositions to act in a particular way. If we think back to the balancing, tight-rope, act we will see that inner resources 'feed' and 'nourish' coping capacities when adverse external factors demand. But inner resources are especially vital when we face inner struggles which like a tornado can suddenly arise out of confusion, inner crises (such as crises of faith), a sense of incoherence between actual (first order) desires and desires about desires (second order desires). An important resource in inner struggles as well as an essential source for inner strength is a person's values and world view; if you know what you stand for, you have reasons to act even under adverse circumstances. In a well-known letter to her niece, Ita Ford shares the sense of meaning of life she had found in El Salvador and encourages her niece to cultivate value-based resilience: "What I'm saying is that I hope you can come to find that which gives life a deep meaning for you, something that energizes you, enthuses you, enables you to keep moving ahead."[68] A sense of deep meaning is an important source of resilience: L.V. Polk, for instance, differentiates between four basic types of resilience, two of which are "internal:" dispositional (having a sense of autonomy, of self), relational, situational and philosophical; dispositional and philosophical types of resilience are connected to the inner; but all of them are decisive in the way we perceive the world and the values we believe in—our *weltanschauung*.[69]

It should not be forgotten that it is our *weltanschauung* which enables us to recognize obstacles as obstacles, equip us to define "adversity" which as a concept is a dependent variable; it needs a reference point: adverse to what? X is adverse for S if X is a "malum" according to the value basis of S. Inner resources generate our points of view, provide us with a clear sense of orientation and the capacity to integrate these aspects into our own personality. This capacity is comparable to the co-ordinates on a map—they determine

66 C.S. Titus, Resilience and the virtue of fortitude: Aquinas in dialogue with the psychosocial sciences, Washington, D.C. 2006, 28; concerning the concept of spiritual resilience see also K.M. Clarke, F. Cardman, Spiritual Resilience in People Who Live Well with Lifelong Disability. *Journal of Religion, Disability and Health* 6 (2002) 23–36.

67 Cf., J.S. Russell, Resilience. *Journal of the Philosophy of Sport* 42,2 (2015) 159–182.

68 Judith M. Noone, The Same Fate as The Poor, 117.

69 L.V. Polk, Toward a middle-range theory of resilience. *Advances in Nursing Science* 19 (1997) 1–13.

the 'course' we chart for self, others and the world around us. A person would take all her inner resources to find orientation.

Those resources responsible for processes of epistemic resilience are: strength of will and one's own convictions, disposition, aspiration, memory and recall, powers of judgment, and breadth and depth of sensory perception. These basic capacities are the prerequisite for a responsive culture to life's four 'big' questions: where to? Where from? Why? How? In seeking answers to these questions we acquire a sense of orientation which as a source of individual inner power sees us through when the going gets tough, and allows us to grow as a result retaining our sense of direction. "Robust identity" is a fundamental element in the dynamics of retaining that sense of priorities and orientation.

One classic element of robust identity leading to epistemic resilience would be that of *fortitude* which in adverse circumstances is the capacity to hold on to what is good and true despite all odds; fortitude is that inner willingness and willpower to not give in or give up. Even in a situation of displacement this virtue allows us to remain committed to an inner moral space thus preventing inner chaos and moral confusion. The constant companions of fortitude are patience and perseverance. Thomas Aquinas tells us that *fortitudo* is needed to fight our fears and the temptation of daredevilry. Pusillanimity and vainglory are the vices against which fortitude has to fight.[70] Fortitude will not avoid or evade difficulties but will instead try to conquer them. The foundations of fortitude need to be seen within a wider framework, within wider perspectives and objectives comprising moral norms, relationships and obligations and a clearly defined sense of commitment. Here again, we can see how the different levels on which the concept of resilience is played out, are interconnected.

I would now like to view epistemic resilience through the eyes of two interlocutors who have expressed deep insights into sources of inner strength: Boethius and Meister Eckhart. Boethius compiled *The Consolation of Philosophy* in the 6th century while serving an unjust prison sentence and awaiting his unlawful execution.[71] He found himself, so to speak, in a situation of utter displacement, and had to cope with the loss of the familiar. In a state of complete despair and confusion, he composes a paper describing how he is visited by the Lady Philosophy who comforts and consoles him in his despair. *The Consolation* reveals a lot about epistemic resilience in as far as external

---

70   Aquinas, Summa Theologica II–II, 123–140; cf., Titus, Resilience and the virtue of fortitude, 143–187. Titus links the capacity of flexibility with self-efficacy and ability to be objective orientated via psychological resilience research.

71   Boethius, The Consolation of Philosophy. London: Victor Watts 1969: Abbrev: "CoP".

conditions and circumstances can be neither an indicator of nor strengthen inner powers of resistance. In order to regain good health, the patient needs to find his voice and articulate his thoughts: "He takes the first step on the road to recovery by recognizing Philosophy and by regaining his ability to speak."[72] Boethius diagnoses himself as suffering from 'sickness of the spirit', as living in limbo minus his true sense of self (a person in need of consolation no longer knows who she is); he languishes in an opaque haze of confusion and no longer knows where he is or where he is headed for. This dual malady of the mind saps him of the strength to resist.

The remedy to this double dilemma lies clearly in the fact that he has to 'pull himself together', in other words: exert some self discipline on his moods and mindlessness; only in guarding and guiding his thoughts will he find the way out of this maze. Like any remedy, care must be taken in administration: small doses, regularly taken and gradually increased as strength returns. First, he needs some sweetener to help the medicine go down, the sweetening sound of soft words of rhetoric, the colder harsher facts of reality can only be given when the patient is stronger. As in any holistic treatment, music is vital in easing the pain of the overstretched mind.[73] The goal of this therapy is for the patient to attain equanimity and steadfastness which requires the close monitoring of thought processes. Lady Philosophy teaches Boethius that he needs to set his house of thoughts in order and keep them tidy and orderly; further, she tells him to stop longing for seeming past happiness.

Nostalgia will only weaken the system—an important lesson in itself—since the patient is no longer in the there and then of the past but in the here and now of the present; it does no good to compare or confuse them. What she is telling him is that inner attitude and perspective are essential for recovery. Lady Philosophy invites him to focus his attention on that which is constant and enduring and not to be deceived by what is fickle and volatile. Equanimity invariably looks to the Most High: the human soul will by necessity be that much freer the more it contemplates upon the Divine Spirit but less so, of course, if it slips back into contemplating physical existence, base servitude is giving in to vice and becoming its slave, divorced from one's own powers

72   T.F. Curley, The Consolation of Philosophy as Work of Literature. *The American Journal of Philology* 108,2 (1987) 343–367, 344. This ability is the capacity to enter dialogue, to take part in the process of dialogue cf., S. Lerer, Boethius and Dialogue. Literary Method in The Consolation of Philosophy. Princeton: Princeton UP 1985, 3ff, 95ff, 124ff.

73   Cf., D.S. Chamberlain, Philosophy of Music in the Consolation of Boethius. *Speculum* 45,1 (1970) 90–97.

of will.[74] It is our powers of reason which enable us to look temperately at the outside world as a whole, at its orderliness, at the faultless nature of life, of human life, which gives us the orientation we need. The healing powers of Philosophy work through viewing human life in its entirety: "Boethius is engaged in a search for meaning through inquiry into natural philosophy. He is consoled when he can see that the events of his life fit into a larger order that gives them significance."[75]

Self-awareness and self-control cannot be taken from us, under any circumstances, as we have seen in the examples of prison experiences: "Consider further, that the feelings of the most fortunate men are the most easily affected, wherefore, unless all their desires are supplied, such men, being unused to all adversity, are cast down by every little care: so small are the troubles which can rob them of complete happiness" (CoP 37). Philosophy's admonishing reminder that we need to bridle wild imagination, stop lamenting and cease complaining is an interesting one from the perspective of epistemic resilience: "With all that great wealth, was your mind never perturbed by torturing care arising from some sense of injustice?" (CoP 63).[76] The blueprint strategy for resilience sketched out for Boethius is one relying on human powers of reason to control both erratic thoughts and emotions. This power is the fruit of looking, seeing, knowing: "What can be as powerless as the blindness of unknowing, of nescience? for now you bring your eyes more watchfully to scan the truth. But what I am going to say is no less plain to the sight" (CoP 97).

Nescience will lead us astray "if men are the more worthless as they are despised by more people, high position makes them all the worse because it

---

74   Cf., CoP 127.

75   W.R. Olmsted, Philosophical Inquiry and Religious Transformation in Boethius' "The Consolation of Philosophy and Augustine's 'Confessions'". *The Journal of Religion* 69,1 (1989) 14–35, 16. Olmsted focuses on the parallels in Augustine's and Boethius' therapeutic approach: "In both works, philosophy liberates the mind from particulars and from the egoism of opinion by enabling it to gain access to a totality that exists in otherness" (17).

76   In this connection, one might ask what role 'lament' can play in the fight for and pursuit of resilience—historical theologian, Georg Fischer, has indicated that it serves as a sign of positive power, reactive force, a sign of life seeking community, testimony of the truth and may be a step towards cognizance (Warum ist mein Schmerz anhaltend und meine Wunde unheilbar? In: H. Hinterhuber et al., eds., Der Mensch in seiner Klage. Anmerkungen aus Theologie und Psychiatrie. Innsbruck: Tyrolia 2006, 150–159). The Book of Job must also be cited as a key text in conjunction with resilience research, as it focuses on the extreme pain and suffering of Job and not the wise words of his pious friends as being a prime source of resilience: it is experiencing God first hand which paves the way from covetous desire to absolute obedience.

cannot make venerable those whom it shews to so many people to be contemptible" (CoP 67), and will lead us to dwell upon deceptive thoughts. Nescience is not only an epistemic *black hole*, a lack of knowledge, primarily pragmatic in nature, it is the inability to do what is right. The corrupted soul will fail to reach the summit, the "highest good" which is guided by strength and disposes of gentleness (CoP 96). Boethius is clearly linking correct thinking with correct doing; linking mental capacity with physical ability; one can understand his reasoning in identifying vice as a sickness of the spirit: "Surely not, for what is weaker or less compelling than the blindness of ignorance? Do they know what they ought to follow, and are they thrown from the straight road by passions?" (CoP 108). The only way the powers of life can be restored and invigorated is to focus on and apply oneself to virtue and elevating the spirit to Hope (CoP 147).

If we sum up the main message in Boethius' *Consolation*, we note that (i) resilience is undermined by sickness of the mind and spirit, loss of self-awareness and the increase in mental confusion; (ii) sickness of the spirit—nescience—has two root causes, erroneous thoughts and wrongful deeds; (iii) the medicine must be administered in small doses and increased slowly; (iv) The remedy lies in disciplining thought and controlling one's emotions, in other words a double-edged process with equanimity as its goal; (v) disciplining thoughts and emotions to attain equanimity involves nurturing Virtue and cultivating a proper ethic of Hope. Boethius is thus addressing an aspect of epistemic resilience rooted in knowing which path to take in life, having a clear sense of orientation in life decisions and acquiring the knowledge and experience to do so.

Meister Eckhart's thesis *The Book of Divine* Consolation[77] is a mid-14th century work written as consolation for Queen Agnes of Hungary whose life was beset by tragic events. The focal point of the work is, of course, the individual human relationship with and to God. It is about making one's home in God, having an inner space that allows for an intimate encounter with God. Master Eckhart's point of reference as a life based on absolute faith in God demands a form of epistemic resilience relying on that "trusting relationship," in other words fiduciary resilience. In contrast to social resilience based on friendship, this is about a relationship to a higher, transcendent being, to the invisible Divine God, which engenders those human qualities, which can, if sought after be found in the divine corners of the human soul. Master Eckhart firmly believes it is imperative that we do not lose sight of the Absolute in life

---

77   Meister Eckhart, Selected Writings. Selected and translated by Oliver Davis. London: Penguin 1994. Abbreviation: "BDC".

particularly in adverse circumstances; only this will guide us in making the right decisions in times of crisis. In the final analysis, we have to ask ourselves what is of the *Highest* and utmost value in our lives? For it is only with an eye fixed on the Highest that we are able to act accordingly.

At the same time, in focusing our gaze on God we are fixing our eyes on the mystery God represents.[78] Strange as it may sound, it is this paradox of looking to veiled clarity that fortifies resilience, the ability to see and acknowledge what is secret. This capacity says Meister Eckhart, deepens that sense of Divine presence making it become clear that: suffering is the result of not keeping God before you at all times and in all things (BDC 58). This might sound too much for the human mind to digest, but does reflect the almost Stoic notion of keeping one's eye fixed on a goal no matter what the fates might throw at it to undermine resolve. One cornerstone of this thought is the image of the righteous man being steadfast in his resolve and Master Eckhart follows this approach in his belief that righteous persons will not allow themselves to be aggrieved—regardless what happens: the art of remaining unmoved in serenity and peace of heart is the sign of a good person (BDC 59). It is the sign of a weak heart when someone can go about his business without a care to the transiency of this world. We can actually detect a universal Buddhist motive here, the one of suffering:[79] suffering is the pain of clinging to notions of how things should be rather than how they are. If we insist on clinging to guile and not truth, we must expect to suffer pain, grief and sorrow. Things that are not from God are bitter and acrid, "nothing can reach the heart which does not first pass through the sweetness of God where it loses all its bitterness" (BDC 88).

Human beings, who want more than God is, have a false sense of priority leading to their suffering great pain. Only in letting go of morbid notions and the yoke of desire can inner space be created *for* God and the heart and mind of that person opened up to God. Eckhart understands those "poor in spirit" as being those who are "bereft" of spirit and consequently: "receptive to all spirit and the spirit of all spirits is God" (BDC 69). Poorness of spirit is, actually, the remedy for sadness since love, joy and peace are the fruits of the spirit. "Possessing nothing, being naked poor and empty, transforms nature. Emptiness draws water uphill (...)," (BDC 69). In other words the empty space of sadness and poorness is a vacuum which will be filled and it is suffering which fills it—it is that inner space every human needs to breathe and live, and

---

78   Cf., B. McGinn, The God Beyond God. Theology and Mysticism in the Thought of Meister Eckhart. *The Journal of Religion* 61,1 (1981) 1–19.

79   Cf., P. Coff, The Inner Journey: Reflections on the Awakening of Mind and Heart in Buddhism and Christianity. *Buddhist-Christian Studies* 11 (1991) 173–195.

the more exposed the soul is, the more able it is to comprehend God. Self-denial and kenosis are the only solution to life's tragedies Meister Eckhart concludes.

The "good" soul knows she owes her life to a Higher order and prays to God that God's will be done. The good person is endowed with immense inner strength based on her trust in God: "A good person should trust God, believe in him and be sure of him, knowing his goodness to be such that it is impossible for God with his goodness and love to permit any suffering or sorrow to befall someone unless they are either spared some greater suffering thereby or God wishes to give them more perfect consolation on earth to make something better out of the situation" (BDC 63).

Apart from the constant reminder to hold dear what is true and shun what is false, in the Christian tradition of battling against sin and resisting temptation, blessed in the conviction that God is on the side of she who suffers, Meister Eckhart also puts forward four singular strategies for tackling the onslaughts of fate: (i) in-depth analysis: misfortune does not happen by chance, even misfortune has a reason (BDC 59); as human beings we should know that nothing in nature can be destroyed unless is has been put there for the purpose of achieving something higher through suffering (BDC 89);[80] (ii) disciplining one's gaze: remember the Good which is in you;[81] (iii) a comparative perspective: think of those who are suffering more than you at this moment (BDC 61); (iv) a conjunctive perspective: think of what could have happened.

Meister Eckhart's *The Book of Divine Consolation* could be described as a guidebook even manual on how to strengthen epistemic resilience; he draws upon elements of the Stoic tradition and there are clear echoes of Buddhist thinking: suffering is the result of a misconceived over-adherence to certain rituals and habits; the only way to fight and overcome suffering is emptying oneself of self for God and clinging to that which is absolute as the sole requisite for life; this will pave the path of steadfastness in accordance with God's will, pursuing such a path is a clear sign of spiritual strength.

We can thus see that there are a range of reference points and indicators within epistemology, philosophy and spiritual traditions. Striving to lead a life in which one does not lose sight of the 'wider' picture of things despite the pitfalls and traps of everyday calamities has undoubtedly passed the test of time.

---

80   This echoes the metaphor of purification and cleansing—everything that we suffer, we do so for God's Will and this suffering will be made sweet through the sweetness of God (BDC 89).

81   More graphically expressed: "If someone who had lent me their jacket, fur coat and cloak took back their cloak, while leaving me the jacket and the fur coat in the cold, then I should properly be grateful to them and relieved" (BDC 75).

In striking such a path we need to pursue and practice our inner resources of orientation, availing ourselves of the spiritual and intellectual tools put at our disposal along the way. It should be mentioned at this point that the pursuit involves stepping across that threshold of theoretical knowledge thus entering the realm of wisdom; this notion of Wisdom is a key factor in reflecting upon epistemic resilience; a Cartesian analysis does not suffice; reflection demands more, it demands we take an in-depth look at both the basics, (the foundations of our lives) and our goals and objectives—where we want to go. Wisdom is the art of distinguishing what is essential from what is not and seeing the big picture. And this is a key to epistemic resilience—if we know what is important and have made this our own it cannot be taken away from us; not now and here, and not then and elsewhere, not in this place and not in a situation of displacement.

CHAPTER 3

Testimonies of Epistemic Resilience in Situations of Displacement

Having explored the concept of resilience and the concept of epistemic resilience I would now like to exemplify the term with three real life examples, three examples of serious displacement which will show that the capacity to be displaced is linked to epistemic resilience and that epistemic resilience is a force of existential value and life-shaping potential. Examples can "illustrate" as well as "demonstrate." This is to say we can "color" our understanding of epistemic resilience, but we can also "deepen" and even "change" it. I will look at the reflections on the (inner) sources of resilience in the works and lives of Ingrid Betancourt, Tiziano Terzani, and Francis Xavier Văn Thuân. All three experienced displacement, finding themselves in both inner and external spaces that they would not have chosen. They may exemplify the fact that a resilient person can see a situation of displacement as an invitation to deal with the essential questions of life; dispossession and displacement are able to intensify certain aspects of life.

3.1 Ingrid Betancourt: Inner Struggle in Captivity

One poignant example of displacement and epistemic resilience is that of Ingrid Betancourt: the Franco-Colombian politician who was held prisoner in the Colombian jungle by FAC rebels from February 2002 to July 2008—six and a half years. A candidate for the Presidency in Colombia, she was suddenly ripped from of her prosperous life and successful career when she was kidnapped. In her book *Even Silence Has an End* Betancourt describes those endless years in abduction and her battle to hold on to her own identity: "In abduction, you lose identity. Without freedom, we lose the compass to our soul. Without individuality, you question "who am I?"[1] Her testimony sketches her inner turmoil and agonising struggle to remain "I" regardless of what her captors did to her; she was determined to remain "unhurt," "inaccessible" and to

---

[1] I. Betancourt, Even Silence Has an End: My Six Years of Captivity in the Colombian Jungle. London: Penguin 2011. I use the following abbreviation for this edition "ESE".

© KONINKLIJKE BRILL NV, LEIDEN, 2017 | DOI 10.1163/9789004342453_005

do this she turned to her own inner resource of "reflection" (ESE 116),[2] clung to her own idea of self (ESE 6), would not afford herself the luxury of self-pity (ESE 9), and constantly devised new plans to escape after each attempt failed (ESE 78, 84, 134).

She knows that as a politician, educated in France, the rebels see her as a foreign middle-class, spoilt brat (ESE 516). In roll-call, she refuses to be reduced to an anonymous number on a list: "We had to count!" (the irony of the usage is particularly poignant) "I found this monstrous. We were losing our identity. They refused to call us by our names. We were nothing more than cargo (...)." Her comrades consider her to be foolishly arrogant in clinging to such minor details: "(...) but I refuse to be denigrated (...) words had a supernatural power, and I feared for our health, our mental balance, our spirits," (ESE 253). One day she discovers to her own horror that she is actually planning ways to murder one of her captors and knows she must overcome such thoughts: "Could I kill? Oh, yes, I could! (...) that afternoon under that wretched rain, I understood that I could be like them," (ESE 387). "The worst would not be to die; the worst would be to become something I abhorred" (ESE 389).[3]

She desperately clings to the dignity she has or has left and is determined, too, to fight for the most basic of human rights—those things we owe each other as fellow human beings against whatever odds, such as not to be forgotten; she calls upon her fellow inmates to observe a minute's silence for Pinchao who is brutally killed in his attempt to flee (ESE 513). At times she feels no better than an animal: "Little by little I was beginning to detach myself from both the small and the big things, for I did not want to be subjugated to my desires or my needs, because having lost the ability to satisfy them made me more a prisoner in my jailors' hand," (ESE 130).

As time passes and the pendulum swings violently between complete hopelessness and inner growth, she makes important discoveries about herself and her own resilience: "I was beginning to understand that humility (...) was the key. I'd got to the bottom of that wheel to understand" (ESE 390). In such conditions, you cannot hide from anyone, not even yourself; all your horrible failings and weaknesses are displayed for all to see: "but in captivity, I discovered my ego suffered the moment I was deprived of something I wanted, (...)

---

2   "I would not permit myself any thoughts at all of my own children" (ESE 116); "I was able to let go of all my thoughts of sadness, regret and uncertainty" (ESE 154).

3   Betancourt sees her struggle to keep her own identity as a battle of wits against the demands of the flesh. She is determined not to haggle over rations, times of day which brought out the worst in her: "I decided to monitor myself (...) I ended up doing just the opposite of what my good resolutions dictated. My only solace was that I had become aware of it" (ESE 297).

I observed a transformation of myself that I did not like. Deprived of every-thing (...) we had the misguided reflex to cling to cling to what was left," (ESE 228). Time is plague and resource: time to look at self—time in which one can only look at self and realize that there is always a choice that can be made, there are always obligations to self which must be kept.

Betancourt realizes that control—self control is imperative for survival as a human being: "(...) I still had the most important freedom of all, no one could take it away from me. That was the freedom to choose what kind of person I wanted to be," (ESE 554). With this comes too the realization that choices made can have a positive effect. We can create and construct our environment even when there seems to be no possibilities open to us. Betancourt notes at one point: "I felt it was time to change. Instead of trying to adapt to my rough conditions, I had to try to become a better person," (ESE 175f). And later: "I observed myself as I never had before, and I understood that spiritual fulfil-ment required a constancy and rigor that I needed to acquire," (ESE 175f).

The realization that we can actively impact our immediate surroundings and be positively affected in the process is linked with an understanding that limits and boundaries are not what they seem to be—there is always the boundlessness of inner space: choice is part of responsibility and responsi-bility is an important element of self-respect. Betancourt knows she does not want "to emerge from the jungle a shrivelled old woman, ravaged by acrimony and hate. I had to change—not adapt (...) I needed wings, I needed to be able to fly far away above this fiendish jungle that thought to transform us into cockroaches," (ESE 261). In using her freedom of choice she learns too the im-portance and value of gratitude. At the end of her fifth year in captivity she suggests they make a list of "all the nice things that have happened to us this year, to thank the heavens," (ESE 562), even though there seems little to be grateful for.

Similar as with Dietrich Bonhoeffer, we sense Betancourt is in awe of grati-tude in circumstances which would seem to be anything but gracious or wor-thy of gratitude. She makes every effort to express her thanks in the face of all that is undesirable—she can see and she can breathe, she is able to feel: "an interlude of joy, (...) a sad, fragile, fleeting joy," (ESE 126, 151). She understands that in keeping herself—mind and body—busy, she can overcome crippling boredom. She weaves belts and bands for her children's birthdays—making haste to be ready on time—well aware that her daughter will not be able to see or receive the make-shift gift. At Christmas she busies herself with mak-ing a nativity scene out of clay; she lovingly makes all the figures and feels re-warded when some of the rebels join in and help, contributing angels and even Christmas lights (ESE 169). Keeping busy also includes praying, and to help her pursue and cultivate regular prayer she makes herself a rosary out of old bits of nylon thread and buttons (ESE 174), she knows she will be better able to focus on prayer if she has something tangible she can hold in her hands.

Betancourt knows she has to keep her physical body fit too and "establishes a methodology" to this aim: "my solitude became a sort of liberation," (ESE 188f). She has little idea of what exercises she might do and in the absence of a manual she "practiced the acrobatics she learned as a child," (ESE 189). Being busy is being active in mind, body and spirit: "In my boredom I read the Bible (…) I would reread passages, and I would discover why they had stayed with me. It was like finding chinks, secret passages, links to other thoughts (…) The Bible became a fascinating world of codes, insinuations and hidden meanings." She meditates upon what she has read while weaving and "thanks to manual activity, my mind entered a state of meditation, and I could reflect on what I had read while my hands were moving," (ESE 140).

Gradually Betancourt's world begins to grow from the inside out; she reflects, ruminates on words, passages she has read in the Bible—this is a core activity in cultivating interiority, especially if done in connection with some manual, mechanical task. She disciplines her mind and thoughts, not allowing herself to dwell on toxic memories or notions, in doing this she is strengthening her own inner resource of resilience. She constructs interiority by focusing on those memories of loved ones shifting her focus away from the her plight in the present, sharpening her wits and stretching her imagination: "I pictured myself leaving (…) I would go straight to papa (…) I would surprise him (…) he would be sitting in his green leather armchair," (ESE 62). Although physical pain is unbearable, the pain in her heart from not being able to forget is much, much worse: "it was the pain in my heart that was aroused, for I was incapable of letting go of my past life, a life I so loved and was no longer mine," (ESE 164). After yet another failed attempt to escape she is able to look into her innermost being and find inner peace and serenity. "They would punish us. Of course (…) that no longer frightened me. I would never give up," (ESE 138); her sense of inner identity grows as she actively works on constructing a meta-level from which she can look at herself and her life: "I observed myself from within, measuring my strength and resistance not according to my ability to fight back but rather to submit to their blows, like a ship that is battered by the tides yet will not sink," (ESE 15). Such power can only come from within, from an inner space that resists destructive forces of displacement.

Betancourt realizes the additional pain she will suffer if she allows 'outside occurrences' to touch her inner self: "I knew in this abominable jungle I had to detach myself from everything to avoid more suffering," (ESE 176), to maintain the interiority she has attained—this includes relationships with fellow

prisoners and guards; it includes too trust—who to trust with what? She refuses to be lulled into a false sense of security even when the reward is tempting, e.g., the chance to send a personal message to her family: ("What I do not
accept is that in addition they manipulate my voice and my thoughts," ESE
180). At the end of a day she goes back over all that has happened, what she
calls *circular thinking*: "I would stop to examine certain moments, I reflected
on the meaning of words such as prudence and humility, (...) I was discovering another way of living, a life based less in action and more in introspection,"
(ESE 190).

Any books she happens to come across she regards as a hidden treasure;
an encyclopaedic dictionary is a "luxury" which she uses to "travel" and break
through the confines of the barbed-wire fence. After browsing randomly, she
develops a more methodological approach to the way she reads and studies:
"following the logic of a treasure hunt. (...) art, religion, medicine, philosophy,
history, aircraft, war heroes," (ESE 188). The dictionary, another prime find was:
"my university in a box (...). This book was vital to me, because it enabled me
to have a short-term goal and cleared me of the underlying guilt inherent in my
condition, that of squandering the best years of my life," (ESE 321). She recounts
her childlike impatience in desperately wanting to read the Harry Potter books
which make their miraculous appearance in the camp—a source or intellectual nourishment which is shared out by means of a strict rota schedule. The
"power" of the imagination creates alternatives to the reality of here-and-now:
"Our thoughts bore us far away (...) beyond the barriers of thick vegetation
(...) to the mystical North, where it is written that God dwells, and where I
imagined he could hear He could hear the silent quest of our hearts only He
could answer," (ESE 170).

The imagination puts distance between self and the agonies of everyday;
imagination can bring some memories so close as to make them seem real
and in the present, thus in recalling past Christmases spent with her family,
Betancourt is able to imagine what Christmas was—is—like, all the more so
since her family cannot know how she is suffering—that gives her solace. At
the same time, imagination can keep things at a distance, give memories a
third-party observer perspective, providing peace of mind and "quiet happiness": "I saw myself as some strange creature, an entity totally distinct from
my present self," (ESE 196f). The power generated by the power of the imagination has strong Janus attributes in that it enables one to look both forward
and backward; it enables her to 'invent projects' to work on together for the
future, *after* captivity (cf. ESE 251). It keeps hope from fading, Betancourt tells
her warder that: "It is my duty to regain my freedom," (ESE 121). This mindset
allows her to distance herself from her enforced suffocating environment and,

set it in a wider context with wider coordinates, the struggle in surviving the here and now; it means she can retain a level of personal pride and dignity which her gaolers cannot take away from her.

The capacity to even consider plans is in itself a source of energy: "It would take us (…) years to get out of this jungle, and that we would have to learn to live in it with no resources but our ingenuity," (ESE 322). Learning to live on ingenuity alone, which we might also term 'hope', is a wonderful and necessary resource for survival, but, at the same time, it poses a threat, because if too much energy is focused on 'hope' alone, then all seeming signs of release which come to nothing can sap one of energy and willpower, and increase the risk of becoming a malleable, manipulative toy in the hands of the rebels. Ingrid Betancourt discovers this in a conversation with one of the Indian guerrillas: "But the Indian had started my dreaming, by pronouncing the word freedom, he'd opened a box that I'd kept double-locked."[4]

Although she knows that what he is saying is all lies, this word *freedom* unleashes a "flood of raving visions that submerged me. I could see my children, my bedroom, my dog, (…) I could smell my mom's perfume, (…) How could I shove all that back into oblivion? I wanted so badly to become myself again," (ESE 374). These images of *box, double-locked, flood*, paint a picture of the inner space she has created to survive; it is space rich in images which have to be tamed and not allowed to run wild, at the same time, it is a personal archive, reservoir of what has been carefully collected through life and must thus be guarded, treasured and looked after.

A further crucial resource as building block of interiority and survival is memory as a door to a treasure of inner space; memory allows for recollection and retrospection. "I drew from an enormous reserve of memories, feeling thankful for the incredible store of happiness I had accumulated over the years," (ESE 186). She is shaken beyond measure when she discovers that a prison camp is to be erected within the 'prison' of the jungle, she has to continually remind herself that she is not a criminal and that she is being held illegally: "I needed this constant reminder to help me not to give in, not to forget that it was my duty to rebel," (ESE 227). She keeps her own thoughts to herself, remaining silent to protect her own self-esteem, and perhaps not to burden others with detailed analyses of her own sufferings: "If you share certain things, they will stay alive in other people's minds," (ESE 237f), so the most "gracious and appropriate" action is to keep quiet. Having said that, it is vital that collective experience is shared in memory swapping as this is the adhesive

---

4 "The Indio had sold me hope in a box. For days I was floating in bliss, the expectation of happiness, being more enjoyable than the happiness itself" (ESE 375).

which holds communities together: "we indulgently listened to one another. (...) Sharing slices of our lives with the others let us see our memories as if we were staring at a movie screen," (ESE 261). Words, poems she has learned by heart allow her to enter her "secret garden" from where she can observe the inhumanities of the world at a safe distance (ESE 55). This too is an essential contribution to constructing sound interiority; in learning things by heart she knows and remembers the lesson taught her by her father with his mesmerizing recitals: "he was arming me for life."

Powers of imagination and memory can extend perspectives beyond horizons to hitherto unknown en*lightened* views of the world which contribute towards the cultivation of inner space. This inner space is "furnished" with thoughts, with hopes, with memories, with all these threads that make a person experience connectedness with a wider world. Notwithstanding, the shifts in mood and mental state which Betancourt moves through underline the ambivalence of thoughts dwelt upon: locked in 'The Cage' she prays in an attempt "to find an explanation, some meaning behind my misfortune. "*Why, why?*" (ESE 168). At the same time, she gains incredible power in her conviction that there is no such thing as chance; this is supported by her deep faith in God. Betancourt turns to prayer for solace, help and guidance again and again (ESE 150f), gradually over the seven years her *weltbild* changes: "I no longer believed in coincidence. Ever since I had been abducted, (...) I had been able to look back over my life like someone who has too much time on her hands. I'd concluded you had to be patient and wait for the purpose of things to become visible. And then coincidence ceased to exist," (ESE 439). And this realization opens a door to a different perception of personal experience: "If God didn't want me to be free, I had to accept that I wasn't ready for freedom. This notion became a lifebuoy," (ESE 466) and opens the door to even wider horizons than imagination; this sense of vastness and expanse gives energy, Betancourt describes the happiness she feels when she hears Pope John Paul on the radio pleading for the release of the prisoners (ESE 176). In moments of greatest distress it is the knowledge of and faith in a world beyond the barbed wire which keeps her going: "with each breathe I suffered, I could not go on, but I had to go on—there were the others, all the others, my children, Mom." (ESE 226).

News from this outside real and remembered world becomes more than special, for Betancourt it is "sacred," even news not about self but about her fellow prisoners. News of the death of loved ones is particularly painful and Betancourt receives news of her father's death while she is held captive: "At the beginning of December, it was Jorge's mother who had passed away then Lucho's, and now Orlando's (...). Without their mothers, my companions felt adrift, dispossessed of the women who had safeguarded the memory of their lives. Now they were projected into a space where to be forgotten by others was to enter the worst of prisons," (ESE 331).

Thus the reciprocal power of memory—of remembering and being remembered—is a key resource of resilience. To know you have not been forgotten, validates your existence in some powerful way: it is uplifting to know—to remember—that there are important people in our lives even if they are beyond our immediate, tangible and social confines. A piece of paper with a letter from home suddenly becomes priceless in the absence of the one who wrote it. Betancourt reads a letter from her mother over and over: "I clung to (it) as to my life," (ESE 341f).

At the very end when she is reunited with her mother, and her years of captivity are over, she has mastered the years of displacement. They have both mastered displacement. They are "survivors, not victims" as commonly depicted in resilience research. She descends the steps of the plane slowly: "We embraced with the energy of victory. A victory that we alone could understand because it was a victory over despair, over oblivion, over resignation, a victory solely over ourselves," (ESE 594). The clear contours of structure in Ingrid Betancourt's epistemic resilience shine through; resilience built on a sense of identity and via a keen sense of utter displacement, understanding the need for self-control, the importance of clinging to choice and sense of responsibility, the need to be physically and mentally active, an awareness of transcendence via powers of imagination and memory.

3.2   Tiziano Terzani: Epistemic Resources in Illness

Displacement can also be experienced in illness, an experience as explicit reminder of a person's vulnerability. Tiziano Terzani was a much-loved journalist and Asia correspondent for "*Der Spiegel*". He was a highly educated man-of-the-world, a globe-trotter, a cosmopolitan, a person "in chosen exile;" there was little he had not experienced in his life. He has constantly been "in between." However, this all meets with an abrupt end when Terzani is told that he has terminal cancer and in his book "*Un Altro Giro Di Giostra*" ("*one more go on the merry-go-round*"), he describes the trials of his illness, of being personally, professionally and socially displaced and the journey illness as displacement takes him on in his last attempt to discover resistance and resilience, and the realization he has to cultivate his own epistemic resources to do so.[5]

---

5   T. Terzani, Un Altro Giro Di Giostra. Milan: Longanesi 2004. I will use the abbreviation "TG" throughout.

Yet again, he finds himself "in between" and displaced "in exile," but in a wholly different sense and way.

Terzani recognizes that this unique condition of terminal cancer is his one and only (last) chance to make a new start, and he devotes the time and energy left to him to do just this: He had now "the peace and quiet to take stock of my life, set new priorities and make major decisions," he felt that he was liberated and could focus on his new challenge without being distracted.[6] He decides to spend three weeks in an Ashram, learn the rudiments of Sanskrit and basically take time out to think about life's big questions: who am I? He gives up his name and becomes a nomad, a 'non-entity;" this really is a new beginning since he had spent a good deal of his life trying to *make* a name for himself. He changes his outer appearance and even has his moustache shaved off. He sets out on this new phase of life by asking himself: what can—what should-I learn? He asked himself whether perhaps this diagnosis of terminal disease had a secret message attached to it: "perhaps I needed to be ill in order to really understand the message!"[7]

Terzani instinctively senses there is something radical at work, and while he is adamant in not allowing himself to be pulled back to his everyday routine, a life with a treadmill of deadline,[8] at the same time there is a strange longing for safety, for that past life, perhaps. But he does not kid himself that there is an eject button sending him back to that old life, his old self ("tornato a essere quello di prima;" TG 30). This extreme and undesired challenge of being totally displaced must be relevant for the here and now as well as for the future, whatever it may bring. This displacement, alias illness is that "point of no return" in his life, and yet it is a new beginning, is indeed the beginning of something new! It is the opportunity to cultivate an inner self which becomes meaningful and necessary, it is an opportunity to try to find—try to hear the melody of the inner life ("la melodia della vita dentro;" TG 23). His sense of interiority stretches and grows in the sudden realization that his spirit is free regardless of circumstances; even if his body is incarcerated, his willpower never can be. He looks back in history to the Tibetan monk Palden Gyatso, who was tortured and imprisoned in solitary confinement for thirty years but survived with his

---

6 "Così potevo, con calma, . . . fare i miei conti, ristabilire le mie priorità e prendere le decisioni necessarie" (TG 09); "Volevo mettere a fuoco la mia mente, non essere distratto da nulla e da nessuno" (TG 10); "Col cancro mi ero conquistato il diritto di non sentirmi più in dovere di nulla, di non avere più sensi di colpa. Finalmente ero libero. Totalmente libero" (TG 14).

7 "Forse c'era un messaggio segreto in questa malattia: m'era venuta perché capissi qualcosa!" (TG 51).

8 "Era l'ultima cosa che volevo fare. Tornare a vivere come prima? Ricadere nella routine?" (TG 149.

spirit unbroken (TG 35). This shining example is all the more meaningful for
Terzani since it underpins his own belief in and practice of meditation (TG 47).

Terzani feels his condition—terminal cancer—is both exodus and a journey
(TG 14); the metaphor of the journey suggests moving forward, growth, healing,
and change and transformation; a journey forces you to take your leave of the
known, it takes you to a new destination and the experiences made along the
way, knitting a sweater of resilience and getting you to that destination—final
port of call—are more meaningful and consequential than the arrival itself.
In setting out into unknown territory we invariably say our 'farewells' in the
hope that those leaving and those left behind will *fare well* and that nothing
untoward will happen to cause injury and prevent return. Being *on the road,
abroad, out and about, en route* can only be really experienced in the doing,
in the going, in "knowledge by acquaintance;" a voyageur is not an armchair
traveller who gathers her 'knowledge' from third hand "novel" accounts and
narrations: there is a disparity between what is related and what is felt, only
he who has travelled can recount his own story and history, his own narrative,
made all the more meaningful when observed in a greater, more meaningful
context, especially now that he has embarked on a journey that brings him to
the brink of his mortality.[9]

Ironically it is this kaleidoscope image of the journey which allows Terzani
to travel back through his life's history and look at the questions which "move"
us all. Terzani is both raconteur and master of metaphor—as the title of the
book bears witness to; his life has been like a ride on a merry-go-round (a
metaphor which came to him suddenly in a sleepless night while in hospital).
He stretches the boundaries of this metaphor still further: he has so far successfully lived the life of a fare-dodger, constantly catching free rides, and now
someone asks to see his ticket, to check if he has paid his "fare": "The ticket
collector was here and with any bit of luck I would pay what I owed and with
even more luck might soon be jumping back on board for yet another go on
the merry-go-round."[10]

Yet another image Terzani battles with is that of the intruder, the unwanted
guest, that "interior visitor" (which sounds as political as it does surreal!), that
"interno visitatore," the tumor in his body (TG 17); he is faced with reconciling

---

9   "Ho deciso di raccontarne la storia, innanzitutto perché so quanto è incoraggiante
     l'esperienza di qualcuno che ha fatto già un pezzo della strada per chi si trovasse ora ad
     affrontarla; e poi perché, a pensarci bene, dopo un po' il viaggio non era più in cerca di
     una cura per il mio cancro, ma per quella malattia che è di tutti: la mortalità" (TG 24).
10   "Bene: ora passava il controllore, pagavo i dovuto e, se mi andava bene, magari riuscivo
     anche a fare . . . un altro giro di giostra" (TG 10).

himself with this "visitor" and perhaps getting to know it better, becoming more acquainted with it. He has to move over, dis-place part of self to make "inner space" for this visitor, thus an experience of displacement is transformed into one of not giving up but of appropriating space. A further image is that of the body as costume—a costume leased to him at birth, to be returned to the owner at the appropriate time in the future (TG 35). These images help Terzani to gain both distance and closeness at the same time, and to place his life in a wider context.

He begins to understand that his own 'little' life is a piece of a bigger jig-saw puzzle rooted in an even wider context, he discovers 'absolute' coordinates, universal denominators, common datum points;[11] he remembers a colleague who had suffered a similar fate.[12] Terzani tries to develop his skills in meta reflection, he tries to stand back and look at himself from the outside, an exercise that can be learnt.[13] Thus, he is constantly trying to perceive and communicate the notion of common destiny; he likes collecting stories about the successes and failures of therapies, cures and recovery (TG 20). He starts looking at and thinking about his life as a complete entity; he goes over individual episodes, phases, ways he does things like what and when he eats, how he breathes, he studies his dreams and those 'bad' habits we all have which doctors tell us cause cancer. Surveying and quantifying his life thus helps him to gain a new perspective which he would not have achieved without the cancer: none of us are just flesh and blood, there is something else besides, but we don't bother about this *something else*, we neither look after it, nor care for it. We are so caught up with satisfying our senses with every imaginable sound, perfume, image that our souls are starving to death and dying of thirst.[14] This widening of the human horizon melts away the icy cold, jagged arrogance of reason (TG 290); prejudices of and in the mind dissipate and disappear.

---

11   "Passai ancora una notte in ospedale, da solo, a riflettere. Pensai a quanti altri prima di me, in quelle stesse stanze, avevano avuto simili notizie e trovai quella compagnia in qualche modo incoraggiante" (TG 09).

12   "... un paio di anni prima l'amico aveva avuto lo stesso tipo di malanno ed era sopravvissuto. L'andai a trovare a Delhi e gli chiesi consiglio" (TG 12).

13   "Riuscire a guardarsi con gli occhi di un sé fuori da sé serve sempre. Ed è un esercizio, questo, che si può imparare" (TG 9); for most of his life as a journalist, Terzani had spent his time watching and observing others, now for a change, he found himself observing a life that concerned him even more, namely, his own (TG 13).

14   "Se oltre al corpo siamo anche qualcos'altro, quel qualcosa non viene però nutrito bene, non viene annaffiato. Mentre i nostri sensi sono continuamente rimpinzati di tutto quel che possono desiderare—suoni, odori, cose da vedere—l'anima, se esiste, fa la fame, è assetata" (TG 289).

Terzani does his utmost to retain control over what he does and does not do on a daily basis, over the things he knows will happen in the course of one day or one week. The doctor advises him to stick to a daily routine, to take regular exercise and not give up his early morning workout (TG 34); habits are "home-building," necessities in an exodus experience; strangely enough this control mechanism is intensified by handing over the controls—so to speak—to the medical experts in charge; he found comfort in the dynamic of unquestioningly obeying all they commanded him to do.[15] Here, too, we find that metaphor of funambulism; one important task on his agenda is finding and keeping some sort of balance, equilibrium that will withstand the onslaughts of everyday (TG 114). The Ashram with its orderly and bright daily rhythm (*regolato, sereno ritmo di vita*) gives him stabilizing support (TG 407).

In a similar manner, he strives to structure his day around certain rituals, for example in California the encounter with the ocean became his daily ritual (TG 272). He extends this ritual of what he himself can control to fortify his body, too with the exuberating experience of never having been this close to his own body before. Like the tight-rope walker, he has to learn to keep his body under control and not allow himself to be totally dictated to by its needs and reactions.[16] This concern with control is chiefly the concern about how he can strengthen his spirit; he asks the doctors if there is anything he can do, spiritual exercises or such, so that the straw he is clinging to will weather the storm: "*perché l'arbusto a cui ero aggrappato resistesse?*" (TG 15). In focusing on self-control, he can, of course, either resist or embrace physical and mental displacement, he can keep the idea of the suffering self and being victim at bay; he has the choice to either play the role of victim, to the limit or to reject it entirely and "instinctively I chose the latter."[17]

Terzani finds strength in coming to terms with a displaced view, an 'outsider' view of cancer and terminal illness: He realizes that a healthy person cannot possibly understand a sick person and that is how it should be. No matter how a person deals with her own fate, a sensation of sluggish inertia (the result of physical weakness) can only be felt by the patient and never by the healthy visitor, nor can a healthy person feel that composure and equanimity no matter

---

15   "C'era, in questo credere nei medici, nel seguire le loro istruzioni, qualcosa di consolante che, avevo l'impressione, m'era di grande aiuto" (TG 34).

16   "Mai avevo dovuto guardare così da vicino il mio corpo e soprattutto imparare a mantenerne il controllo, a esserne padrone, a non farmi troppo dominare dalle sue richieste, i suoi dolori, le sue palpitazioni e i suoi urti di vomito" (TG 13).

17   "D'altro canto che alternative avevo, a parte quella di fare o non fare la vittima? Per istinto preferivo non farla" (TG 51).

how hard she tries to sympathize and share in the patient's suffering. In fact, quite the reverse is true: a healthy human being will interpret such an attitude as resignation and will as a result feel duty-bound to help or save the patient. But there is a logic in this seeming madness and one part of that might be that he or she is preparing herself mentally for what lies ahead, that inevitable end.[18]

This admission of a gaping chasm between the world of the fit and healthy and that of the sick and suffering enables Terzani to claim a special status in his condition as patient and at the same time it equips him to be in a better position to deal with the wise words of advice, demands (both reasonable and unreasonable) put upon him by those around him in that other world. Realizing he has a right to a special status gives him the strength to fight for his own way of experiencing life which is contrary to the ongoing conspiracy between well-meaning friends and relatives, people who are determined to convince you that your condition it is only temporary, you will soon get over it and that recovery is the most wonderful thing you can possibly look forward to. And they are all involved in this conspiracy: the doctors and nurses, family and friends; all with the best intentions in the world and all very worried that there is someone who does not want to be "normal" again.[19] Terzani does not want to go back to life as it was before, and resists attempts to put him back, re-place him in his old life and feels he has a right to refuse it.

Terzani makes a new start, he takes time and effort to develop and deepen friendships; his stamina is fortified through these close relationships, through confidence and trust. These are social sources of resilience, strengthened by his inner attitudes. He also gains strength through his own inquisitiveness and love of the Arts, through living in a vast world he can enter any time he pleases. Art remains a constant in this displacement process. Art is a language he makes his own: it seeks neither profit nor gain, does not have to complete some task, serves no real function and achieves no goals—he ponders. Art consoles us, elates our soul, gives us orientation. Art heals. We are not merely the sum of what we eat and the air we breathe. We are the tales we have heard, the fairy

---

18   "Chi è sano non può capire chi è malato ed è giusto che sia così. C'è nel malato, qualunque sia il suo atteggiamento nei confronti della malattia, un torpore fatto di debolezza, ma anche di serenità, che il sano, pur con tutta la simpatia, non può provare. Anzi, il sano prende quell'atteggiamento per rassegnazione e crede sia suo dovere aiutare il malato a combatterlo. Ma la malattia ha una sua logica, forse anche quella di preparare psicologicamente chi l'ha addosso alla sua possible fine" (TG 70).

19   "... perché attorno al malato si crea una sorta di benevola congiura di tutti quelli che gli vogliono far apparire la malattia come uno stato transitorio, passato, e il ritorno al ‚prima‘ come la cosa più auspicabile. E i congiurati sono tutti: i medici, la famiglia, i migliori amici. Tutti in buona fede. Tutti preoccupati che uno non voglia tornare ‘normale'" (TG 149).

stories we were told at bedtime and dreamt about, the books we read and the music we listen to, and we are the feelings inspired by a painting, a sculpture, a poem.[20] Art requires fantasy and challenges our powers of imagination—a major source of resistance: what we all need is fantasy; we need it to turn our lives around, to free us from those rigid ruts we have become entrenched in and which we know do us no good.[21]

His inquisitiveness drives him to want to find out more about natural cures and complementary medicine: he uses Eastern wisdom and his own personal experience as his foundation stone. In his thirst and quest for alternative points of view and perspectives he is reinforcing his own powers of resistance. During a visit to Dharamsala, where the Dalai Lama lives in exile, he writes: "*A volte cambiare punto di vista serve*" (TG 219: "A change of perspective can often help a lot"), and that is the key to cultivating epistemic resilience. He consciously rethinks and in conversations with his son Folco goes over his life—life, its lessons, its meaning, its depth. This matter of "putting matters into perspective" and "finding a wider horizon" have helped him throughout his life with its many adventures, but especially in times of crises.[22]

In this long and detailed testimony, seven moments in strengthening resilience stand out—that attitude of mind which is prepared for a new beginning and in which there is no going back; the leitmotif of life as journey incorporating all the "places visited"—life's expectations and experiences the new path taken; attitude of mind as the ability to see life in its entirety, perceiving the greater picture of which it is a part and the role of one's own giving, taking and letting be; actively schooling one's control over the structures, rhythms and values of one's life, and strengthening the foundations we build our lives upon; having a realistic down-to-earth attitude in the way we tackle and deal with the challenges we come up against; the supporting role of friendship and mutual trust evolving out of those friendships; being inquisitive and clinging to an unbiased attitude, cultivating one's own powers of imagination and a love of Art in all its forms. This openness to life's tangible and intangible treasures allows "displacement" to be transformed into an invitation to personal

---

20   "L'arte ci consola, ci solleva, l'arte ci orienta. L'arte ci cura. Noi non siamo solo quel che mangiamo e l'aria che respiriamo. Siamo anche le storie che abbiamo sentito, le favole con cui ci hanno addormentati da bambini, i libri che abbiamo letto, la musica che abbiamo ascoltato e le emozioni che un quadro, una statua, una poesia ci hanno dato" (TG 138).

21   "Quello di cui oggi abbiamo tutti bisogno è la fantasia per ripensare la nostra vita, per uscire dagli schemi, per non ripetere ciò che sappiamo essere sbagliato" (TG 246).

22   T. Terzani, La Fine è il mio inizio. Un padre racconta al figlio il grande viaggio della vita. Milan: Longanesi 2006.

growth, thus adapting the person to the new challenges. All these moments are decisively linked with those inner factors of attitude of mind, personal convictions, feelings and sense of judgment.

3.3 Francis Xavier Văn Thuân: Living Out of Hope

The third example I would like to present brings us back to the displacement of imprisonment. It teaches the lesson that the capacity to be displaced cannot be separated from hope; contours of hope as resource of epistemic resilience can be clearly identified in the life and works of Francis Xavier Văn Thuân.[23] First Bishop, later ordained Cardinal, he was invited by Pope John Paul II to preach the Spiritual Easter Exercises in Rome in 2000, in the light of Xavier Văn Thuân having undergone such extreme life experiences. Thus it was that the Vietnamese priest was able to conclude these Exercises with:

> Exactly twenty-four years ago on March 18, 1976 (...). I was taken by force from my residence in Cay Vong and put in solitary confinement. (...) Twenty-four years ago I never would have imagined that today, on exactly the same date, I would conclude preaching the spiritual exercises in the Vatican (TH xix).

It is against this background that even "against all hope" miracles can and do happen if we are able to hope, cling to this hope and cultivate it actively which is exactly what Francis Văn Thuân *chose* to do.

Recently nominated Bishop of Saigon he was arrested in 1975 (taken away from his place by force) and would spend the next 13 years in prison of which 9 years were to be in solitary confinement. He was then expelled from Vietnam in 1991 having been under house arrest since 1988. He continued to work in the Vatican until he died in 2002. If one word could sum up his life's works it would be: Hope. This is the thread running through all his writings and spiritual works. In his paraenetical notes and prayers written during imprisonment and in later Exercises in which he draws on the memories and experiences of imprisonment, Văn Thuân grapples with the meaning of Hope. I would like to consider and pursue his discoveries. Hope relies on strict discipline of mind which requires: i) obedience, gratitude and joy, goals; ii) hard work, a sense of the here and now; iii) reasons, trust; iv) signs.

---

23   I use the following texts by Francis Văn Thuân, The Road to Hope. A Gospel from Prison. Boston, Mass 2001 (RH); idem, Testimony of Hope. Boston, Mass 2000 (TH); idem, Prayers of Hope. Boston, Mass 2002 (PH).

(i) Hope is strengthened in the way we master our thoughts. Here, we could imagine thoughts to be furniture of our inner space, ways of furnishing our interiority. There is choice and freedom involved in the furniture we imagine. Like the circus trainer we have to learn to control the tiger of our own inner will (RH 85). Văn Thuân uses this image to underline the importance of directing Hope towards a fixed goal and not allowing it to be led astray by volatile folly, choosing to be obedient—choosing to obey than being obeyed. Rather like the tiger, it is a disciplined will which is strong. Likewise, spending too much time dwelling upon the negative aspects of life can only lead to complete despair; I must actively and deliberately take steps to prevent this and: "put my trust in your love and abandon myself to you" (PH 7). We may all have a goal we wish to strive for but it demands being fearless, not dillydallying along the way and not giving up at the first obstacle (RH 9; RH 65). Not only is it unwise to spend too much time thinking about our failures, but we will never be able to gain renewal since: we are always in need of beginning again. We always have to be aiming at our conversion if we do, our hearts will grow old and we will lose all hope without love (cf. PH 31; RH 39, RH 149).

It is an immature attitude of mind which would tell us we cannot do or change anything, a weak "I'm-made-like-that-I-can't-help-it" perspective will prevent us becoming true children of God; we do have a choice, and we can do something (RH 47). Hope cannot wither if we know we have to constantly "reconstruct and reinforce"—let go of the past (PH 88f), begin again (PH 90f). Văn Thuân discovers the potential destructiveness of nostalgia, of a sentimental longing for the way things have been in a world where history is built on the dynamics of change. There is the possibility of growth precisely because we cannot stay in the same inner space forever, we need to, have to be displaced somewhere along the way if we are to move forwards and develop.

"Holiness is continuously joyful," but this does not come unbidden, or by chance, it has to be consciously cultivated and tended to daily. Hope and joy are equal (and essential) travelling companions (RH 119). Hope requires a coordinates which can be chartered and steered towards; hope has to have a definite destination; travelling without point and purpose can only end in calamity. The point and purpose of the journey—of hope in exile—is a source of renewed vigor, and strength needs to overcome the storms of fear and anxiety (cf. RH 9).

Fearlessness is a vital tool in tackling one's own notions and thoughts; metaphorically speaking Văn Thuân underlines the need to be aware of "opportunities to make sacrifice" in our everyday lives instead of complaining of the burden and load we think we are bearing. A turn around in thought is a turn around in attitude; fear can be transformed into fearlessness via sacrifice.[24] Văn Thuân knows that we need to "step beyond" what we hear on the radio or read in the papers which might dishearten us fully: any news we hear we should put before God in "heartfelt" prayer (RH 145) and the most useful tool in this regard is to contemplate "eternity"—putting and seeing things in perspective (RH 159f; cf. RH 222).[25] This should not be an excuse for adopting the "I-can't-help-it" attitude outlined above, we must remember that: "Perhaps I am only a grain of sand, but every grain has its own place" (PH 9),[26] and this will give our life meaning and direction, all the more so if we can see ourselves as part of the narrative of a wider human genealogy, knowing that: "we are part of a history greater than we are" (TH 4), there are those that have gone before and those who will come after us pursuing the same commitment. This knowledge of eternity is a source of strength for our own temporal lives; my life may be short but it is different from any other and as such can make a "difference", be a sign since "a sign is a witness," the sign may be silent, it may only demand being silently present, but therein lies its power (PH 24).

Văn Thuân firmly believes that a single human, one single saintly being can make a huge difference to society because a saint is not only able to see beyond her own limits but is like a guiding star for others, she "indicates the way that leads to God" (cf. PH 72; cf. TH 59).[27] Francis Văn Thuân also uses the image of the *salt of the earth* in describing the role of mission and those called upon to bring hope to those "in the midst of a humanity that has lost hope" (RH 217). When a saint relinquishes everything "then the authenticity of (*his*) interior life will be evident to others" (RH 19), a saint will draw on her own innermost resources and find nourishment for her own spirituality of hope.

---

24   An allegorical view of the world can be expressed as follows: "If you were being tortured, you could adopt one of two attitudes: 'This person is destroying me', or 'By this person I am becoming a sacrifice'" (RH 33). Similarly, when he was taken captive and on board a ship with other captives: "I understood that at this point, on this ship, in this prison, was my most beautiful cathedral, and that these prisoners, without exception, were the people of God entrusted to my pastoral care" (TH 79); an allegorical view of the world is at the same time a Eucharistic view of the world, too. He finds comfort in a Eucharistic Christ (TH 133), suffering is not the defeat it is often made out to be, but in thinking of the death of Jesus on the cross it is the most important moment imaginable (TH 205).

25   For the believer death is not "a void of darkness" but a fulfilment of lifelong hope (RH 155).

26   The purpose of life becomes all the more meaningful in knowing that the Holy Spirit "can use any kind of person as an instrument in his grace" (TH 177). The "finest service you can render to God" and the greatest source of hope is to help others nurture their own faith in God (RH 140).

27   An important lesson lies in martyrdom—cf., TH 107.

One particularly nourishing resource for hope is gratitude; hope and gratitude are inextricably linked since gratitude springs from that self-same allegorical perspective of the world. Văn Thuân is able to teach a communist
policeman hymns because he had asked Văn Thuân to help him brush up his
Latin. The policeman sings the hymns and Francis Văn Thuân finds strength
in hearing them sung: he realizes that the Holy Spirit is using a communist
policeman to help a weak imprisoned bishop pray (TH 122). Văn Thuân does
in fact begin to wonder about all the gifts we all receive free, each day and yet
we never think to give thanks, never think to express our gratitude (cf. PH 12);
gratitude should also be shown for the mentors, role models and uplifting
people we meet in our lives who give us the strength to go on (TH 59). Văn
Thuân cites countless examples of things and people he is grateful to and for:
he is grateful for being able to receive Holy Communion (TH 131), and thankful for the strangest of experiences such as the fish wrapped in an old copy
of the *Osservatore romano* which he is given by a policewoman while he is
under house arrest: this newspaper would have been confiscated at the post
office and sent along with other papers to the market place as packing material. These few sheets of paper were more nourishing for his hope than any fish
could be, for he was reminded that he was still part of a worldwide congregation of fellow believers (TH 155).

Sources of gratitude such as these are usually stored away in our memories
and can be picked out and perused at will: in this way thoughts and memories
enabled Francis Văn Thuân to consciously and systematically build his own
congregation by means of his 'hall of spiritual memories' even in displacement. He remembers St. Paul, while in prison like himself, had written letters
to various members of the congregation, and so he does as Paul did and begins
to also write down his thoughts for a world outside of his cell inviting them to
share in his insights (TH 56).

(ii) Hope is hard work and demanding in control and perseverance; it has
to be firmly focused and well anchored; hope demands constant attention
and regular prayer; in Văn Thuân's language, "the person of hope is a person
of prayer" (RH 221). It is worth noting at this point that it is not only inner
hope which needs care and attention but also those "silent depths of being"
which nurture hope for it is in the "secret recesses" of the heart and mind that
"important projects" are born (RH 117). For such projects to become reality
and bear fruit, it is vital we remain in the hope of here and now—it is only
by remaining steadfast in *now* that we are not drawn into the pitfalls of past
memory or the unrealities of the future: holiness is built in the present and
this is why we should "treasure the present moment" (PH 111; RH 187). With
this in mind, we will not put off what can be done now in this moment of

time; if we are aware of the moment and live in that same moment, we will be equipped to deal with the same (TH 57).

Hope is an adventure which begins *now* regardless of place or displacement and we should be aware that this is the only time we have available to us (TH 51). Experiencing the present moment in prison was especially different: "I no longer had a schedule; I experienced the truth of the Vietnamese proverb: One day in prison is worth a thousand autumns in freedom." Imprisonment is one long moment waiting for freedom (TH 52). At the same time he learns that it is no good sitting back and waiting for things to happen, one has to actively "do" something.[28] The road of hope is to be travelled one step at a time, like any other road—each step may be both the first and the last—both are equally important. Every moment should be lived as if it was the only, the first and last moment of our life (TH 57). The present should be our meridian, our gauge, our map of time, directing us forward.

Savoring the present and making the best possible use of it is a true source of hope, for only in living this moment as the one and only can we hope for the future; the present is the seed of a future, a future with a promise. A promise is not a weather forecast, it is the fertile ground on which hope grows which is a promise in itself. The covenant between God and Abraham was the promise of a Promised Land—based on the hope of a bountiful, abundant land. Abraham is thus symbolic of a promise as the seed of hope which enables Abraham to make a new start. Abraham pursues a Divine promise and in doing so undergoes spiritual transformation; this transformation, in turn, depends on Abraham's being and living in this moment- every moment, every morning has the potential for a new beginning (RH 10). Abraham willingly and heartily embraces the Divine command to allow himself to be displaced.

Only by mindfully paying attention to the here and now can we "hope" to structure sound interiority. When we spend too much time and effort on nitty picky details, on doing nothing in particular, we overlook and forget the

---

28   During his imprisonment Francis Văn Thuân suffers hard times: "my mind was racked with many confused feelings: sadness, fear, tension … The great distance that lay between my people and me broke my heart. In the darkness of this terrible night, in the middle of an ocean of anguish, I slowly woke up. 'I have to face reality', I told myself. 'I am in prison. If I wait for the opportune moment to do something really great, how many times will such occasions actually present themselves? Only one thing comes with certainty: death. I have to take advantage of the occasions that present themselves everyday. I have to accomplish ordinary actions in an extraordinary way" (TH 52). This exemplary attitude of achieving something exceptional by means of something ordinary is another testimony of a culture of hope which depends more on the "how" than the "what" in life.

underlying point and purpose; what we seem to be doing merely "masks the interior void" (PH 78). On being put into prison Francis Văn Thuân was stripped of all vestiges of priesthood—he was displaced both literally and metaphorically. He was to be called mister and treated no differently to any other prisoner: "Without warning, I was asked, also on God's part, to return to the essentials," (TH 13)—at the same time, he found it much easier to "make a choice for God" in the here and now without the outward signs he had hitherto been accustomed to (TH 45). He could not make compromises, there was nothing to hide behind. However, it was this external void which helped him accept displacement and become truly acquainted with the essentials of interiority, of the "essence of prayer" (TH 117).

Hope, as previously outlined, needs a solid foundation stone; a central supporting pillar of point and purpose: without this pillar hope is in danger of collapsing (cf. RH 219). Văn Thuân finds sense and purpose in knowing he is never alone; the Holy Ghost is there to strengthen him (TH 187), Jesus Christ is at his side to accompany him and Christ's love to sustain him (TH 46; cf. TH 72). Faith such as this should not be read as a sign of resignation, as some kind of waiting for Godot. Hope demands more, hope is not passive, it is in fact very active; it requires both effort and single-mindedness. Hope must be actively "turned on" to *work*. When asked how life could be rebuilt in a scarred and wounded country Văn Thuân gives a straightforward, "simple" answer: "work, intelligence, union, tradition" (PH 83). Hope is not something we pluck from a tree in passing, "if you wish to advance in hope (. . .), you must study" (RH 127): in other words, lethargy and lackadaisicalness are dangerous stumbling blocks on the way to hope (RH 129).

A further obstacle standing in the way of true service, and indeed the spirit of a new beginning, is self-satisfaction (RH 16). It is lots of tiny steps together with those "day-to-day" sacrifices, plus a good degree of stubbornness and sheer tenacity which pave the way to cultivating hope (RH 15); and we shouldn't be afraid of those little steps or those modest beginnings, "do not despise small things" (RH 224; RH 187). Every human being could do no better in life than to "practice one virtue every year" with determination, you would see an improvement in both attitude and actions, and more importantly this would go towards strengthening hope (RH 19).

(iii) Hope requires reasons. Francis Văn Thuân's reason for hope is his faith which is not the result of human speculation but an existential certainty. (cf. TH 13f; RH 59); when asked by his fellow inmates why had had left everything behind to "follow Jesus", he is reminded of peter's words to Christ on being asked "why?"; "Lord, to whom can we go?" (Joh 6.68; TH 61). The question in the answer indicates the empty words and false hopes in the world, and Francis Văn Thuân warns, too, of those false hopes which in the face of social injustice many of us turn and have turned to throughout the centuries (TH 135); at the end of the day false hopes cannot fulfil what they promise: true hope will never let you down, because it is founded on rock and *the* rock is *the* fundamental foundation stone.

Hope also has to do with what we trust in, what is worthy of our trust and faith in a God who keeps his promises, provides the power and the trust we need to metaphorically follow Abraham in the desert (TH 41; RH 2). The more powerful and trustworthy the source of hope is, the more prepared we are to take risks for that hope. An act of trust always involves taking a risk and the question is: is it worth it? When hope is not fulfilled, trust is tested to its limits. In the sixth chapter of the section entitled "the Adventure of Hope" Francis Văn Thuân examines the role and significance of that second person relationship between himself and God and how it can be tested to the limit. While in solitary confinement, his own trust in God is tested almost to breaking point and he is forced to distinguish between God and works of God. Some days the electric lights would be left on 24/7, on other occasions he would be left in complete darkness for days on end. Suffering such torment almost to insanity he realizes "in the depths of my heart" that he has to choose God alone and not God's works to survive, go on and thrive (TH 42). The reason for hope must be God alone and not his works.

(iv) Hope depends on signs. As laid out at the beginning of this chapter, inner space and external place are interconnected. Invisible hope requires visible reference points, visible expression. Let me give an example from a Latin American context—Father Lawrence Schanberger recounts an experience of an earthquake in Talcahuano, Chile. Because of the imminent tidal wave, he was asked by the pastor to advise the people to leave their homes and go up to the nearby hills. A group of the people reacted to this call with the response: 'Before we go we want to take the statue of the Blessed Mother from our small chapel and have a procession on the beach.' And this is what they did, giving a tangible expression to their hope and confidence.[29] The inner lives of individuals, families and communities with all their hopes need to be expressed, desire to be expressed. We have seen how a culture of interiority can be constructed, and for Francis Văn Thuân silence, "inner silence", is the most important building block of all (RH 19). Even though he has no books to hand, no one to talk to, he recalls all the passages from the Bible he knows off by heart and it is these 300 quotes that accompany him through the depths and isolation of imprisonment (TH 62f): seen thus we can perhaps understand that under such

---

29   Joseph A. Heim, M.M, What They Taught Us, 49.

circumstances every word "counts,"[30] for body and soul. Meditating upon just one word in captivity can provide more strength than reading whole chapters under normal circumstances (TH 76); Francis Văn Thuân spends the three day journey, below decks on board ship meditating on the Passion of Christ and trying to comfort his fellow prisoners (TH 118f).

When word gets out that indeed one copy of the New Testament has been smuggled into the prison, it is meticulously divided up into tiny sections, single sheets, and distributed among the prisoners who then learn their "text" off by heart before passing it on to their neighbor (TH 65). In those darkest wee hours of the night, the sound of individual prisoners reciting their part echoed around the prison for all to hear and share in. Here was solid, audible hope indeed, often backed up by liturgical songs and hymns which Francis Văn Thuân had learnt in his early childhood and could now pass on to others: a prisoners' chorus like no other (TH 118; TH 123). These two signs were further strengthened by the Eucharist which he was able to celebrate with three drops of wine and one drop of water: "(…) without the Eucharist we cannot live God's life" (TH xix; cf. TH 130).

Father Parick Reilly underwent a similar experience in China when he was forced to spend 14 months in solitary confinement without even a bed to lie on, and without extra clothes to cover himself from the cold. His only wish "was to say just one more Mass before I died," and he managed to get bread and grapes to use for the one precious moment of consecration when his guards where distracted.[31] The meaning of the Eucharist can be tentatively grasped in those situations. It is a sacrament, a connection between the tangible and the intangible, the visible and the invisible—with the tangible and the visible being indispensable. Similarly, Archbishop Văn Thuân managed to make himself a small cross which he carried on his person: these outward signs were essential for survival and strength in displacement (TH 72). These physical, tangible signs were testimonies of an inner intangible hope. Francis Văn Thuân would wear this cross close to his own heart until he died as a sign of his deep inner conviction that Jesus' love can and does touch and change men's hearts.

---

30   The things you learn by heart cannot be taken away from you, Francis Văn Thuân realizes
      this when he is taken prisoner along with many others and forced to leave his home;
      he is reminded of a verse in Acts which gives him the support he needs "And now as a
      captive to the Spirit, I am on my way to Jerusalem, not knowing what will happen to me
      there,"(Acts. 20:22–23).

31   Aidan Clerkin, Brendan Clerkin, eds., A Road Less Travelled. Tales of the Irish Missionaries.
      Portland, OR: Four Courts Press 2011, 167.

These examples show, I believe, that the capacity to be displaced, the capacity to grow in the face of circumstances throwing a person out of her routine, depends on inner resources, on strengths from within; this is an important aspect of resilience which I suggested calling "epistemic resilience." An understanding of this concept is predicated on a "deep" understanding of the human person with her inner richness.

CHAPTER 4

Structures of Inner Being*

Displacement requires epistemic resilience, i.e. resilience from within; aid workers as well as missionaries, for example, often work in remote regions; quite often, these places are rough, contexts of hardship and suffering: "Aid workers routinely work in under resourced contexts, face exposures to personal and communal trauma, and are challenged with considerable human suffering."[1] That is why resilience has been identified as a key factor in the well-being of aid personnel.[2] In a sense, they have no choice but to be resilient.

This has been confirmed in a qualitative study by Christina Montaiuti who interviewed aid workers about their resilience; one participant said in the interview: "Actually, because we don't really choose to be alive at the beginning, so, later on it becomes our responsibility to keep your life and survive. And then if you are an adult, you are responsible for other people. So, by the end it's not something that you choose but by the end you need to keep life continued, certain quality and certain things that you fight for. So, this is a—I mean this is my opinion about life. I mean, it's about also responsibility."[3] There is no option but to be resilient.

A chief component of the kind of resilience required in the missionary experience is internal resilience, the capacity to cope with adversity through cognitive processing. Meaning-making is an essential building block to this kind of resilience, and needs to be nurtured by a person's internal sources. I suggest calling this type of resilience (as opposed to social or structural resilience): "epistemic resilience," i.e. resilience based on epistemic resources such as beliefs and hopes, faith and memories. The capacity to engage in meaning-making is one pillar of the capacity to be displaced. Aid work is demanding and happens under adverse conditions which at first glance make no meaning

---

*   Biblical quotes taken from: New Revised Standard Version Bible: Anglicized Edition (will be abbreviated as: NRSV throughout) Popular Text Edition edited by Oxford University Press: Oxford, October 1995.

1   Cynthia B. Eriksson et al., Social support, organizational support, and religious support in relation to burnout in expatriate humanitarian aid workers. *Mental Health, Religion & Culture* 12,7 (2009) 671–686, at 671.

2   Cynthia B. Eriksson et al., Predeployment Mental Health and Trauma Exposure of Expatriate Humanitarian aid Workers: Risk and Resilience Factors. *Traumatology* April 16, 2012.

3   Christina Montaiuti, The Effect of Meaning-Making on Resilience Among Aid Workers. A Phenomenological Analysis. PhD Dissertation. Minneapolis, Mn: Walden University. March 2013, 152.

but can fill the people involved with a sense of purpose.[4] This sense of purpose found in displacement can be confirmed outwardly both socially and politically, but it is nurtured by inner sources, resources from within.

Epistemic resilience is "resilience from within." But what does that mean: "within," "inner"? The idea of interiority has been recognized as one of Christianity's main contributions to our cultural and intellectual history, a contribution which has been influential in identity and self-understanding. Interiority confirms the fact that human persons are beings which can only be described via language which similarly presumes that beyond the aspect of the visually obvious there is a complex world of memories and emotions, powers of thought and reflection, desires and attitudes at work under the surface, in the innermost being of an individual. These assumptions are imperative if we are to define 'self'—Jerold Seigel puts forward the idea that reflexivity is the defining principle in constructing the modern concept of self.[5] This perception of ourselves and others as individual beings has become an integral part of our modern-day understanding of self. The concept of "epistemic resilience" would not be possible without this commitment to a concept of interiority.

The idea of "inner depth" within the Christian tradition, an important factor in considering the capacity to be displaced, has in turn been shaped by biblical "background languages," as I would like to call the tradition we find reflected in the Books of the Hebrew Bible as well as in the New Testament. In order to get a fuller understanding of the concept of interiority, it might be useful to take a brief look at human nature as portrayed in the languages we find in the Bible.

4.1   Biblical Background Languages

The Hebrew Bible is a collection of books not short of experiences of displacement; it could be argued, as we have seen, that a major factor in the cultivation of a sense of the inner has always been and continues to be the experience of exile. Let us take a cursory look at the semantic contexts provided by the Jewish and Christian Scriptures. We will see building blocks for a particular understanding of the human person, a peculiar anthropology committed to a deep understanding of inner sources.

---

4   See Roslyn Thomas' PhD Dissertation, from stress to sense of coherence: psychological experiences of humanitarian workers in complex humanitarian emergencies. Oxford: University of Oxford 2008.

5   J. Seigel, The Idea of the Self. Thought and Experience in Western Europe since the Seventeenth Century. Cambridge: Cambridge University Press 2005, 7–17.

In the Hebrew Bible the most relevant sources for an understanding of interiority can be found in the Wisdom literature. The Book of Psalms perhaps more than any of the other Books is consummate in its attention to existential depth and intensity; we tangibly sense the human condition in prayer before God. In Psalms we discover the core facets of human interiority; those essential structures of the heart and soul finding expression through language spanning the wide spectrum of the human state from the *perturbed* soul seeking solace and comfort (Psalm 6:4; 42:6; 43:5) to an *exultant* soul awakening to a new dawn (Ps 57:9), filled with that steadfast feeling of gratitude and confidence; we come across a soul *hungry and thirsty* (Ps 107:9) seeking nourishment which it finds in a "rich feast" (Ps 63:6), but also a soul which has had more than its fill of that which is unhealthy (Ps 123:4).

The Book of Wisdom takes up three key aspects from Psalms, consolidating them with more: first of all, human thoughts are described as an inner activity, thoughts may be *perverse* (Wis 1:3) or *foolish* (Wis 1:5), but no matter how hard we try, we cannot keep them secret from God for He witnesses all our innermost thoughts and feelings (Wis 1:6). Unrighteous thinking and wrongful ideas will cut us off from God: secondly, we find in the Book of Wisdom a macro theory based on and rooted in that innermost of human spaces: the soul. The souls of the righteous are in the hands of God and can never be tormented (Wis 3:1); the souls of the righteous receive their just rewards, special favors will be shown them for their faithfulness (Wis 3:13); the unfaithful never know who formed them, who "inspired them with active souls" and "breathed a living spirit into them," (Wis 15:11); nor do the unfaithful know that their soul is *borrowed* and when the time comes, will have to return it (Wis 15:8). Pictures such as these are paramount in our understanding of the basis of our framework theory: the soul as that innermost human space bears witness to the fact that we are not of this world and can, therefore, not remain in this world; thirdly, the Book of Wisdom gives a detailed description of the spirit of wisdom which abides in a true and uncorrupted soul and reflects those attributes which a pure and good soul requires; the spirit of wisdom is gentle, intelligent, manifold, subtle, and undefiled, loving what is good, more beautiful than the sun (Wis 7:22). She bears good fruit; her purity of heart is reflected in her integrity, steadfastness and beneficence, in other words, she focuses on purely that which is good and for the sake of all that is good.

In the Book of Proverbs the heart is that place where memory abides; that inner sanctuary in which God's commandments and laws should be kept treasured (Prov 3:1).[6] This space is neither static nor passive, it can be shaped and formed depending on individual human will and conviction to follow and

---

6   Cf., Proverbs 7:3; 22:18.

uphold God's commandments in accordance with his will. However, that inner being, that inward space is fragile and needs to be protected; the heart needs looking after, never to be forsaken (Prov 4:2–4), this reminds us of the shepherd and his duty to his flock; just as the shepherd never lets the sheep out of his sight, we should be vigilant and guard what is good in our heart so that it does not become dark and perverted, longing to sow only seeds of discord and intent on devising evil plans (Prov 6:14,18): the only way to deal with dark tendencies is to wield the "rod of discipline" on the mind, heart and soul (Prov 22:15; 23:12). Discipline is reliant on the willingness of will of the person to be disciplined; beneath the question of will, purity of mind and heart is an imperative, a state not to be achieved without inner struggles and battles.

As we have seen the heart is a central "organ" of body and soul; it needs to be nurtured and nourished and as such gives us a thirst for life in its most quintessential form: it is this thirst which "commands" our outlook on and relationship to life. The heart, is that inner space providing our certainty of being and as such it: 1) needs protecting from undesirable intruders, 2) reflects and reveals our innermost feelings, sometimes at odds with each other and sometimes battling for dominance, 3) decides and determines when and how we act and react to the human actions of 'other'—it expresses itself in our sympathy and understanding for the predicament of that 'other'. The heart by nature is not strong and needs to be fortified and guarded.

The question is how? This takes us back to interiority where memory, wisdom, knowledge, aspirations, will and trust abide; this innermost core of personality is the clearest indication of being, a being protected by integrity which in turn requires God's laws. God can see into our hearts and minds, and it is this inner integrity based on a deep closeness to God that protects the heart and allows it to flourish. This closeness and unity with God is expressed in the gospel of John:

> Abide in me as I abide in you. Just as the branch cannot bear fruit by itself unless it abides in the vine, neither can you unless you abide in me (. . .). Those who abide in me and I in them bear much fruit, because apart from me you can do nothing . . . If you abide in me, and my words abide in you, ask for whatever you wish, and it will be done for you (John 15:4–5;7).

"Abiding" can be reconstructed as a core category to characterize the theological dimension of the relationship between God and the human person.[7] The motif can be found in books of the Hebrew Bible and is deepened in the books of the New Testament. In other words, the Wisdom literature opens up a whole

---

7   Ben Quash has offered a rich analysis of the term from a theological perspective—B. Quash, Abiding. The Archbishop of Canterbury's Lent Book 2013. London: Bloomsbury 2012.

new vista of what we as human beings are, presenting us with the mystery of human life and revealing ways in which we can surpass even ourselves. It provides the framework in which the Christian view of the 'humanness of being' continues to unfold in the Gospels.

The Sermon on the Mount marks a turning point in perspective going beyond outward signs of obedience e.g., in observing laws and commandments and acknowledges that inner level of nature as the very essence—'heart'—of being itself. The Sermon on the Mount brings to the fore the aspect of a "secret" attitude of mind which may harbor erroneous thoughts "anyone who covets a woman has already committed adultery with her in his heart," (Mt 5:28), but more importantly in praying and fasting: an interior attitude—without need of outward justification—which Augustine would later focus on: God knows our hearts. The supremacy of inner-being is reflected not so much in passive purity as in the active rule of the inner with regard to purity and impurity of mind, Jesus says: 'it is not what goes into the mouth that defiles a person, but it is what comes out of the mouth that defiles' (Mt 15:11). The things we speak aloud are the expression of that which lies at the heart of our being. The heart is where we 'store' our thoughts and attitudes, and the heart is the seat of memory and recall. From Luke 2:19, we know that Mary treasured the shepherds' words and pondered upon them in her heart. Similarly, the Gospels remind us that the heart can have or adopt particular attributes: we read that it may be ruled by hardness, be troubled or anxious, but may also be joyful. This unseen inner space is the source of our character, a bona fide place of integrity. Jesus voices this teaching in his admonition of the Pharisees: "Woe to you, scribes and Pharisees, hypocrites! For you are like white-washed tombs, which on the outside look beautiful, but inside (...) are full of bones of the dead and all kinds of filth," (Mt 23:27).

We only begin to fully grasp the import of "being" when we realize how a person can be "inwardly" stirred; on the road to Emmaus, the disciples are moved and guided by what they see and hear: "Were not our hearts burning within us?" (Lk. 24:32). From the Gospel of St. John, we know that Jesus was "greatly disturbed in spirit and deeply moved," when Martha weeps at the death of her brother Lazarus; he feared the hour of his own death, in knowing Judas Iscariot would betray him. But the heart is also an "abode" in which forces can move in and govern the way we act and think. The heart may be "possessed by evil spirits," but can be a dwelling place where both Jesus and God would want to live, thus making it a point of union and communion with God who wants to reside in us. This union with God finds expression—similar to the example of Mary—in God's word abiding in us. Thus, discipleship signifies an inner conversion, a transformation of the heart in which certain principles—inherent laws—become manifest.

St. Luke's Gospel describes Jesus as being one such governing principle, a telling statement about displacement, inner growth and development:

> When the unclean spirit has gone out of a person, it wanders through waterless regions looking for a resting place, but not finding any, it says, 'I will return to my house from which I came.' When it comes, it finds it swept and put in order. Then it goes and brings seven other spirits more evil than itself, and they enter and live there; and the last state of that person is worse than the first. (Lk 11:24–26).

What exactly does this tell us? That inner being has to be kept clean and tidy, and this often demands displacement as a means of purification, the inner space is vulnerable and can be defiled, our own inner growth and development can be lastingly stunted, beyond repair.

Proceeding on from the Gospels, Paul's Epistles define us as beings with the capacity of comprehension. Paul alludes to the same images: God knows our hearts (Acts 1:24;15:8), and we may experience intense pain as a result: describing how in Peter's Pentecost sermon "they were cut to the heart". He describes the Lord as a 'place' where we take landmark decisions and as such needs to be purged and cleansed by faith. The language Paul uses to illustrate inwardness becomes noticeably more intense and compact, and propels our perception of the emerging picture of human nature forward. It is in Paul's Letters to the Romans that this image takes on real shape and substance; Romans is at heart a confession of inner-being: God knows the human heart, searches it and sees our spirit—sees us as we really are yet at the same time we as humans are incapable of knowing the 'mind' of God, which is important in considering the inscrutability of God's will. It is the heart that harbors and generates human passions and desires, and it is here that we will find the reasons for our 'human' impulse, the incentives of our actions and deeds. True 'repentance' is forged in the heart, repentance demanding a turnaround—a "circumcision of the heart." It can be filled with God's love given through the Holy Spirit, or, as described in the seventh chapter of Romans, filled with evil making us a slave of sin—sin rooted in the flesh rather than in the 'mind' and which will lead us astray: in other words the passions and desires of our hearts set us on a road which we would not walk 'willingly.' We never cease to not do what we want to do, but invariably do what we do *not* want to do, "it is no longer *I* that do it, but sin that dwells within me," (Romans 7:17). Here Paul is clearly describing the aspect of displacement in all its levels, meanings, point and purpose. In Romans, Paul is reminding us that the heart is the seat of conscience and is the center of our moral sense of judgment, those inner attitudes and frames of mind which are not displaced when external circumstances shift the outer world as we know it.

In his later Letters, Paul develops his use of metaphor, e.g., in his admonishment and reminder that our inner-being is a temple to God in which He dwells, and that the Holy Spirit fills and forms our hearts, will and desires 1 Cor 3:16; Phil 2:13,2; Thess 3:5). There is an "inner space" in the human person that provides refuge, is an inner center, an inner "locus of control," if paradoxically speaking we hand over this space to God. The idea that God knows our innermost thoughts is repeated, and Paul instructs Timothy that having a conscience is an integral part of being human, which needs to be actively cultivated and nurtured; it is here that our innermost desires and passions take root—and can be employed to motivate and power our actions (1 Cor 7:37). He drives home the point that we are our own renewable source of energy: "even though our outer nature is wasting away, our inner nature is being renewed day by day," (2 Cor 4:16). At one point in his Letter to the Ephesians, Paul refers to the "eyes of the heart", which he prays will be enlightened by God. This is again close the idea of conscience. This idea of "conscience" was hugely influential for the Christian understanding of a person's inner life. Conscience, like "the heart," can be darkened and needs renewal; it has properly been called "perception of the heart" and the "sentiment of the understanding."[8]

4.2   Inwardness and Augustine's *Confessions*

'Inwardness' is the hallmark of modern identity as put forward by Charles Taylor in his in-depth study of the modern-day self.[9] Without an understanding of inwardness we would not have been able to develop a language, a vocabulary of deep emotions such as "grief" or psychological phenomena such as "depression" or "burn out." Taylor draws our attention to the fact that seeing other as self with all his/her innermost complexities inherent in individual identity is a typically modern concept. Likewise, it is this depth and complexity of 'self' which denies scientific definition wholesale, because the subject of any scientific study has to be identified and described objectively, regardless of subjective interpretation, regardless of point of reference and regardless of framework environment. None of this can be applied in analyzing *self* in *other*,

---

8   J. Butler, Five Sermons. New York: Bobbs Merrill 1950, 82.
9   C. Taylor, Sources of the Self. The Making of modern Identity. Cambridge, Mass: Harvard University Press 1994; cf., K. Flasch, Wert der Innerlichkeit. In: H. Joas, K. Wiegandt (eds.), Die kulturellen Werte Europas. Frankfurt/Main: Fischer 2005, 219–236.

and to a certain degree even eludes any exhaustive examination of own self.[10]
The feeling or notion of self must go beyond any neutral observation of being
or categorization of the practicalities involved. Attempting to identify identity
is an attempt to define a place or space from which I can make a statement
and which in turn I would like to be addressed. A key work, even a turning
point in the historical development of understanding human interiority, are
Augustine's *Confessiones*. Ever since the reception of the Confessions, the idea
of inwardness and the rich interior life of the human person has become part
of the understanding of the human condition.[11]

Augustine describes both himself and humankind in general as beings that
have infinite inner-depth and rich resources at their disposal. The imagery
Augustine uses to illustrate inwardness of being is revealing: the house (C 1.5)
the heart as vessel containing and conveying a plethora of things (C X.35) ar-
able land (C II.3), the image of the battleground (C VIII.8). We see images of
place and space at work here, supporting the argument that inner space is fundamental in coping with outer displacement. While the image of the house
conveys the idea of untold rooms within, an idea which was outlined in the
16th century by Teresa of Avila in '*The Interior Castle*', the image of a field to
be ploughed suggests the labor and toil involved in attaining inwardness. The
image of the battleground is perhaps the most dramatic and reflects the battle
being fought out in our own inner being. This inner space of interiority is, according to Augustine, the 'core' of human being; it is that inner space in which
we can find God and the place 'where God makes himself known to me' (C 1.2).[12]
This inner space is also the seat of that sense which perceives the voice of God,
'et clamasti de longinquo: ego sum qui sum. et audivi, sicut auditor in corde'
(C VII.10). Augustine talks about 'the ears of my heart' (C 1.5). God is the true
'heart' of inward being, more inner than inner" (C III.6). Hence, God knows us

---

10   Taylor, Sources of the Self, 2.2.

11   Augustine, Confessions. Ed. J. O'Donnell. Oxford: Oxford University Press 1992
      (Abbreviation: C); cf., P. Carey, Augustine's Invention of the Inner Self. Oxford: Oxford
      University Press 2000. Carey reconstructs the Platonic school of thought as seen by
      Augustine in order to examine the originality of Augustine's ideas. While Augustine
      undoubtedly had a decisive influence on the development of the notion of inwardness,
      one might dispute how original Augustine's ideas were. Carey depicts the soul accord-
      ing to Plato's idea of Hell and Plotin's 'sphere revolving around the inner source of intel-
      ligibility'—all metaphors of space with the inner palace as the key metaphor as used
      by Augustine whom he sees as a bridge between linking Plato and und Descartes; cf.,
      Michael Tkacz's review in *Journal of the History of Philosophy* 39,4 (2001) 584–585.

12   'Quis locus est in me, quoveniat in me deus meus? quo deus veniat in me, deus, qui fecit
      caelum et terram?' (C 1.2).

better than we can ever know ourselves, since fathoming the profundity of our own inwardness let alone others is beyond us.

As immeasurable as our inner being may be, it is not without structure: it is the seat of diverse powers (will, memory, reason), but also divergent moods and emotions (craving and lust, joy, fear, regret and grief (c x.14). The soul as inner space can be depicted as 'active agent' as well as backdrop and set where the events of life are 'staged' and come to pass. A central force in Augustine's reading of the soul is the will: "I knew I had a will, of that I was as sure as I knew I lived; I was also equally sure that if I really wanted or refused something, nobody but myself wanted or refused it, and gradually I came to realize that this must be the source of my own sin" (c vii.3).[13] Human will is very much influenced by its overall level of purity or impurity; it is a will unto itself generating and controlling its own power, making it independent (c viii.9).[14] It is a sick soul that gives rise to a divided will, torn apart by indecision. A divided will becomes a weakened will, resilience from within can only be strengthened if the will is not torn but clearly committed and focused. Similar to the heart, the 'will' has to be monitored and controlled since it is the driving force behind all action. When this driving force of the soul is flawed, acts of violence can result (c iv.15).

Next to the will, Augustine reserves a special place for memory—*memoria*— as part of inner being in his tenth book.[15] We have seen in Ingrid Betancourt's case that she relied on memories and remembering as an important resilience-strengthening source. Augustine claims that it is memory that drives the thinking process: thinking collects and orders random ideas (c x.11). He is continually amazed by that rich inner homogeneity of memory which harnesses the heterogeneity of thought. Memory plays a central role in Augustine's analysis of the heart of being and the core of interiority. In one place, he mentions having made the journey to the seat of the soul, 'which is in my own memory' ('intravi ad ipsius animi mei sedem quae illi est in memoria mea, quoniam sui quoque meminit animus," c x.25). Personal memory serves as meta-memory: 'I remember having remembered' (c x.13). Memory is also the place in which

---

13   "... quod tam sciebam me habere voluntatem quam me vivere. itaque cum aliquid vellem
      aut nollem, non alium quam me velle ac nolle certissimus eram, et ibi esse causam pecca-
      ti mei iam iamque advertebam" (c vii.3).

14   See Augustine's *De Civitate Dei* xi (the will acts on its own accord).

15   Cf., R. Sorabji, Self. Ancient and Modern Insights about Individuality, Life and Death.
      Oxford: Oxford University Press 2005, 99–100; cf., N. Fischer, Einleitung, in Aurelius
      Augustinus, Suche nach dem wahren Leben, (Hamburg, Meiner, 2006), pp. xiii–xci.

we are confronted by ourselves (C X.8).[16] Finding rapport with self, is perhaps *the* cornerstone in a culture of interiority.

So saying, Augustine's *Confessions* present us with a rich tapestry of inwardness which can bestow human life with depth and unique meaning.[17] Inwardly our abilities and powers are caught up in a fight for prominence; and it is from here that action taken is decided upon, made up of striving, judgement and memory. However, the governing factor remains the *structure* of inner-being which can be moulded, fashioned and shaped, and which is subject to inherent laws which can at the same time be specified. Ultimately however inexhaustible resources of inner-being may be, they remain inaccessible without the Grace of God; he knows our soul better than we do ourselves and it is this knowing which can lead us as beings to Truth and Salvation. This concept of understanding will have an impact on the way we think about and regard ourselves, the concept of subjectivity has to be defined in the light of this inner wealth. An active agent bases his or her actions on emotions, ideas, aspirations, ambitions and perception, which can only be expressed in the complex language found in interiority.

The key points from Augustine's *Confessions* we need to remember for our purposes here in this enquiry are his insights into the richness of the inner life of a human person, the vitality and dynamics of inwardness with its forces and motions, the fact that the inner life can be ordered and analyzed on the basis of internal laws. Epistemic resilience can be strengthened by respecting those laws; the capacity to be displaced can also be strengthened by the same laws, the same knowledge and the same inner dynamics. Epistemic resilience enables us to integrate experience with memory and knowledge, too; Cynthia Stuhlmiller, to give an example, examined the effects of rescue work after the San Francisco earthquake of October 17, 1989; she identified "meaning-making" and the integration of the experience and activities within a wider framework as crucial in this exceptional situation[18] which displaced people, even professionals, from their routine work. Indeed, epistemic resilience is a fact-of-life factor and not merely an academic notion.

---

16   "ibi mihi et ipse occurro, meque recolo, quid, quando et ubi egerim quoque modo, cum agerem, affectus fuerim" (C X.8).

17   Cf., Ch.T. Mathewes, Augustinian Anthropology: Interior intimo meo. *The Journal of Religious Ethics* 27,2 (1999) 195–221. Mathewes points out that Augustine's seemingly incoherent anthropology does shed new light on our understanding of 'agency' and autonomy as seen as the basis of interiority.

18   C.M. Stuhlmiller, Occupational Meanings and Coping Practices of Rescue Workers in an Earthquake Disaster. *Western Journal of Nursing Research* 16,3 (1994) 268–287.

4.3   John Cassian and the Inner Order of the Soul

While Augustine's *Confessions*, provide us with a ground-breaking change in the perception of the human condition, similar ideas about interiority are underpinned in contemporary writings of the same period. Far from being an autobiographical 'confession' Augustine's work is one of a number of texts penned at the end of 4th century aiming to summate and synthesize spiritual life and values. An important topos at that time, undeniably important for the study of displacement, is the topos of the desert. The desert has been presented as a place of transition in some biblical sources (Exodus, Gospels), as a place of deprivation of external sources that forces people to rely on their inner resources. Displacement is a "desert experience."

With this in mind, I would now like to turn to John Cassian (ca 360–435) whose broad knowledge of spiritual teachings and doctrines affords us deep insight into the mystagogical wisdom and practices of early Christianity. Cassian's writings attest that rather than an indefinable, hazy 'something', inwardness has clear structure and capacity which can be shaped by its own decisions and disciplined by self. This point—the structure of the inner—will be a key issue in our exploration of epistemic resilience.

Cassian's teacher was Evagrius Ponticus. Evagrius portrays inwardness as being shaped by memory, reflection and emotion. Inner growth depends on inner dynamics and the way we deal with them and in this, prayer provides sustenance for the spirit in the way a virtuous approach to life nourishes the soul. Regular pursuit and single-minded commitment to prayer will regulate inner-being positively, but only with God's help. Fear of God is the starting point for a correct—proper—approach to inner purpose and design.[19]

John Cassian was particularly interested in healthy inner growth and how it could be encouraged in Hesychast monastic life in Palestine and Egypt. In this study, he pursued dialogue and discourse with Desert Fathers. Both in *De institutis coenibiorum* (ca 420) and *Collationes patrum* (ca 426–428) Cassian gives us insight into what he learns, outlining a doctrine of cultivating inner spirituality, both in the fabric and texture of human inwardness.[20]

---

19   See Evagrius Ponticus, The Prakticos. Chapters on Prayer. Cistercian Studies. 1972.

20   I use the following edition: John Cassian, The Conferences. Translated and annotated by Boniface Ramsey. Mahwah, NJ 1997; The Twelve Books of John Cassian on the Institutes of the Coenobia. Translation and Notes by Edgar C.S. Gibson. A Select Library of Nicene and Post-Nicene Fathers of the Christian Church. Second Series, Vol. 11. New York 1894. I quote using the edition-independent way of referring to Book and Section. Abbreviations: "Coll" for *Conferences* (*Collationes*), "Inst" for *Institutes*.

Cassian learnt from the spiritual masters of the time that there is a real need to work on inward-being, that one's inner life must be tackled resolutely and forcefully on the basis of the redeeming wisdom that inner being can be 're'-constructed if pursued wholeheartedly (Coll 1.1). Anyone entertaining the idea of seeking inner strength, has to be gripped by a passion for life so profound as to create the power and energy to achieve it, (Coll 14.9). This presupposes a reflective attitude to life per se; only by concentrating on this ultimate life-objective can the things encountered along the way be put into the context of 'a' lifetime as a whole and are not overly 'weighted' (Coll 1.2; 1.5). We have to be able to see life in its entirety; an entirety which provides an overall framework for the day-to-day challenges we come up against and determines how much attention they should or should not be given.

Primary goals of the spiritual life are 'purity of heart,' (Coll 1.4) and inner peace of spirit (Coll 9.2). 'Purity of heart' is that state of inner preparedness and vigilance which will not be swayed by outside vicissitudes, and marks the meeting point of inner power and physical capacity supplementing and complimenting each other in focusing on what is good. There is no doubt in Cassian's mind that inner-being has a wide range of attributes: single-mind-edness, conscience and memory which have to be cleansed and purified to align themselves with God. It is a state by which each attribute is judged on its own merit and all attributes together as a single unity; any source of disturbance and distraction is tracked, eliminated and the 'state' put back in order.

Cassian believes in the law of a mutual dependence between the interior and the exterior. In his *collationes*, Cassian maintains that inner spirit can be affected and changed if not firmly anchored by outside forces (Coll 1.5), and goes on to assert that everything depends on the inner state—constitution—of spirit (Coll 1.13). An astute eye can see inner state of spirit via the 'state'-outer mantle-of 'body' (Coll 7.15). It works both ways, not only are externals impacted by inner nature but externals affect inner spirit, too. In creating a culture of inwardness, external forces and structures have to be activated to support and further growth. Worries which lie heavily on the heart will show in agitation (Coll 24.5) and the state of inner exhaustion and weariness of spirit—acedia—will grow worse the more one gives into disquiet and tries to escape from it (Coll 24.5). *Acedia* is a term (and phenomenon) relevant to the exploration of epistemic resilience since it describes inner dryness, spiritual exhaustion, inertia of the inner.[21] Acedia is causally linked to impatience and over-ambitiousness and the burden of shouldering tasks and burdens too

---

21   See, Siegfried Wenzel, The Sin of Sloth: Acedia in Medieval Thought and Literature. Chapel Hill, NC: The University of North Carolina Press 1960.

heavy. Acedia (lack of "kedos", i.e. "care") describes a sense of inertia and passivity in the face of the vastness of a task. This state, close to today's burn out syndrome, will break all powers of inner resistance because acedia is a form of extreme ennui which blocks inner impulse and incentive. Acedia induces listlessness and aridity of spirit. Acedia causes both restlessness and lethargy (Inst 10.6). Acedia is a sign that inner resources have been exhausted, that inner wells have dried out. One feels "in the wrong place" and "out of place," because of a loss of inner home.

Cassian pays particular attention to this phenomenon of inner dryness,—he is concerned with the role of cognition in the way inwardness is structured and constructed. Ideas and thoughts are the outward expression of an inner frame of mind and leave an indelible impression. Cassian regards the human spirit as something restless, driven by its nomadic instinct to roam (Coll 7.4); it is 'moved' by trains of thought, can decide which to ponder upon and which to reject outright. (Coll 1.17): the thinking process is in itself a decision-making process in sorting out which thoughts are worthy of attention and which not.

Cassian emphasizes that it is impossible for the soul to remain in calm contemplation if the heart is caught up in a whirlwind of worldly issues (Coll 20.9), the focal point of inwardness needs to be built upon its own inner framework and structure. Cassian draws our attention to the importance of being mindful of the 'thoughts we think about;' we would be well advised to guard our thoughts well, a task requiring guidance of self which in turn demands a focused view of things: we should not let our eyes wander from our purpose for a moment (Coll 24.6) and in focusing on God, the spirit has a fixed point of reference, which provides reliable support for the thinking process (Coll 24.6).

We are free agents in choosing what to think and we can govern the peace of heart such thoughts embody (Inst 8.17). It is crucial that the thinking process be monitored for a lasting balanced attitude of inwardness. If we allow a bad habit to take root and gain the upper hand, it will spark a chain of other bad habits wreaking inner havoc in the soul: overindulgence often signals the first step of a disorientated quest for sensual pleasures; this in turn triggers inordinate craving which turns to anger, anger to sadness, sadness to inner fatigue, and fatigue to acedia (Coll 5.10). Vanity and pride are so intertwined that the incitement of one invariably provokes and promotes the other (Coll 5.10).

Such connections point to the structure and order of the soul. The eight wrong attitudes of the soul (described as eight demons) are interlinked so that the tackling of one affects the others. These "demons" or misplaced attitudes weaken epistemic resilience; they are closely interrelated and follow a particular internal order, almost a hierarchical pyramid: it is vanity and pride which come to the fore and gain momentum precisely when the other weaknesses of the soul are being disciplined. This is a sad fact, but if vanity is left to flourish unchecked the other fruits of the soul will invariably perish (Coll 14.9). Vanity will poison the soul (Inst 11.15) while pride is considered as the root of all evil i.e., 'original sin' (Inst 11.15). Overindulgence and lack of moderation demand abstinence, which means regular doses of attention be given to the condition of the soul (cf. Coll 5.3). But it is envy which is the most difficult 'malcontentment' to cure (Coll 18.16) simply because envy is aroused by the attitude of mind which will cure the other maladies: virtuousness. Ironically virtuousness is the mindset we seek to attain but which becomes the subject of envy when we are unsuccessful in our endeavors.

It is also part of the order of the inner that the failures of the soul which weaken epistemic resilience can be systematically scrutinized. Cassian underlines a basic law in dynamics: anything in motion cannot be stopped because like a snowball it gathers and gains in momentum once set in motion. These inner demons are able to worm their way into our soul because they are not readily recognizable (Coll 7.10), revealing that the soul acquires—learns—powers of reception born of negligence and complacency. However, the person affected (afflicted) only has him or herself to blame and no one else beside, because nothing can enter and take over the soul completely unobserved. Forces may be as diverse as they are dissimilar; each individual is vulnerable to different things (cf. Coll 7.15). The concept of "temptations" as well as "failures of the soul" provide windows into a person's inner struggles.

The key virtue and corner stone of personal growth (and inner stability and epistemic resilience) is, in Cassian's eyes, humility (Coll 4.15; Inst 12.23). Without humility perfection of the soul cannot be attained; the road to perfection is navigated according to the way we interpret our own weaknesses and it is this on which the overall tenor or 'mindfulness' relies (Coll 5.14). On the road to self-awareness, to growth, we must discover which part of our soul is damaged and distorted—'corrupt' (Coll 24.16), to be able to eliminate it. In being mindful of signs of illness and disease an essential attitude is mindfulness of silence—remaining silent—(cf. Coll 10.9) accompanied by prayer. True to his teacher, Evagrius, Cassian firmly believes that prayer is a prerequisite on the journey to inner-growth and as such he lays out the necessary guidelines for 'proper' prayer: day-to-day worries and cares have to be put aside—completely; strong feelings e.g., of anger, equally ignored or rebuked (Coll 9.3). However, how we prepare ourselves for prayer is of vital importance, too, and in this we are free to draw up our own "rules of preparation." No matter what has been playing on our minds, and no matter how successfully we manage to put it aside beforehand, it will return during prayer (Coll 9.3). Therefore, the right attitude of mind can yield constant, uninterrupted prayer which 'steels' the soul.

The way we 'educate' and look after our soul is no meager task; from small and tender beginnings, the soul will grow, slowly but surely (Coll 10.8); but it is a process exacting patience and persistence. Cassian frequently turns to the metaphor of 'doing battle' and 'wrestling' for true inwardness: a battle to keep our personal desires and ambitions in check to be able to take a real step forward. Thus, in summary, the three main elements which make the heart steadfast and strong are thought, attention and prayer (Coll 10.14). This will lay the foundation for spiritual firmness; those hit hardest by temptation are those lacking firm foundations, not only in the big things we do in life, but in the little everyday tasks we perform as well (cf. Coll 4.21).

According to Cassian, the soul can have different properties, it may be beautiful or ugly, judged according to its degree or lack of virtuousness (Coll 4.3). The soul may be healthy or ailing; should the latter be the case, then medication can only be prescribed after it has been examined—a correct diagnosis requires good guidance before it can be reached (Coll 24.14). The rich tapestry of images Cassian weaves to reflect human inner-being contains such metaphors as the millstone (Coll 1.18): inner being hates being idle in the same way as a millstone constantly needs grain to grind, but in the way the miller chooses the grain to be ground, we are free to choose what our soul needs to keep it busy. This image is not new, but Cassian employs it to illustrate the restlessness of the human soul—a soul forced to roam in its own thoughts and memories. The metaphor of the millstone also emphasizes the 'grind' of repetition; in cogitating and contemplating on what goes through the mind over and over again.

However, one remedy is ruminating upon a single verse from the Bible which will keep the mind busy and focused. Another image Cassian employs is the one of the house (Coll 6.17), which should only be built on 'good,' solid foundations. Similar to the proverbial house built on sand and the house built on rock, the seemingly sudden collapse of a house is not so unexpected after all since it will not collapse for no reason at all: the foundations are bad or rotten. However, Cassian takes this metaphor one step further: negligence of the spirit is akin to neglecting a house and leaving the roof in such a bad state of repair as to let the rain in. Once a roof is no longer impervious to the rain, rot will set in and left unchecked will result in the roof 'falling in' and the house 'falling down'. A third image I would like to mention is the image of the feather (Coll 9.4): the soul is like a feather in its natural lightness—lifted ever upwards.

Just as a feather can be weighed down and grounded by dust and dirt, the soul can be burdened by 'grime' and 'filth'. The soul should not be 'contaminated' with thoughts and notions which will drag it down into the mire, but be kept clean, light and transparent in its endeavors to rise up to God.

If we reflect upon Cassian's multi-layered illustration of inner structure, we cannot overlook the fact that building inner-being means making decisions, investing power properly and nurturing a deep longing to attain peace of spirit, an honest nature and purity of heart. This is a matter of agency, a matter of choice. Building up the inner space is too important to be left to chance. Experiences of displacement, as we have seen in the examples of Tiziano Terzani, Ingrid Betancourt, and Francis Xavier Văn Thuân, call for discipline of mind and soul to cultivate the inner. Sister Maria del Rey, for instance, describes her missionary experience in Peru highlighting the prayer routine of the sisters in their prayer room at 5.15 am before going to the chapel; she finds enthusiastic words to describe this cultivation of the inner:

> Here alone, in all the world, is a man really and truly a man. Stripped of accidentals like money and position and education, he stands forth as a single unit of humanity—a man made to know, love and serve God in this world and to be happy with Him in the next.[22]

After this quiet time the sisters would go out and face adversities and suffering. The inner space allows full presence in and full attention to the outer space; it fosters the capacity to be displaced, the capacity to be and even flourish in the desert. John Cassian presents some clear ideas about the dynamics of fortifying the inner, in striving for purity of heart. In achieving this, we should be 'particular' in what we think about and how much time and energy we devote to it because attitude and approach is essential: only this will prevent us from losing our 'balance' (on the tight-rope) or losing our foothold on the steep climb. To strengthen this inner structure still further, we must hold onto images which soothe and ease the soul e.g., the image of the floating feather, the picture of the millstone turning, turning, and the picture of the house with the rotten roof. Epistemic resilience is weakened by inappropriate attitudes and orientations (demons) that are interconnected so that weakness in one area leads to weaknesses in other areas. Control of thought, attention and prayer are three main sources for refilling the inner wells.

---

22   Sister Maria In & Out the Andes: Mission Trails From Yucatan to Chile. New York: Charles Scribner's Sons 1955, 83.

4.4   Interiority and the "Deep Self"

Biblical background languages as well as early Christian writers like Augustine and Cassian have shown that the human person can be characterized by rich interiority which can be ordered and follows certain spiritual laws. Epistemic resilience is strengthened by inner wealth and inner order. Nevertheless, having a rich inner life or having access to the riches of one's inner life may not be a given. Our inner lives are precious, our inner lives are fragile—Bill Russell Edmonds talks about "the experience of a moral injury" when working as a soldier in Iraq, his inner life had been changed: "In May 2006, I left Iraq with no visible wounds. But something had changed inside. It just took me a long time to realize it."[23] Ever since then he has had to live with "this inner contradiction, the yawning chasm between my desire and my life experience."[24] The landscape of his inner life had changed, he had to cope with inner chaos, forces at work in his soul, forces he could not control. In experiencing extreme displacement quite literally in the desert he was unable to cultivate the capacity to cope with the experience; perhaps he was not given ample opportunity to access any skills he might have had. Doubly distressing is the sense of displacement when one returns to a known, a given, familiar environment one has lost the inner capacity to "be" in. Bill Russell Edmonds had to learn how to get in touch with his inner life again. Having access to one's own inner treasures and inner order is not an unearned privilege.

Let us explore an example: in his semi-autobiographical book *The Invention of Solitude*, Paul Auster describes his father as a man who seemed to have no sense of inner depth at all.[25] Paul Auster characterize his father as being "absent" (IS 6), strangely absent from the lives of those who were—or should have been—close to him and, even more strangely, seemed to be absent without leave from his own life, too. Auster also sees his father as a 'solitary' figure (IS 17), not having to see himself as seen by others; Paul Auster's father—Sam—lived in his own home like a stranger, he was a tourist in his own life;[26] he seemed to have no real passion for anything (IS 6); he lacked imagination (IS 27), and the

---

23   B.R. Edmonds, God is not here. A Soldier's Struggle with Torture, Trauma, and the Moral Injuries of War. New York: Pegasus Books 2015, 20 (remark on moral injury on p. 21).

24   Ibd., 96f.

25   P. Auster, The Invention of Solitude. Abbrev: "IS" for purposes of this text.

26   "His house was just one of many stopping places in a restless, unmoored existence, and this lack of center had the effect of turning him into a perpetual outsider, a tourist of his own life. You never had the feeling that he could be located" (IS 9). Auster describes his father at another point as being: "implacably neutral on the surface, his behavior was so flatly predictable, that everything he did came as a surprise" (IS 21).

world passed him leaving him untouched, like water off a duck's back (IS 7), he preferred to stay on the surface, on the outside of things and not get involved (IS 15).[27] It was almost as if he was divested of interiority (IS 20). Like someone entering an exam completely unprepared was the way he wandered through his existence (IS 11): he was not the least interested in the subject to be studied, had no desire to sit down and learn for the exam; he didn't seem to care and chose instead to follow a monotonous daily routine which, according to his son, Paul, was less to do with lack or loss of memory than just not giving a damn (IS 9).[28] It comes as no surprise that he could not cope with change, with new life factors; he remained polite, respectable and aloof—keeping everything and everyone at arm's length. Paul remembers the time he took his first-born, Sam's first grandchild, to visit:

> Daniel was just two weeks old when (*my father*) first laid eyes on him, (…). My father pulled up in his car, saw my wife putting the baby into the carriage for a nap, and walked over to say hello. He poked his head into the carriage for a tenth of a second, straightened up and said to her, 'A beautiful baby. Good luck with it', and then proceeded to walk on into the house (…). He might just as well have been talking about a stranger's baby encountered in line at the supermarket. (IS 20).

The occasion was more of a brief encounter than a family celebration; Sam was courteous and civil, but that was all; he followed a strict code of proper conduct but there was no authenticity in his reaction or in what he said—there was no sign of his being moved inwardly. He gave the impression of wanting to escape from the here and now (IS 58). And yet in everyday life he was amazingly practical and went about his duties and met obligations in a world where everything had to be in a certain place and was to be had for a certain price (IS 57). The impression he conveyed was of someone who was unaware of his own inner being, someone who had no idea what interiority was let alone how to go about finding it; and all those human dreams, hopes, convictions, inner feelings and desires were missing—buried.

---

27 The idea of a life without depth was completely alien to Paul Auster—"your existence is confined to a narrow space in which you are constantly forced to reveal yourself—and therefore, constantly obliged to look into yourself, to examine your own depths" (IS 15).

28 Auster saw this negligence as the dominant feature in the life of his father both in the way he treated himself and those around him. The house he continued to live in after his divorce fell into a state of disrepair and he didn't seem to care or even notice. Auster sees this as the image of his father's life.

Paul's father was head of the family, but randomly so, without much thought of himself, his wife and children; he treated them like relatives on a visit. Later on, Paul found out that as a child his father had been severely traumatized: he had witnessed his mother murdering his own father, an experience which cut Sam Auster off from himself. He went on functioning at a superficial level but void of inner life and feeling. Denied of inner self as source of epistemic resilience, he had lost the depth we all need to be able to delve into when we are faced with new challenges. Depth and interiority are intertwined and cannot be divorced from each other; without the one or the other, we can only *react*. An individual who can react will be deeply affected by what has happened—it will impact and form inner self, nudge it onwards. Experiences are 'deep' in that they have a deep impact on the structure of our heart and soul and our capacity to be displaced, and help us to see the world around us as it truly is.

Inner wealth is not a given; the Christian tradition provides a language and spiritual laws to look into the structure of the inner. If the inner is not structured or if a person does not have access to her life, as in the case of Samuel Auster, this person will not able to cultivate resilience from within. Deep insights into the profundity of the inner life can be found in a particular passage of Edith Stein's *opus magnum* "Finite and Eternal Being."[29] Edith Stein is undoubtedly one of the greatest Christian philosophers of the 20th century. She connects Thomism, Carmelite spirituality as well as phenomenological philosophy in an original way and is uniquely placed to contribute to the exploration of the structure of the inner. Edith Stein defines interiority as that which makes us human beings; it makes who we are: "I"—the signature of our own person (EES 334); this "I" is not static but needs to work its way towards self-awareness (something Sam Auster was incapable of doing after witnessing what he did) and learn to know self. It is through "I" that I see, perceive and understand the world, from my own point of view; "I" also gives me my own tool box to chisel and create my own life, which is mine and mine alone (EES 335). Thus seen, interiority is most pronounced in a human life which has had the chance to develop *my* intellectual and spiritual capabilities (EES 393). Freedom of spirit unlocks the door to new experiences and discoveries—which already exist in that inner "I" (EES 336).

We access the outside world with our powers of perception; much of what I see in the outside world is registered and stored in *my* mind as numbers and percentages of some kind or another, but *my* interior world demands a

---

29   Edith Stein, Endliches und ewiges Sein. Versuch eines Aufstiegs zum Sinn des Seins. Freiburg/
        Br: Herder 1950 (Edith Steins Werke. Edited H.L. Gelber, R. Leuven. Band II). Abbreviation:
        "EES." A helpful English translation of the passage most relevant to this project can be found
        as E. Stein, The Interiority of the Soul. Logos 8,2 (Spring 2005) 183–193.

different type of awareness—attention and concentration; it is not immediately or wholly accessible to me but it is *my* personal mission to dig as deep as possible. The human spirit is not visible to itself, but this does not mean that it is wholly invisible, it needs to be elucidated but should not be penetrated completely.[30]

It is interesting to note that acknowledging one's own inner limits is in itself a lesson in discovering self. When I am pushed to my own limits, the experience of being unable to cope is a valuable lesson, a valid contribution to *my*self (EES 338). Hence crossroad challenges and decision-making enable us to find more of self. In fact the spirit is duty-bound to cultivate that inner plane of interiority which in turn shapes and fashions our outside world. Edith Stein refers to inner self as the center of own being (EES 341). The soul has to first take hold—take possession—of its own being: the soul is striving after its own self (cf. EES 395).

On this journey to inner fulfilment, the soul does not dictate or direct the actions and words of the body, as if directing some play on a stage, but plays its own part in finding being in that self. It acts in tune with the dynamics of an inner world unseen by but not detached from the outside world. En route to its destination, it will be shaped, moulded and formed in its own unique way. This dual role of shaping and being shaped reveals that the human soul has a life of its own: it is not something between intangible spirit and tangible matter, it is its own creation; not a reflection of a created spirit but a creative spirit in its own right (EES 393). On its journey the soul takes strength from silent prayer and meditation; this disentangles it from the lure of external provocation; its power source is God and only God (cf. EES 408f). This life-giving energy source also requires regular inputs of bright sunshine, the sight of a lush green meadow, hearing the joyful laugh of a child or a word of encouragement (EES 400).

These outside stimuli can only be truly perceived by the inner soul and it is this mindful watching, noticing and perceiving, anew and afresh which is a core life mission. However, the more we seek to stick to this path and the more progress we make, the more energy we require to do so, this means that progress relies on our seeking and sourcing, seeing and perceiving valuable resources both in daily encounters with those we meet along the way and our experiencing personal displacement in the landscape we find ourselves at any one particular moment in time. How do we differentiate between what we should take with us and what we should leave by the wayside? Like the shepherd we need to be on our guard, watchful and vigilant, recognizing the good

---

30   "Der Menschengeist ist für sich selbst sichtbar, aber nicht restlos durchsichtig; er vermag
      anderes zu erhellen, aber nicht völlig zu durchdringen" (EES 336).

and beautiful and realizing that these alone are God-given gifts; we should re-alize and know that we do not suffice for our own growth and development; withdrawing into inner self and being oblivious to the outside world—letting it go by in the same way as Paul Auster's father—is a hindrance and not a help on this journey; we need to be alert and receptive for new cultures, new life-giving sources. This symbiotic process of looking out and seeking within, al-lowing at the same time that inner space to be moulded and shaped enables each unique individual to lead a life of freedom dependent on plumbing those depths of interiority.

Similar to Augustine, memory and capacity of recall play a significant part in the structure building of the soul for Edith Stein. It is memory which ensures that nothing meaningful is lost; it can recall, relive and retrieve events and situations in the past but free of the context and ties existent at the time of occurrence. "The length of time something is kept in the memory largely depends on the initial impact and degree of impact on the life of the indi-vidual in question. At the same time, one decisive factor in level of memory is the depth at which it was sensed and perceived which in turn depends on the 'depth of perception' at the time the event took place," (EES 401). Here we have a singular description of what any individual requires to cope with and grow in a displacement experience.

Memory remembers and stores the things that penetrate to the depths of the soul, this process is supported by a sort of filing and sifting system which structures the absorption capacity of the memory and arranges memories ac-cording to their weight and significance. Edith Stein highlights the dynam-ics at work in shaping that inner self and distinguished between two types of thinking processes, the one skimming the surface of experience and awareness and the other probing deep down into innermost structures of perception and comprehension. Someone who can delve into such depths of thought is also able to draw on a similarly deep treasure-trove of resources. Those who see and hear without much thought or consideration to the subject will not be able to draw on such a wealth of resources. The soul will resonate in harmony with what the eye or ear perceives; it will be so inwardly moved, it will not be able to do otherwise.

Of course, whether or not human powers of thinking merely scratch the surface or dig deeper, depends on a person's powers of imagination. Edith Stein cites an example: In the summer of 1914 the assassination of Archduke Ferdinand is announced (EES 401). Two people who hear this news react in two distinct ways: the one carries on with his daily chores untouched, unperturbed by what he has heard, the other is shocked to her inmost core (EES 402); the one is unaware and unconcerned of the consequences of this item of news; the other is all too aware of the implications of the act, the disruption it will cause and from the moment of hearing the announcement lives in anxious anticipation of what must undoubtedly come (EES 402). This is a deep and powerful example illustrating a difference between "deep" and "shallow" reception," "deep" and "shallow" self. It is the repercussions sensed by the inner eye that decide whether an experience is "deep" or not, whether it can be processed in deep learning or not.

How we react has less to do with *what* we think than *how* we think. Why does such news leave an indelible impression on *you* and not on *me*? If we view the *scenery* of our own life's stage, if we consciously (and continuously) dwell upon aspects which impact the very structure of our own role on that stage, those aspects tend to be the things which concern us as individuals and reveal the depth or shallowness of the life we live: deep people are inwardly touched and moved by what goes on around them which also suggests a willingness on their part to be touched, moulded and shaped by experience. It does go without saying that this bears a higher risk of being hurt by that *scenery*; yet, at the same time it affords stronger powers of resistance, too.

Edith Stein analyzes the wider significance of such capacities; the unique spiritual life of each individual is embedded in a wider universal context and it is this wider context which motivates the soul to act. Edith Stein makes it clear that a spiritual life depends on both meaning and purpose, and the power to be motivated. The simple question of "why?" triggers the soul into action: it is our human obligation to seek meaning and purpose in life and not drift with the crowd. Again we come back to the idea of freedom, freedom to act—or not to act. Are we responsive to what we see, to the challenges life sets us? Responsiveness at its basic level is answering a call one hears, whereby we need to distinguish between degrees of *hearing* and if we are "free" to hear and react as we see fit. The answering process is intertwined with the freedoms we as human beings have at our disposal.

Responsiveness is also a matter of meaning-making capacities; these capacities are proven under duress. Steven Schwartzberg and Ronnie Janoff-Bulman, for example, showed that grief shatters and challenges patterns of meaning-making and assumptions about meaning.[31] It requires inner strength (and paradoxically, openness to the real, i.e. flexibility) to respond to adverse experiences. The key to this inner strength has to do with our inner core. Edith Stein maintains that universal existence is human life with a clearly defined

31   Steven S. Schwartzberg and Ronnie Janoff-Bulman, Grief and the Search for Meaning: Exploring the Assumptive Worlds of Bereaved College Students. *Journal of Social and Clinical Psychology* 10,3 (1991) 270–288.

inner core, a core with an equally clear focus, but this is a rare commodity in any human being. People may often have an outlook on life emanating from the inner ego excited by trivial sensationalism and rarely shocked by world disasters and if they are, then only temporarily, soon distracted and returning to their old habits of superficial detachment (EES 404). Universal existence is guided by its inner strengths and sources which will hold sense of being in the balance without allowing it to be knocked off course (completely displaced) by sensationalistic news reports. That sense of universal existence will ponder on the real depth and significance of what goes on in the world and set it in a wider context; it will relate to and arrange the things it perceives according to their common importance.

While some individuals may briefly be aware of the depths of inner soul, some will never experience even this (EES 404), and never truly feel that power guiding them imperturbably towards a worthwhile goal; they will never know the agency of responsibility. A person who can draw on depths of inner knowledge and *trust-worthy* experience will reveal an inner depth and breadth of soul beyond the boundaries of self (EES 405). And this is the person who will most probably be a candidate for epistemic resilience based on a deep experience of her own depth. This will allow a person to "drink from her own wells."

4.5   A Word of Warning

Since this book is about epistemic resilience as the core of the capacity to be displaced, it pays particular attention to the inner aspects of human life and the inner life of a person; there is a risk here and it should be explicitly mentioned: it is the risk of reducing resilience to epistemic resilience and the person to her interiority. Rowan Williams however points out some dangers of this concept in his essay on '*Interiority and Epiphany*;' the fiction we easily succumb to is the myth that we each have a hidden inner 'kernel' with an external husk, a husk which needs to be pulled away to reveal the kernel inside. Rowan Williams argues that: 'My sense of the 'hiddenness' of another self is something I develop in the ordinary difficulty of conversation and negotiation.'[32] Or in plainer terms: 'The exchanges of conversation and negotiation *are* the essence of what is going on, not unsatisfactory translations of a more fundamental script.'[33] Interiority is a sense of self and a way of speaking to and talking about others,

---

32   R. Williams, 'Interiority and Epiphany', in: R. Williams, On Christian Theology. Oxford: Blackwell, 2000, pp. 239–264, 240.

33   Ibd., 241.

and being human; similarly, awareness of my own hiddenness is revealed in exchanges which arise in conversation. Interiority is not so much a realm to be discovered than the result of a process of dialogue. Walter Davis express- es this view when he writes: 'No depth exists in subject until it is created. No *a priori* identity awaits us (...) Inwardness is a process of becoming, a work, the labor of the negative. The self is not a substance one unearths by peeling away layers until one gets to the core, but an integrity one struggles to bring into existence.'[34] Reflection upon sense of self—my own and other—must never be divorced from social and material processes of reflection. Identity is gener- ated in interrelation between self and other, as 'self among other selves'.

With this in mind, we can now turn to sources of epistemic resilience— sources that are cultivated within a social and even political context.

---

34   W.A. Davis, Inwardness and Existence. Milwaukee, MI: University of Wisconsin Press
      1989, 105.

CHAPTER 5

Strengthening the Powers of Resilience: Voices from the *Philokalia*

The Christian tradition has developed a new way of thinking about the inner; our inner life can and ought to be structured, even if it is an effort and struggle to do so. A well-ordered interiority provides rich resources for building epistemic resilience; if "the inner house" is well kept, one can find building-blocks of resilience within oneself. The "threshold of resilience" differs from person to person; some people need more inner strengths to cope with a particular situation than others. Some people can live with a lack of organization and structural clarity, others struggle. When mission doctor Albert Schweitzer first arrived at his destination, Lambarene, he had to learn how to deal with what he called *Unzuverlässigkeit* (unrealibility).[1] He was frustrated, but had to preserve his morale; this required inner strength. When South African writer Lewis Nikosi first arrived in New York in January 1961 he experienced the city as hard, cold, tough, brutal and as "the loneliest city in th world."[2] He found himself in a desert having to pull together all his inner strength.

The missionary experience can ask a person to use all her inner resources. Italian Jesuit priest Vincenzo De Francisco served the Italian community in Melbourne in the 1920s and was deeply discouraged by his first encounters. "They would view me with suspicion, and snap at me, 'Why are you here?', 'What do you think you're doing?'." He had to endure, he had to nurture patience and hope, he understood that it takes time to build trust and respect; but he was able to fall back on his inner sense of purpose and mission.[3] He dealt with his experience of displacement by creating and cultivating inner space. This cultivation of the inner is a way of practicing epistemic resilience. The Christian tradition has a wealth of literary resources to motivate, give

---

1 Albert Schweitzer, A., Zwischen Wasser und Urwald: Erlebnisse und Beobachtungen eines Arztes im Urwalde Äquatorialafrikas. Bern: P. Haupt 1922, 31 and 62 respectively.
2 Lewis Nkosi, Encounter with New York. In: M. Robinson, ed., Altogether Elsewhere. Boston: Faber and Faber 1994, 289–298, at 292.
3 Vincenzo De Francesco, Letters to Naples. A Neapolitan writes home about his work in Melbourne 1919–1928. Ballan, Australia: Connor Court 2010, 12.

strength to fall back on when we find ourselves in a desert of displacement. Such a treasure chest as this is the *Philokalia*.

The *Philokalia* are a collection of early Orthodox Christian texts written between the first and 14th century and put together in the 18th century.[4] Establishing and developing inner strength and powers of resistance in times of adversity is the central theme running through most of these texts. The *Philokalia* could actually be read as a study guide in epistemic resilience based on the experiences of spiritual masters. Silent prayer is often seen as the true spiritual path to inner-growth, a path best trodden alone, in solitude and silence. The recognition of solitude as a source of strength is not only a Christian idea: Donald Winnicott published an article in 1958 on "The Capacity to be Alone."[5] An article in which he underlines the importance of this capacity for maturing and growth, and presents this idea as a corrective thought to the dominating discourse on the importance of social skills.

A similar thought can be found in Anthony Storr's book *Solitude*. Here again we find suggestions of "being alone" as a contributory factor to a contented life and personal fulfilment.[6] Storr connects the capacity to be alone with inner security and inner strength: "The capacity to be alone ... becomes linked with self-discovery and self-realization; with becoming aware of one's deepest needs, feelings, and impulses."[7] Against this background he cites creative spirits like Newton, Kant, Wittgenstein who found their creative force in solitude. The ability to retreat into and to be alone with oneself opens up the possibility to gain and cultivate independence from external conditions; "the capacity to be alone is a valuable resource when changes of mental attitude are required."[8] The capacity to be displaced cannot be separated from the capacity to be alone. The capacity to be alone has been recognized as a source for creativity, intimacy, and spirituality including imaginative involvement in multiple realities, self-transformation and the reconstitution of cognitive structures.[9] This is precisely the idea at the root of (now returning to the wisdom of the spiritual

---

4   Edition used: The Philokalia. The Complete Text compiled by St. Nicodemos of the Holy Mountain and St. Macarios of Corinth. Vol. I. Transl. and edited by G.E.H. Palmer, Ph. Sherrard, K. Ware. London: Faber and Faber 1983.

5   D. Winnicott, The Capacity to be alone. In: D. Winnicott, The Maturational Process and the Facilitating Environment. London 1969.

6   A. Storr, Solitude. London 1997 (orig: The School of Genius. London 1988).

7   Ibd., 21.

8   Ibd., 29.

9   Christopher R. Long, James R. Averill, Solitude: An Exploration of Benefits of Being Alone. *Journal for the Theory of Social Behaviour* 33:1 (2003) 21–44.

tradition developed in many writings) the *Philokalia*; the idea of conversion, repentance, growth and a commitment to a new life shaped by the inner.

The motifs of desert, solitude, and silence are important building blocks of early Christian writing. The capacity to be displaced was discussed in the discourses on the desert experience. Desert, solitude and silence are archetypical settings of hardship and purification. In the second book of his "Twenty-four Discourses", St Peter of Damascus writes about the constant struggle encountered in spiritual battles advising that, "in spiritual warfare it is impossible to find a place anywhere in creation in which a battle is not being waged. In the desert there are wild beasts and demons and other malefic and terrifying things; in places of solitude and stillness there are demons (...)."[10] At the same time, solitude is a privileged spiritual situation; deserts are environments with little stimulation; they provide space to practice inwardness and the turning or re-turning to inner self.

The desert is the perfect place for solitude; John Cassian mentioned solitude in his *Collationes* as a way to finding peace of the soul (Col I:7) and a road towards perfection (Col XVIII:16), since a solitary state allows special communion with God (Col II:2). He is, however, also aware of the challenges of solitude with its lack of fraternal admonishment and communal correction (Col V:14). There are special temptations a hermit is confronted with such as the loss of all sense of proportion, the loss of a life with "feet on the ground" (Col IX:15), and deception and self-deception (Col XIX:10). In other words, solitude as experience and desert as space are places of painful growth, flourishing in adversity—training grounds for epistemic resilience.

A discussion on the capacity to be displaced can benefit from a discussion of the desert. Irish missionary Brendan Payne found himself in a desert, literally and figuratively when he arrived in the Turkana desert in Kenya; "The landscape was barren, hot, shimmering, the sun beating down. It was widely accepted that the Turkana Desert was one of the toughest postings."[11] And on top of this was the challenge of coping with his own inner mental landscape given his keen experience of displacement and loneliness. The desert is a special place for encounter and growth because of solitude, as we have already discussed, but it is also a difficult place to live in since it does not offer much in the way of water, food, shelter or human company. One's own identity is not supported externally and sheer survival is threatened. A desert is vast expanse of seeming nothingness; it is a place that requires resilience as beautifully described in Antoine de Saint-Exupery's 1935 book

---

10   Peter of Damaskos, Twenty-Four Discourses, Book II, V (Patient Endurance).

11   A. Clerkin, B. Clerkin, A Road Less Travelled, 73.

Wind, Sand and Stars. Surviving in the desert is a struggle, both internally and externally.[12] Living in the desert requires the capacity to lead a solitary life and accept the mental and physical demands of solitude and absolute peace which are inseparably linked with developing a way of life centered on inner-spirituality. The heart comes into its own as a safe-haven in solitude and silence, and its prayers become the mainstay source of inner stability and heart-felt joy, which in turn can generate inner-strength on the path to steadfast inner-peace. In the following section, I will refer to three writers, who each in their own right created a correlation between the state of the inner self and outward resilience: St. Isaiah the Solitary, St. Mark the Ascetic, St. Hesychios the Priest.

5.1 On Guarding the Intellect: St. Isaiah the Solitary

Isaiah the Solitary is thought to have lived in the first half of the 5th century and to have written a short but profound text *On Guarding the Intellect* (27 texts: 27 chapters or paragraphs).[13] In this concise work we can find advice on how to strengthen epistemic resilience and it seems its author was primarily concerned with helping his pupils face and tackle adverse challenges. The four main guiding principles can be outlined as follows: (i) the role of anger; (ii) the significance of formed conscience; (iii) the focus on the divine and the fearlessness based on fear of God; and (iv) constant watchfulness.

(i) Isaiah emphasizes the importance of anger in cleansing the heart. We need to purify our thoughts from all beliefs that are directed against knowledge of God (IGI 24:27). Adverse circumstances have to be faced fairly and squarely with righteous anger (IGI 1:22). What is being addressed here is the idea of both resoluteness on the one hand and the power of protest on the other, both of which have to be set in motion by every possible means to fight evil (IGI 2:22). Anger is described as being a 'natural' force rooted in human passion, a force "in accordance with nature." Anger is therefore regarded as a natural 'weapon' in the human toolkit of defense which should not be abandoned since one has to be able to 'fight' what is wrong. Job's experience is quoted as an example of well-placed anger that serves resilience; inner life must retain access to the power of righteous anger. Nonetheless, anger needs to be controlled and directed i.e., used rationally and justly, not blindly. Being

---

12 See J. Allain-Chapman, Resilient Pastors. London: SPCK 2012, esp. ch. 3.

13 I will quote from the above-mentioned edition of the *Philokalia* (volume 1), paragraph and page number using the abbreviation "IGI."

able to channel anger depends on a strong resolve to choose good and forego bad. When someone knows why and what direction she has chosen to take, she can set out along the hard and rugged path to Goodness equipped to overcome hardships on the way and strengthened by the assurance of what she is doing. Prayer is the foundation for the appropriate attitude that allows a person to deal well with anger.

(ii) A key to inner strength is a clear sense of moral direction—the main source of this direction is conscience; conscience needs to be formed:

> In the fear of God let us keep our attention fixed within ourselves, until our conscience achieves its freedom. Then there will be a union between it and us, and thereafter it will be our guardian, showing us each thing that we must uproot. But if we do not obey our conscience, it will abandon us and we shall fall into the hands of our enemies, who will never let us go. (IGI 3:22–23).

Our "fear of God", set within a wider framework of life, is a benchmark standard to measure our thoughts and deeds against, we have to form our conscience since it is the basis for epistemic resilience and itself "an adversary because it opposes us" when we wish to give in to desires not formed in accordance with a God-fearing attitude (IGI 3:23). A properly formed conscience will be a major source of epistemic resilience since it not only gives us a sense of direction but also a motivation to walk down a road chosen. We will revisit this point under the heading of existential commitments. Conscience will remind a person of the good path; this inner voice points to an inner struggle and as long as there is an inner moral struggle, a person is not free (IGI 18:25). The key point of living with a formed conscience is to allow one's conscience to steer and hold on to this course (IGI 23:27).

(iii) Epistemic resilience is strengthened by focusing on Divine help—fear of God creates the ground for fearlessness since "Fear not" is the message of God to an intellect submitted to God. "When the intellect hears these words of reassurance [Fear not], it says boldly to its enemies: 'Who would fight with me? Let him stand against me'" (IGI 5:23). A person who puts her trust in God is never alone. These are key elements of existential commitments: fostering epistemic resilience, in looking at our life as a whole, in its entirety, including the way ahead, trusting in the certainty that we have a companion as we go, acknowledging our own helplessness in being incapable of 'going it' alone and being forced to see our own limits. With this in mind, epistemic resilience can be nurtured and developed despite (and if we consider the capacity to be displaced perhaps exactly because of) all odds. And an additional point, in understanding the framework in which we act out our lives, we also have to realize that we can turn round and start again at any point in time, make a fresh start, reset the compass: "When a man abandons his sins and returns to God, his repentance regenerates him and renews him entirely," (IGI 22:26).

Discovering that we have—are given—opportunities to re-take our bearings, helps us in fortifying epistemic resilience. This discovery requires us to focus on our encounter with God in our soul and thus master independence from external circumstances. "Curiosity" and "distraction" are two obstacles to be overcome when struggling to remain focused on God (IGI 23:27). Isaiah compares our human senses with the "gates of the soul" that have to be carefully guarded (IGI 7:23). In other words, inner strength is responsible for watching over weakening factors and forces at work in our experience of the senses (IGI 12:24). This is a helpful thought: Epistemic resilience can be strengthened by a wholesome diet of sensory experiences. If we manage to set our hope on invisible things, we gain independence from the visible world (IGI 8:23), in other words, a person with faith-based epistemic resilience embraces a sacramental view of the universe, and is able to connect the visible with the invisible (which we will discuss in chapter seven).

A soul freed from external pressures will find peace, "Sabbath rest" (IGI 10:24), e.g., in offering up genuine prayer (IGI 13:24).[14] In connection with prayer, Isaiah's text is rich in imagery: "In storms and squalls we need a pilot, and in this present life we need prayer; for we are susceptible to the provocations of our thoughts, both good and bad," (IGI 24:27). These images of the ship, pilot and squalls speak volumes and reveal a deep understanding of what adversity really is and what surmounting it involves: we are literally at the mercy of the elements in adversity, life is akin to walking on shifting sand and not going under. This demands our setting clear goals, keeping a tight hold on the tiller and not allowing ourselves to drift with the tide. The soul may be tossed about like a boat in the raging tempest of feelings and emotions, but will remain steadfast, unmoved in the eye of the storm if it keeps its sights on the horizon, (steers clear of the rocks) and focuses on the course set. The one crucial resource here is absolute trust in God; a trust in a greater power beyond known territory.

---

14   Isaiah is slightly ambiguous with regard to inner peace and permanent watchfulness: He does recognize the idea of inner peace (if a person has attained dispassion: IGI 18:26), but persists in warnings about constant watchfulness.

(iv) Peace found by the intellect, however, can only be maintained with an attitude of constant watchfulness; there is no place for complacency in peace of mind (IGI 11:24). The heart of the text lies in the constant reminder that we have to be vigilant. Vigilance means always being mindful of one's innermost thoughts and feelings in the soul. One of the keys to vigilance is self-awareness. Self-awareness is the fruit of self-scrutiny which, according to the *Philokalia*, is "in the sight of God" (IGI 20, 26). Achieving self-awareness means looking into one's own heart and heeding one's own sense(s), thus a meta perspective related to our own inner self and the way we deal with the world around us (cf., IGI 12:24).

Inner reflection, deep in the shelter of the heart will become the conscious contemplation of life, of one's own inner self as a fountain of strength and resilience. Isaiah's understanding of the inner life (similar to his predecessors and successors in Christian tradition literature) is an image of constant battle. Any person fighting with ordering her desires must be prepared for a struggle (IGI 14:25). In the spirit of early Christian writing, a false sense of security or inner pride can undermine all efforts to achieve this goal at any time, and it is exactly that feeling of having 'made it' and 'got to the top', of being safe and sound, home and dry which makes us vulnerable: "The demons cunningly withdraw for a time in the hope that we will cease to guard our heart, thinking we have now attained peace; then they suddenly attack our unhappy soul and seize it like a sparrow" (IGI 11:24). Hence the key to epistemic resilience is watchfulness both to our senses and to our thoughts.

This idea of guarding one's thought is an idea that can be found in many different cultures and traditions, including the Stoic tradition with its emphasis on discipline of the mind, as expressed in Marc Aurel's *Meditations*. We must resist shameful thoughts and immediately call to mind divine matters if a shameful thought enters our thinking (IGI 27:28). "Remember that God sees all your thoughts, and then you will never sin" (IGI 27:28). Isaiah the Solitary urges his readers to know their thoughts and the nature of their thoughts: "When a man has an exact knowledge about the nature of thoughts, he recognizes those which are about to enter and defile him, troubling the intellect with distractions and making it lazy," (IGI 12:24). Self-knowledge, as an aspect of epistemic resilience, can be cultivated by daily examination of self and inner attitude in the sight of God (IGI 20:26). Isaiah exhorts his readers not to leave their hearts "unguarded" (IGI 15:25), to discover what is in the heart (IGI 20:26) and to "be attentive to your heart" (IGI 21:26), "(...) to yourself" (IGI 22:25). Only such watchfulness will help us to distinguish between good and evil (IGI 24:27).

Summing up, we can say that in this text attributed to Isaiah the Solitary, powers of resistance are of central importance because life is a continual struggle to achieve inner growth in the face of adverse forces trying to 'lead us astray' from the true path. Fortifying epistemic resilience lies in not just dodging crises, but in actually facing them, taking them on board and coming out alive or even invigorated on the other side. Secondly, when adversity strikes, the effective use of anger will help us keep things in perspective and acknowledge our dependency on outside help and support. Thirdly, growth is rooted in self-awareness; being able to judge and assess the external and inner powers of persuasion, and fourthly, the significance of clarity of mind, disciplining our own thoughts and remaining focused. The culmination of the four elements of anger, conscience, focus, and watchfulness can be expressed in one word: inwardness. Inwardness is the key to dealing with external adversity and external deprivation as we have seen in the example of Archbishop Francis Xaver Văn Thuân. Isaiah expresses this thought in the following words: "We have practiced virtue and done what is right, turning our desire towards God and His will, and directing our incensive power, or wrath, against the devil and sin. What then do we still lack? Inward meditation" (IGI 26:28).

5.2 Outside Pressures and Inner Growth: St. Mark the Ascetic

Our second interlocutor in the *Philokalia* is Mark the Ascetic who is thought to have written the three works "On the Spiritual Law—200 Texts," "On Those Who Think that They are Made Righteous by Works—226 Texts," and "Letter to Nicolas the Solitary;" I will focus on the first two works.[15] St. Mark probably died in the first half of 5th century having served as Abbot and later living as an anchorite. He is often referred to as Mark the Monk, or Mark the Hermit. His works focus on how to face and deal with life's trials and tribulations, and this is the main reason for analyzing Mark's words in our discussion on epistemic resilience. Some of his motifs and insights are similar to Isaiah's teachings: The importance of second-order desires, i.e. control over desires (SL 176:122), and self-control (SL 134:119), the significance and weight

---

15 Source abbreviations: SL: On the Spiritual Law (quotes by text number, followed by page number); MRW: On Those Who Think That They are Made Righteous by Works (quotes by text number, followed by page number).

of thoughts[16] as reason and cause of sin (SL 119:118; 180:182), the major role of examination of conscience in a healthy spiritual life (SL 70:114; SL 185:123), the firm belief in divine providence (SL 3:110; SL 47:113).

Again and again we find in the *Philokalia* this motif of controlling thoughts: if our condition changes, it does so because of a change in the inner situation; and the inner situation changes because of a change in "quality of our thoughts" (SL 160:121). That is why you need to "guard your mind" (SL 163:121). Thoughts need to be categorized; types of thought differentiated between: some people savor the content of a thought, others the cause; in the case of involuntary thoughts, people tend to love the cause more, otherwise such thoughts would not emerge (MWR 86:132). Thoughts can be arranged according to their depth and tangibility: if thoughts are accompanied by vivid images, this suggests they have been endorsed and their entry permitted, so to speak (SL 141:119f). Thoughts tend to be restless, and they project this restlessness on to the soul which is why they have to be guarded carefully; Mark uses a vibrant image to describe the power of thoughts: "Like a young calf which, in its search for grazing, finds itself on a ledge surrounded by precipices, the soul is gradually led astray by its thoughts" (MWR 74:131). Like thoughts, memory must be guarded, too. Memory plays an important role in the cultivation of attitudes— St Mark warns against the involuntary presence of former sins in the memory (SL 139:119), and he warns against images stored in memory since they can be more harmful than images formed spontaneously out of of perniciousness (SL 182:122). St. Mark does not advise deliberately recalling sins to memory (MWR 133:136), or going over past sins in detail when making a confession to God (MWR 153:138).

I would like to focus attention on the admonitions, instructions and guidance of this spiritual teacher under four main points: (i) the connection between inner growth and external hardship; (ii) spiritual laws; (iii) hardship as teacher and giver-of-strength; and (iv) reasons for hardships.

(i) Hardship is the trials and tribulations, misfortunes and insurmountable obstacles, and being lured away from the path to spirituality, in other words, those situations and forces which distract or displace us and make us lose sight of the straight path of goodness; but these situations can in fact be the tools for, the milestones on the way to, inner growth. Situations that require epistemic resilience are opportunities for growth. True love, that is the bond with a *bonum*, has to undergo the acid test of tribulation, to be cleansed, purified

---

16   "Every thought has its weight and measure in God's sight" (SL 87:116: cf., SL 111:118); "Never belittle the significance of your thoughts, for not one escapes God's notice" (SL 89:116: see also SL 168:121 on this point).

and grow (SL 65:114). Overcoming hardship despite all odds means practicing patience and endurance, taking us further along the path to finding inner-strength. No virtue can be of any practical value if it cannot withstand the ordeal of hardship (SL 66, 1114).

This is a point worth thinking about: building character on living a life of virtue, does in turn mean hard work; virtues can only be acquired and strengthened by confronting and tackling hardships and unforeseen challenges face-on: if there are no stumbling blocks, there can be no inner growth. This in itself is a good reason why we should be ready and prepared for affliction (SL 51:113), and humbly open to the possibility of temptation;[17] building a life on a view that those afflictions and adverse experiences we meet along the way are a "part of" life and not something directed "against" life. Afflictions can bring blessings (SL 42:113), it is all a matter of inner attitude. In fact, opposing adversity is in Mark's eyes opposing God (MWR 197:142). Unexpected affliction is a test of our human "metal" and "steel" and should be tackled as such: "Every event is like a bazaar. He who knows how to bargain makes a good profit, he who does not makes a loss," (MWR 212:144). Maneuvering hurdles is a necessary part of moving ahead—obstacles do not hinder, they are a vital part of growth. Misfortune helps to remedy a bad character, just "as the bitterness of absinth helps a poor appetite" (SL 115:118). Unexpected trials are sent by God as invitations to practice an ascetic life (MWR 8:125f).

The way we deal with adversity says a lot about who we are and where we are. The way we react reveals something about our own human will (MWR 204:143). Any individual will come up against his or her own 'inclinations' when the temptation arises or forcefully invades. So, inner growth and overcoming hardships are linked in three ways: an ordeal will test our level of inner growth, an ordeal is a 'golden' opportunity to grow still more since we can only cope with ever bigger challenges by overcoming them; ordeals provide a mirror for us to see ourselves, recognize who we really are and in this realization grow still further.

(ii) If one wants to deal with adversities properly, one needs to be aware of spiritual laws that provide the framework within which we struggle to grow. St. Mark presents his readers and listeners with insights into these spiritual laws, insights into the order of the spiritual dimension of a person's life, an order with its own rules and mechanisms. In this regard, I want to mention five such laws:

---

17   "He who says he knows all the devil's tricks falls unknowingly into his trap" (SL 166:121).

The primacy of interiority, in the sense that God sees and judges intention (SL 184:122); a person may be "outwardly humble, but inwardly arrogant"
(SL 36:113), expressing the idea that private attitudes and individual inner life
are more important than behavior and conduct which everyone may observe
and judge character by. In this, St. Mark is implying that "we get what we
deserve," the things that happen to us often happen as a direct result of our
inner state (MWR 67:131). This also implies that external events and experience
say something about our inner state of being.

The primacy of action over theoretical ideas (SL 85:116; SL 86:116), is the conviction that everything is firmly established but only becomes part of a person's life situation "by being put into practice" (MWR 12:126).

The importance of small beginnings ("Everything that happens has a small
beginning, and grows the more it is nourished," SL 171:122), and proper attention to detail ("The devil belittles small sins; otherwise he cannot lead us into
greater ones," SL 94:116). This law reveals a lot about the logics of space: if you
give space to something by establishing it in the framework of your regular
routines and habits—it will grow; this notion also links back to the idea that
the involuntary follows the voluntary.[18] A voluntary action can lead to habits
that over time become chains of bondage, forcing a person into a condition of
being enslaved to a way of acting or thinking.

The logic of resilience is based on hopeful prospects; a correlation between
present strength and future hope: "The greater a man's faith that Christ will
reward him, the greater his readiness to endure every injustice" (SL 44:113),[19]
which is a summons to adopt a vision of the future when facing adversity;
"accept present afflictions for the sake of future blessings" (SL 156:121; MWR
168:140f). If a person has a clear concept of future as well as a clear sense of
transcendent criteria, i.e. outlooks on life that transcend the current situation
and allow for the capacity to be displaced and to consider life per se regardless
of context, the person can remain steadfast in the midst of adversity.[20]

---

18   "If, as Scripture teaches, everything involuntary has its cause in what is voluntary,
      man has no greater enemy than himself" (MWR 104:133); a similar thought is expressed
      in MWR 190:142.

19   "When harmed, insulted or persecuted by someone, do not think of the present but wait
      for the future, and you will find he has brought you much good, not only in this life but
      also in the life to come" (SL 114:118).

20   "When you suffer some dishonor from men, recognize at once the glory that will be given
      you by God. Then you will not be saddened or upset by the dishonor" (MWR 68:131); see
      also MWR 187:141.

There is a connection between body and soul, in the sense that the intellect can only be still if the body is still as well (MWR 31:128), and also in the sense that suffering of the one (either body or soul) can benefit the other (MWR 46:129). Mental strife cannot be overcome if one is physically sluggish or in a state of inertia (MWR 45:129). This is where being physically fit plays a vital role in fighting adversity. Mark makes it clear, too, that physical challenges are indispensable not only for inner growth but also for our whole approach to life (MWR 46:129). Our lack of moderation, excessive enjoyment, intemperance, in other words, overindulging—in the transient luxuries of everyday life can only weaken our inner self (MWR 128:135).

(iii)   Hardships are invitations to grow; this was the inner attitude Vaclav Havel cultivated in prison; this is a common motif in framing the missionary experience. All things considered, one has to say 'yes' to testing times because they help us to grow and tackle the next—even bigger—obstacle which may lie just around the corner. Hardship is a lesson to be learnt, and we all need to be prepared to learn from the lesson: "he who willingly accepts chastening by affliction is not dominated by evil thoughts" (MWR 208:143). Hardship is a "good" teacher; hardships propel virtues forward, keeps them well oiled, up and running, so to speak. Times of distress teach us: "to practice the ascetic life," (MWR 8:125f). And learning to love having to make an effort plays a major role in how we put what we learn to good use. (MWR 7:125).

Wanting to learn without making an effort makes us self-satisfied and over-confident, we lose all sense of proportion; as the saying goes: pride before a fall. And if we fall, we fail to overcome, to 'resist' the temptations of life, we literally 'go astray', wander from the straight and narrow; nor do we learn the key lesson Mark prescribes: "patiently accept affliction," (MWR 56:130). Obstacles should be taken on board because hardships and afflictions create opportunities. Opportunities are real invitations to grow; they are not vague possibilities, but concrete situations that invite a particular response. This idea of 'spiritual opportunities' can be found again and again in Mark's line of thinking. He describes the testing of Abraham (Gen 22:11f)—an image which Kierkegaard came back to repeatedly—as a chance to prove perfect faith (MWR 203f, 143). God knew abominable test Abraham was confronted with was a chance for him to develop and grow. This in itself is a (spiritual) skill—to be able to transform (terrible) situations into (spiritual) opportunities.

The ability to transform a chance situation into an opportunity—*carpe diem*—is what one might also call 'serendipity'. At one particular point, Mark makes this quite clear when talking about spiritual law: "Pray that temptation may not come to you; but when it comes, accept it as your due and not undeserved," (SL 164:121). "Acceptance" is not only the realistic attitude of working with reality, but also a spiritual attitude of trusting that reality expresses a providential and thus beneficial logic. Each and every situation calls for a personal response and is a personal invitation to grow. We should not try to 'pass the buck' as if it had nothing to do with us, not blame others for your own misfortune (MWR 56:130). This is an interesting point, hardship and ordeals can be turned around, upside down if we acknowledge them to be the result of our own doing if we 'own up to' and thus accept full 'ownership' of them. "When tested by some trial you should try to find out not why or through whom it came, but only how to endure it gratefully, without distress or rancor," (MWR 198:142). Seen thus hardship can be a beneficial teacher and this brings us to the role and power of "agency" and "ownership."

Recognizing ownership and accepting agency will reinforce our powers of resistance and thus cultivate and nourish epistemic resilience.

(iv) Epistemic resilience is strengthened by acknowledging roots and reasons, causes and sources. Mark also gives 'inner' reasons for a person having to suffer hardship. These reasons reveal a lot about Mark beyond his non-ascetic, Christian view of things: in saying why such painful occurrences happen, he places blind ignorance at the top of the list (MWR 105:133). From this point of view, it is even comforting to know that if hardship is borne with dignity, accepted without question, it does 'teach us a lesson.' Seen in this light, 'how' is easier to accept than 'why' something untoward happens. Someone who spends and wastes their time on trivia, is investing vast amounts of time and effort on petty details and loses sight of the bigger picture of things in the process, is predestined to plunge into 'an abyss' of misfortune, a 'slough of despond.' Mark underlines this idea by noting that "When the devil finds someone preoccupied needlessly with bodily things, he first deprives him of the hard-won fruits of spiritual knowledge" (MWR 173:140).

To no longer notice the quintessential things in life must have disastrous consequences for two reasons: one, the power of the lesson taught by 'disaster' is absolutely essential; two, ignorance is *not* bliss since it robs us of our competence to deal with disasters, making them that much more painful and impossible to bear. A second source of 'catastrophes' is skepticism (MWR 105:133); skepticism is comparable to a lack of trust, akin to feeling completely alone in the world, made worse by being suspicious of anything which might soothe the pain or look vaguely like a 'rescue plan'. Skepticism as loss of wisdom and inner security denies us of our 'coping' faculties. In his "Letter to Nicolas the Solitary" Mark notes jealousy and envy as a third source and reason for inner weakness, "the mindset of avarice" as the root cause of personal ordeals.[21]

By fixing our gaze on what really counts, there is little danger of our being distracted away from our chosen path. A fourth reason is, we often bring unwanted challenges on ourselves by our own flippant behavior and shallow attitude of mind.[22] Flippancy is not only a sign of our failure to appreciate what is important in life, it also indicates a lack of consideration and basic disregard for others. These reasons as to how personal tribulations may come about, why such 'incidents' in life occur, all express the same message: tribulations do not appear out of the blue, and while they may not be instantly explainable, they do say a lot about the underlying framework or context in which they happen Knowing the kind of circumstances and clearly recognizing the 'breeding ground' which can lead to such 'incidents'— can actually help us to overcome them and to strengthen our epistemic resilience.

In summing up, we can say that there is a connection between inner growth and external hardship that can be unfolded according to spiritual laws; hardships happen for a reason and they are our own private tutors in teaching us a lesson and even providing us with sources of strength. If we take stock of the resources and skills Mark lists as needed to vanquish catastrophes and tackle challenges, we would have to bear in mind the root causes: ignorance and skepticism, jealousy and carelessness. Therefore the tools required to deal with these challenges would be finding ways to acquire wisdom and knowledge, to focus on what matters, to determine one's own path to goodness, and to take to heart the seriousness and necessity of adhering to an orderly life in spirituality. The path to goodness can only be completed by living a life of asceticism, by constantly probing one's innermost thoughts, being aware at all times of the true meaning of salvation, showing discernment and judiciousness, employing diligence and zeal centered on God.

The key to inner strength is prayer (MWR 172:140). Afflictions have to be met with a prayerful attitude (MWR 9:126). This is also a 21st century experience. In two interviews with aid workers, Christina Montaiuti was told about the

---

21 St. Mark the Ascetic, Letter to Nicolas the Solitary. In: *Philokalia* Volume 1, 147–161.
22 Ibd.

importance of prayer. One interviewee who worked in difficult contexts explicitly told her: "Well, I learnt at a very early age that prayer is very important and that is the foundation in which I base everything—almost everything that I do in my life. It starts off with a conversation with God and from that I—yeah, that's the basis of it."[23]

Paying attention to one's own innermost-being proves, once again, to be the decisive tool in building resistance, together with clearly understanding the natural order of things, comprehending the laws of life, working tirelessly to avoid the trap of complacency and idleness, and pursuing discourse with like-minded spiritual friends. The key elements of epistemic resilience are prayer, patience, and a true perception of temporality—that all things pass and that there is a future ahead of us. Having a sense of futurity helps greatly in cultivating epistemic resilience (SL 156:121; MWR 141:137; MWR 168:139f). A sense of futurity will take away any feelings of bitterness or resentment if we feel we have been wronged (SL 114:118). We have seen this sense of futurity in Ingrid Betancourt and her vision of being free; Viktor Frankl similarly cultivated this hope of futurity by imagining a life in freedom.

Mark uses the image of a sea voyage, similar to the one used by Isaiah the Solitary, to drive his message home that inner calm enables us to distance ourselves from the immediacy of suffering: just as sailors, in the hope of gain, gladly endure the burning heat of the sun we, too, should feel encouraged to endure hardship with the prospect of a future destination in mind, so that the spiritual journey through the here and now, daunting though it may be, provides us with a view of what is ahead, of future salvation. This is the unambiguous pattern of life giving us the power to bear life's contingencies, those unforeseen events. The resources we need to deal with such adversity and boost our powers of resistance and epistemic resilience are: prayer, forbearance, remembering the good things of the past and looking ahead to the future.

5.3   The Magnitude of Watchfulness: Hesychios the Priest

Hesychios the Priest is our third 'guide' from the *Philokalia* in the search of a deeper understanding of epistemic resilience. My reference point here is the treatise "On Watchfulness and Holiness." The authorship is not entirely clear

---

23   C. Montaiuti, The Effect of Meaning-Making on Resilience, 155.

(probably not Hesychios of Jerusalem who lived in the 5th century). The text may have been written in the 7th or 8th century by a monk in Sinai, but historical details and evidence are elusive. Fact is, that we have a meaningful text at our disposal in which the notion of the "Jesus prayer" is mentioned for the first time in the context of the *Philokalia*. It is also fact that the text we are dealing with here offers interesting insights into the whole question of epistemic resilience. I would like to reconstruct Hesychios' main insights into epistemic resilience using the following categories: (i) spiritual warfare; (ii) self-examination and self-control; and (iii) attentiveness and stillness of soul.

(i) Hesychios describes our life on earth in terms of spiritual warfare—we are constantly involved in a battle, being torn apart and having to fend off dangerous thoughts and influences (OWH 6:163). The art of spiritual growth consists, I would suggest, in developing inner firmness without complacency, and maintaining a spirit of watchful attentiveness based on peace of mind. The way epistemic resilience is primarily understood in Hesychios' writings is in terms of "resisting destructive inner forces" rather than coping with external adversities. But here again there is the law of connection between the inner and the outer. The weapons to be used in spiritual warfare are humility, fasting, prayer and an attitude of watchfulness (OHW 12:64). Humility is understanding one's vulnerability and a commitment to shaping the relevance of reality, i.e. to accepting reality. Fasting is connected with physical control, control over the body, but also self-discipline in more general terms, as in personal strength and firmness. Prayer is habit-forming and soul-building.

The attitude of watchfulness is an awareness of spiritual challenges. On one occasion Hesychios uses the image of a spider as an example for "stillness of heart." (OHW 27:66). The spider is forever building a center for its warfare, and pursues a strategy that allows it to rest rather than putting the spider into the position of a hectic hunter. The idea here is that the soul needs a center, a place, space where it can remain calm in the eye of the storm, in the midst of spiritual warfare. Again, an inner center provides a basis for coping with displacement. Displacement and desert experiences, as we have seen, bring out specific challenges. There is no doubt that spiritual warfare is serious, threatening the balance of the soul. Attentiveness to destructive influences to the soul and clearly directed prayers (that is, prayers directed against the attackers) are the means to reach this goal (OHW 105:180). Here again the image of the spider is helpful: remain focused and maintain a clear central focal point from which to fight the fight against unhealthy thoughts and self-destructive desires.

Reciting the "Jesus-prayer" Hesychios suggests, is one of the strongest weapons we have at our disposal, a prayer that gives undivided attention to the Lord, falling into a prayer rhythm, pursuing a habit of the heart by constant repetition (OHW 4:60; OHW 102:179f).

One further important aspect of spiritual warfare are strategies dealing with evil thoughts. Evil thoughts appear in the intellect—it is difficult to control their appearing, but the moment they do we have a choice regarding our response; we can deliberately send other, counter, thoughts to "chase after it," (OHW 2:162) in order that we may "rebuke ourselves truthfully and unemotionally," (OHW 138:186). We are free to invite certain thoughts (and prohibit others) to enter our mind and hearts even more deeply (watchfulness acts like a doorkeeper in this respect: OHW 18:165)—"it is impossible for sin to enter the heart without first knocking at its door," (OHW 45:170). So, in spiritual warfare the first step is noticing evil an thought popping into our intellect, the second is allowing (or denying) the destructive thought to co-habit with other thoughts, the third is clear acceptance (or denial)—"assent to the provocation," followed by the fourth step, concrete action (OHW 46:170).

This is a strategy mentioned by an international aid worker who is constantly confronted with suffering and disaster:

> I know that if I just do things without thinking how to survive and how to keep me mentally sane, I would break down in the long run, because there's so much shit that I've seen and been involved in and people dying and all that stuff. (…) It would break down as any normal human being would. But what I do is (…) I have certain principles that I keep to. I understand that I need to think positively. (…) So, I always think positively.[24]

Controlling one's thoughts is now commonly recognized as a means to building up inner strength and to fighting destructive forces.

There is a clear order of destructiveness in the logic of evil, which enables us to equip ourselves for battle, to plan our spiritual warfare strategy. It helps to have a quick and keen intellect able to perceive and judge the destructive forces that enter a person's inner life (OHW 22:165). Spiritual warfare is not only an affair of the heart, but to use Hesychios' language, also involves intellect; there is a need to understand the logic of destructiveness as well as the nature of the thoughts and forces invading one's inner life. Hesychios

---

24   C. Montaiuti, The Effect of Meaning-Making on Resilience, 156.

is particularly aware of dangerous fantasies ("The demons always lead us into sin by means of deceitful fantasies": OHW 118:182)—this is an interesting statement about the imagination as a double-edged sword: on the one hand we can employ our imagination to build up inner strength by accessing treasures stored in the mind, on the other hand our imagination can lead us astray or serve as a vehicle of escapism, of opting out of confrontation. Mental images can be destructive or at least distracting which is why the soul (rather like the in and out boxes of e-mails) needs emptying in order to make space for stillness and tranquility (OHW 89:177). Spiritual warfare is the art of controlling of one's own thoughts and having one's priorities clear. Epistemic resilience is required to fend off dangerous influences, but also to build a strong bulwark against warfare: it is both "means" and "end."

(ii) One of the main notions underpinning a cultivation of inwardness and inner strength, shared by theology and philosophy alike, is the art of self-examination. Socrates is sometimes credited with being the first major thinker in the West to advocate a culture of reflection, to live an examined life. He is even quoted as saying that the unexamined life is not worth living (Apology 38a). Robert Nozick in his explorations of self-examination also mentions Aristotle's *Ethics*, Marcus Aurelius' *Meditations*, and Montaigne's *Essais* as philosophical examples of exercises in self-examination.[25] Self-examination as exercise establishing a well-defined center for interiority will at the same time lead to a clear sense of one's concerns and commitments; thus it contributes to epistemic resilience by building "a spider's web" and by looking at the world from a clear focal point similar to a spider's perspective, to use Hesychios' own imagery he underlines the importance of self-examination in his own terms as a key source of inner strength.

We should review our sins as well as our previous way of life (OHW 52:171), in other words we should appropriate our history and our experience by meta-reflection and growth-oriented judgment. We need to develop, "a view over our whole spiritual life" (OHW 76:175). At the end of each day—and this is a habit-formation process—we should review our deeds and omissions (OHW 65:174). This exercise will help to make sense of the diffuse impressions of the day, it will help us to get a sense of inner order as well as a sense of growth according to stable criteria. We should "note and weigh our actions," "each hour of the day," and "in the evening we should do what we can to free ourselves from the burden of them by means of repentance," (OHW 124:183). Self-examination is hard work, many destructive forces are hidden in the soul, their causes and

---

25   R. Nozick, The Examined Life. New York: Simon and Schuster 1989, 15.

cases have to be revealed (OHW 72:175) in a process of "soul-digging" (not Hesychios' term, but not inappropriate for what he is suggesting).

A useful way to encourage this process of self-examination is to look through the lens of "the eight principal evil thoughts" (OHW 177:193), a motif probably best developed by John Cassian where we find the eight principal vices of avarice, anger, sadness, acedia, vainglory, pride, gluttony and fornication. Since pride and complacency are considered to be spiritually dangerous attitudes as they make a person fall into the trap of carelessness, it is not surprising Hesychios upholds and encourages a self-critical attitude as a means for inner strength—the task of moral judgment is to prompt the soul's power to make us self-critical (OHW 34:168). The lens of the eight principal sources of evil thoughts help us to order and make our judgments, which are complex since self-examination is also the examination of the inner soul.

Hesychios uses the image of a mirror that helps us to see not only our own face, but also the faces of all the others present, i.e. "the demons" (forces active in the soul: OHW 23:166). The recommended "model for stillness of heart" is "the man who holds a mirror into which he looks," (OHW 48:171). Systematic self-examination is a key to epistemic resilience and inner strength; self-examination is, however, but the first step. The second step, to make it more tangible, is self-control. Self-examination and self-control are connected, in the sense that concentrating on one's inner life will help a person "acquire self-restraint," (OHW 68:174). One element of self-control, as mentioned above, is control over one's body (OHW 33:168). "The practice of the ascetic life begins with self-control," (OHW 66:174). A good starting point is "self-control in food and drink," (OHW 165:191). Self-examination and self-control are two key pillars in cultivating inner strength.

(iii) The most important category that Hesychios propounds is the category of "watchfulness." It is a deep disposition that allows liberation from evil thoughts, words, and actions (OHW 1:162). It is the effort involved in focusing and of "keeping your attention humbly in your heart," (OHW 29:166). Watchfulness can be nourished by centering one's attention on Jesus (OHW 16:165; 97:178),[26] and by thinking of one's own death (OHW 17:165; 95:178; 155:189). Based on watchfulness and the prayer of Jesus Christ, "inner vigilance and unfathomable stillness of soul" can be reached (OHW 10:164). Translated into more secular terms this could mean: epistemic resilience is built up through having a clear focus and center through having a perspective of life per se and an attitude

---

26   OHW 97:178 beautifully states: "A certain God-given equilibrium is produced in our intellect through the constant remembrance and invocation of our Lord Jesus Christ."

towards one's existence as a whole, gaining a sense of proportion through our understanding of mortality and life boundaries. The aim is to attain constant attentiveness as "the heart's stillness, unbroken by any thought," (OHW 5:163)[27] and to reach watchfulness as "continual fixing and halting of thoughts at the entrance to the heart," (OHW 6:163).

So "thought control" is an intellectual as well as a spiritual challenge, part and parcel of self-examination and self-control. The sense of what is important is the key to self-examination, self-control and thought control as three dimensions of epistemic resilience: "The more closely attentive you are to your mind, the greater the longing with which you will pray to Jesus: and the more carelessly you examine your mind, the farther you will separate yourself from Him," (OHW 90:177). Epistemic resilience is strengthened by protecting and accessing "the inner shrine of the soul," (OHW 21:65).

An inner center, to use a more secular language, an "internal locus of control" is important, especially when dealing with challenging situations such as the realities of development work.[28] Paul Hoggett, Marjorie Mayo and Chris Miller provide an example from an interview with a development worker:

> I really think about the shit that, you know when you go and do community development on estates and you go to meeting after meeting and you get abused and people tell you you're stealing their resources and all kinds of things. They accuse you of heinous things and treat you like a piece of shit and you have nowhere to go with that.[29]

Hogett, Mayo and Miller suggest strengthening this inner center through the cultivation of two further capacities: the capacity to stay with complexity, i.e. the capacity to contain emotional complexity and to take the standpoint of the other without losing one's own position, and the capacity for self-authorization, i.e. the capacity to take a stand and to remain able to act even in ambiguous situations.[30] These capacities help to build and sustain reflective practices and to consolidate the inner center, the "inner shrine," to use Hesychios' language.

---

27   Cf., OHW 20:165 where attentiveness is described as the presupposition to keep one's heart "clear of all thoughts."

28   Paul Hoggett, Marjorie Mayo and Chris Miller, The dilemmas of development work. Ethical challenges in regeneration. Bristol: Policy Press 2009, 64.

29   Ibd., 60.

30   Ibd., 68.

This inner shrine, according to Hesychios, is not simply "there;" it is part of spiritual warfare. Even in quiet times, the inner life is threatened—epistemic resilience is needed as a protection from dangers that threaten inner stability (stillness) and inner order (harmony). The soul is fragile, it can be easily poisoned (OHW 44:70). Sin, when it wounds a person's heart, withers the heart completely (OHW 78:175). This is why attentiveness and watchfulness are vital. The Jesus-prayer is recommended as a remedy to evil thoughts and emotions that poison the soul (OHW 188:196)—Hesychios draws a comparison with food eaten:

> Noxious foods can give trouble when taken into the body; but as soon as he feels the pain, the person who has eaten them can quickly tame some emetic and be unharmed. Similarly, once the intellect that has imbibed evil thoughts senses their bitterness, it can easily expel them and get rid of them completely by means of the Jesus Prayer, (OHW 188:196).

This analogy contains a key metaphor: the food we eat determines our physical condition and levels of immunity—resistance. The food we choose to eat depends on the knowledge we have at our disposal about the food and our level of self-discipline, the choice also depends on the availability of the food we—our bodies—need. This is how we build up our physical immune system, we choose not too overindulge or gorge ourselves on certain foods purely for the reason that it is unhealthy and not good for us. By constantly monitoring and checking what we eat, we can protect and practice 'body-building' (in the true sense of the word), and minimize health problems in later life related to old-age. But this demands a high level of mental and moral discipline, above all: self-control and moderation (in all things), and the same goes for matters of the mind: all those impressions bombarding the mind and soul from without are just as nutritious (or not) as food is for the body. Filtering these impressions e.g., by cultivating a particular attitude of mind, impulse and way of thinking and building spiritual strength are inseparably bound with exercising prudent diligence at all times, since this will impact both the external and inner forces of the mind. It is important to recognize the harmful effects, the 'bitterness' some thoughts can cause.

This realization can only be achieved by practicing to think about what we really need to, (not losing sight of God, not forgetting our own death). Here is a reason for the special place of the Jesus prayer. The Jesus prayer can serve as purification: "Just as snow will not produce a name, or water a fire, or the thorn-bush a fig, so a person's heart will not be freed from demonic thoughts, words and actions until it has first purified itself inwardly," (OHW 122:183). On numerous occasions Hesychios also cites loose speech as a threat to inner stability (OHW 32:167f; 51:171; 127:184; 185:195). Words are powerful, they shape our inner landscape. Similarly powerful are attitudes—watchfulness is to be cultivated as a deeply rooted commitment, supported by habits such as self-examination, since "in virtue as in vice, constancy is the mother of habit," (OHW 97:178). We should strive for "firmness of character," (OHW 141:186). That is why it is vital we look at the habits that constitute our way of life. Attitudes can quickly turn into habits; Hesychios has a clear sense of the most dangerous dispositions: "The intellect is made blind by these three passions: avarice, self-esteem and sensual pleasure," (OHW 57:172). A key beginning of destructiveness is carelessness (OHW 30:167); it leads to forgetfulness of the inner struggle, this forgetfulness leads to negligence, and negligence to indifference, laziness and unnatural desire (OHW 32:168). Carelessness is a sign of impurity, i.e. of evil thoughts having entered the soul. Watchfulness is the best protection from both carelessness and evil thoughts. Epistemic resilience is nourished by watchfulness.

Summing up, we could say that Hesychios reminds us of the central meaning of "attentiveness" and "watchfulness" as the basis for successful spiritual warfare, cultivated by self-examination, thought-control and self-control leading to stillness of the soul. Watchfulness governed by reason is the constant state of awareness of one's inner spiritual self. This is practical "hands on" advice; the Ursuline sisters, to give an example, who left the security of their cloistered convent in Ohio to embark on a mission in Montana encountered a difficult place ("Sister Sacred Heart commented that 'Everyone walks in the middle of the road; it is a better plan, for many people use the side of the street for the slop sink.' She also observed that 'Every second store is a saloon. We have not met six Catholic men (Montana Catholics they call themselves) who are not saloon keepers, gamblers and the like.'"); the Ursuline sisters built a small chapel in the house that served as their new convent and obtained special permission to keep the Blessed Sacrament, "night and day."[31] The Blessed Sacrament served as a center for watchfulness and attentiveness.

Epistemic resilience is reinforced in the same way as our physical immune system might be built up and strengthened. Being able to articulate and communicate one's thoughts and fears, being conscious of and expressing our own humility, and always keeping sight of what really matters—sight empowered by prayer—and being relentlessly reminded of our own death are the main ingredients in fortifying powers of epistemic resilience. Next to the image of the spider Hesychios' image of "sailing across the sea of the intellect," (OHW 150:188) and becoming entangled in nets of evil thoughts (OHW 152:89), underpin this strong idea of the inner life. A person's interiority is a like the sea obeying laws but also trapped in its own dynamics. Epistemic resilience is the

---

31   S.H. Schrems, Uncommon Women, Unmarked Trails, 45.

ability to have a strong net without being caught up in it and to have a 'calm' inner sea for a prosperous voyage.

It has, I hope, become clear that the *Philokalia* encompasses a rich treasure of insights for our enquiry of epistemic resilience reminding us of the importance of focus and attentiveness. Inner focus ("inner space") helps us to cope with and grow in displacement. The overall message of the *Philokalia* is: human persons have an inner life with richness and depth which needs to be properly ordered; ordering the inner life is not an impossible or super-human task, it is possible but demanding and exacting, it is a life-long challenge to keep our interiority on course and strengthen our capacity to be displaced to avoid the pitfalls and traps of the nets and spiders' webs daily life throws at us.

CHAPTER 6

Cultivating Interiority: Thinking and Therapeutic Arguments

Displacement can lead to confusion and yet at the same time be an intense experience; resilience is not only the ability to absorb shocks and bounce back, but also the ability "to move between different states of temporary equilibrium", for example in contexts and periods of crisis and disturbance, while at the same time maintaining system functionality.[1] The ability to "move between" is an indispensable skill in the capacity to be displaced, particularly since displacement can lead to inner exhaustion. Leanne Olson, who worked as an international relief worker, was deeply frustrated when working in Bosnia in 1995: "I'm fed up, worn out, completely frustrated. I am so *tired* of this. I just want to give up and go home."—and again a few weeks later: "All I want to do right now is go home. The problem is, I don't even know where that is any more."[2] She had had her share of intense experiences, but also exposure to the agony of war where things fall irreparably apart and that was too much for her to cope with. In such circumstances the question of inner resources and inner balance becomes salient.

When working in Liberia, again in a context of violence, Leanne (like Betancourt) found refuge in reading: "I went through about fifty novels while I was in Liberia."[3] Reading (with all the risks of escapism) is a way of cultivating one's inner being, is a way of building an inner "stage" where events and encounters with interlocutors can be acted out. The *Philokalia*, as we have seen, encourages the cultivation of the inner; the *lectio divina* is one well-established way if cultivating interiority through the act of reading.

Our inner lives are sensitive and fragile. Our inner lives can be intense and confusing, rich yet locked up, but also deep and accessible. Interiority can be structured and it can be reconstructed in a particular language, for example in a language that has been shaped by the Jewish-Christian tradition. The voices from the *Philokalia* underline the core point that interiority must be nurtured

---

1 Mark Duffield, Challenging environments: Danger, resilience and the aid industry. *Security Dialogue* 43,5 (2012) 475–492, at 481.

2 Leanne Olson, A Cruel Paradise. Journals of an International Relief Worker. Toronto: Insomniac Press 1999, 119 and 132 respectively.

3 Ibd., 51.

© KONINKLIJKE BRILL NV, LEIDEN, 2017 | DOI 10.1163/9789004342453_008

to survive and flourish and the nourishment it requires equally demands resolve and patience over time—a life time; inner being can be fashioned and
formed but epistemic resources require thought, memory and resources such
as faith and hope to be exercised vigilantly and prudently. It is in a missionary experience in the widest sense of its meaning that countless individuals
are tossed into the unknown of displacement and who intentionally choose to
work on their inner lives.

The missionary experience invites a person to be resilient and one element
of that resilience is a multi-dimensional life. "The missionaries have never
been one-dimensional people. Historically, many have achieved legendary status across a range of fields."[4] A one-dimensional person, famously described
my Herbert Marcuse in his *One-dimensional Man*, assessed all experiences
through one focal lens (consumerism and materialism) and is not open to the
many facets of reality and the many aspects of the human person. A missionary, in contrast, will find herself invited to look beyond the microscope-lens
view of life she might have hitherto experienced and instead look at the whole
person in all her dimensions,[5] and pay attention to all the nuances of her own
life. This approach to building life on several pillars is promising for the cultivation of resilience. A key challenge when dealing with multi-dimensionality is
the question of integration. How to integrate experiences? The answer to this
question can be found in reflection, in the capacity to "hold on to oneself," in
reflective practices and reflexivity.[6] Epistemic resilience can be nurtured by
cognitive processes, by epistemic labor.

This chapter will look at two important building blocks in the cultivation
of epistemic resilience, namely thinking and remembering, thought and
memory. I am not concerned here with the actual cognitive process of thinking
and remembering but more with the notion of cultivating a disciplined mind,
learning life lessons with the tools to hand. In this chapter I would like to inves-
tigate thought and learning as one essential epistemic resource in cultivating
interiority with particular focus on the therapeutic aspects it provides.

---

4   A. Clerkin, B. Clerkin, A Road Less Travelled, 16.
5   R.R. Winter, head of an Indian mission from 1863–1891, summarized this point succinctly:
    "We have had to try to solve the hard problem of how we can get down to the minds of these
    people, so as to make them *care for* us and our message, so that our work may not be a mere
    scratching of the surface, but such that it will reach down to the heart of the human feeling.
    In such cases we should try to come before the people, not merely as preachers of a new
    religion, a capacity in which they care for us little enough, but that, as friends and sympathiz-
    ers we should aim at benefitting *the whole man*" (Robert A. Bickers, Rosemary Seton, eds.,
    Missionary Encounters. Sources and Issues. Surrey, UK: Curzon Press 1996, 187).
6   Hoggett, Mayo, Miller, The dilemma of development work, 69–70.

6.1   Thinking as Remedy in Times of Crisis

Thinking can be healing; "real" thinking is silent, inward-looking and essential for building hardy, reliable resilience. Thinking is sparked in situations and places one would least expect, as was the case with the 48-year-old advertising manager, Jean Louis Cianni; the airline he had been doing PR for went bankrupt overnight and with it his well-paid, challenging job. He was displaced, felt violently out of place. Suddenly he had no income, too much time on his hands and not a thing to do: the world of unemployment.[7] At first he was optimistic that he would soon find an equally well-paid and challenging job; but after three years this attitude changed to one of despondency and weary numbness. He had fallen to the bottom rung of the ladder—as low as it gets, he experiences this state of unemployment as his social death sentence and quotes Rosset who sums up his own condition in a nutshell talking about a crisis of social identity threatening the fragile building one had built.[8] The framework of certainties of an everyday working life had vanished into thin air; he compares the loss of all those aspects which had made life worth living to the loss of his own identity, living like a robot at the peripheries of himself ("je me vivais comme une sorte de robot décalé à la périphérie de moi-même", PR 27), to being lost in a desert (PR 26): gone were well-known reference points, landmark structures providing orientation, life's little rituals, social status, *hyperactive* work and recognition (PR 32, 199); all lost and gone.

In his second year of unemployment, he feels we is drowning in a grey sea strewn with the wreckage of nostalgia, regret and sorrow at the loss of all he had previously known, had, and been. He drifts in this sea of lethargy, no longer wanting to voice an opinion on anything as he can no longer get his bearings due to the dense grey fog around him. In other words, all Cianni's generative and regenerative powers of orientation necessary for epistemic resilience have run dry. What burdens him more than anything else is his complete loss of individual identity, which he terms his Hades of redundancy, the black shadows of depersonalization akin to excommunication—for he who descends into the Underworld of jobseekers, must be prepared to forego his identity which will gradually moulder and rot. He metamorphoses into a dead soul among the living (PR 59f).[9]

---

7   J.L. Cianni, La philosophie comme remède au chomage. Paris: Albin Michel 2007. I will use
    the abbreviation "PR" throughout.

8   "Chaque fois que se produit une crise d'indentité, c'est l'identité sociale qui est la première à
    craquer et à menacer le fragile èdifice de ce qu'on croit éprouver comme moi" (PR 7).

9   "Moi aussi, j'attends de revenir...J'erre dans l'Hades du chomage, tapi dans ce que Kundera
    appelle le 'pénombre de dépersonnalisation'" (PR 51).

Unable to tackle anything, he immures himself in study, incapable of doing anything constructive at all. It is here that he rediscovers his first love: Philosophy which he had been passionate about before embarking on a career in advertising.

> One morning," Cianni writes, "when I was feeling particularly dispirited I took off to the library, a place I had spent a lot of time as a student of Philosophy. For some reason I followed my own intuition, perhaps the Stoics—those masters of resilience even against all odds—could help me to endure my miserable never-ending feeling of wretchedness (…). First off the doses of this medicine were small but (…) [I] was soon savoring the soothing powers of Philosophy.[10]

He discovers perfect conversation partners who become his confidants in personal inner matters: Cianni takes on each philosopher he comes up against one by one with combative disbelief and then the *lumière* of understanding when he takes his leave and moves on to the next giant in the history of philosophy. Seneca, Spinoza, Pascal, Heidegger, Diderot—in getting to grips with these men's lives, he is forced to relive, rethink his own life though their words of wisdom. He also learns that he is not alone in his sufferings and twists of fate; he learns that human "suffering" knows no century and respects no profession, striking 'even' philosophers in her ravaging exploits. So it is that Cianni is able to relive his own experience in the words and voice of fellow sufferers in years previously and countries far away from home. His reading does not deepen his existing wounds, quite the reverse, he finds solace, comfort and identifies parallel circumstances to be fought against and won. His reading and thinking give him both the strength to fortify his own resilience and to understand why it had/s to be so.

In his admiration of their singular inner fights and outer battles, he begins to perceive his own small life as part of a wider, bigger puzzle of things and the cold light-of-day reality it would have been had it continued: he sees his mental life bathing in an ocean of indifference ("Ma vie mentale baignait dans une océan indifference," PR 120–121). His life changes—changed by his courtship with philosophy, the deep thinking it demands and the delights it brings. It goes without saying that the discipline needed to really think about what he was reading will not have been as easy as it sounds in print. In an exercise of self-observation, Cianni finds out how difficult it is to have a decent

---

10   "Un matin plus difficile que les autres, je suis retourné vers ma bibliothèque d'ancien
        étudiant en philosophie. Une intitution me guidait: penseurs de l'endurance et de la re-
        sistance à tous les coups du sort, les stoiciens m'aideraient a affronter mon interminable
        épreuvre. (…) Á petites doses au début puis bientôt sans moderation," (PR 8).

conversation with self particularly when esteem of that same self is low; he has to conclude that he is contributing to the erosion of that dwindling self esteem, and the work to build it back up again will be enormous.[11]

In his *scepticisme* he finds a partner in crime in Sextus Empiricus who offers relief to his mental torture and agony—allowing truth to find him during his meditations without force.[12] This turn-around in inner attitude enables him to discover the strangeness of love (l'étrangeté de l'amour) through Abelard, to see the world in a fresh light. The downward spiral of the spirit is a real mental condition which had begun to take its toll physically, too. Philosophy provides the remedy, the strategic "therapeutic arguments" he needs to regain his spiritual heath. Cianni overcomes his *Angst*; he regains his self-confidence and mental calm with the kind care of philosophy, who quite literally is his therapist.

He begins to savor the essence of and delve into the wisdom of so-called *therapeutic arguments*. He is familiar with the masters of contemplation and the healing properties of their words. One key lesson he learns from the radical thinking of the Stoics is to expect the worst and be prepared for everything and anything; he learns too that he has to get the dose of "big ideas" right: Nietzsche was of the firm opinion that you should approach major problems as you would a cold bath: jump in and then jump out as quickly as you can (PR 13). And it is this objective we will be pursuing in our present enquiry into interiority: we will reflect on life and death before plunging into deep thoughts on greatness of soul and finally diving into the comforting words of bright hope-giving knowledge. We need to realize that growing strong has to do with opening up to other perspectives—this is the antidote, the linctus Philosophy prescribes for survival. Philosophy's therapeutic approach relies on that *connaissance de soi*, that "hybrid identity" of life and death which is the corner stone of survival (PR 13f).

In his *Apologetics*, Socrates tells Plato to worry less about what people have and more about what they are. Cianni's own shift in thinking from *having* to *being* is acquired via Montaigne's Neo-stoic way of thinking: to be more precise, Cianni adopts Montaigne's three key "strategies" which he proceeds to try out (PR 158f): first, watchfulness, turning one's gaze away from the past; second, having a 'physical take on things' (including one's own predicament,

---

11   "Ces questions m'ont longtemps tourmenté. La therapie philosophique m'a permis de la reformuler et, ce faisant, d'en réduire L'intensité coulourouse. La lecture de Montaigne a lus précisément introduit une pointe d'humour dans le couple intérieur malade-médecin" (PR 166).

12   "Je fais de même. Je ne cherche plus rien, je laisse la vérité advenir au hasard de mes méditations" (PR 128).

examining it with the trained eye of a doctor); and thirdly, using one's imaginative powers to soar above the void of emptiness. These are the instruments of therapeutic thinking and they enable Cianni to gradually gain a clearer perspective of his life. He finds it therapeutically beneficial to actually think about the *Angst* which tortures him and ponder upon where the source may lie: I might be afraid of all those nasty, despicable, horrible little gods, my parents, my friends, my children, my colleagues, both the real and the imagined which dwell on the outside world or within me in my innermost being—in other words everyone and everything (cf. PR 113). And he finds out that it is healing and helpful to enter "inner dialogues," an important way of building inner wealth on the basis of "interior interlocutors," as we have also seen in the example of François-Xavier Nguyễn Văn Thuận. This is both a way to gain distance from, and a way to remain close to reality.

In thus putting mileage between himself and his former (working) life, Cianni is able to deconstruct that life: If I think back to how it was, I am aware of an illusion which as a chief executive was more important than anything else at all—day in, day out (cf. PR 68f). He still sticks to those daily rituals and habits developed in childhood and necessary in working life except he is no longer a slave to those habits; he remembers the fragrance of his wife's French perfume, his sons' designer deodorants, but now when he looks in the bathroom mirror he is faced with an identity crisis: "Qui est celui qui regarde? Celui qui est regardé?" (PR 79). This is clearly a "problème d'identité, problème d'image" (PR 71), and it does not stop there, crises have a habit of spreading and this one is no different, in chapter 5 headed "De la perte des amis" ("On the loss of friends") he realizes that friends do not always remain friends when a crisis erupts; whereas you may have been *in* a while before, you are now *out* and that is unacceptable (PR 82f).

With the help of an expert on time, namely Augustine, Cianni rediscovers the value of time; it takes on a whole different meaning. He reflects upon God as the ultimate goal (PR 95). This puts time in an entirely different perspective. While at work, he had measured time according to business meetings, agenda and priority: "(…) leurs urgences, leur priorités, leurs retards, quand ce n'est pas leur simple et insupportable presence" (PR 96f). He is reminded of the hierarchy, inhumanity, masochism and handicap of time (cf. PR 96). Now, he feels time has expanded, slowed down, shifted its axis: When I write down what I am actually thinking about, I sense time differently in that I am consciously choosing to do what I am doing in any one moment. There is not fuss, no bother, no conditions to fulfil and no other purpose than in the doing (cf. PR 99).[13] Similar to the bathroom mirror experience, Cianni knows he has to reinvent

---

13   "Quand j'écris mes méditations, j'habite un autre temps. Je choisis mon activité" (PR 99).

himself, seek his own unique identity, his-self. He discovers too that he can
be productive in his thinking in a way hitherto unknown to him. Interestingly
it is the philosophy of scepticism which helps him to deconstruct his former
way life, with its empty habits and fears (PR ch. 7)—he manages to develop a
healthy attitude of disinterest, even complacency in distancing himself from
his judgmental attitudes of thinking. And the language of love found in the
exchange of letters between Abelard and Heloise prove to be enlightening in
remembering his own lost loves and past love affairs; he gains a new sense of
orientation which empowers him to move on since he discovers something
important about himself (PR 142).

Cianni rediscovers the power and clout of "the question" in philosophy,
he rediscovers how to formulate questions anew, in a way that is less painful
particularly those questions pertaining to quintessential matter such as self
and remnants of what might have once been self. He invariably turns to the
question of *why* and *what now*; he had grown up with the ethos of you-need-
to-work-hard-to-get-a-good-life, which in the light of his predicament and enlightened perspective suggested that everything had been an absolute waste
of time, didn't it? Cianni's contemplative philosophical thinking may not have
solved all his problems but it does come up with the correct diagnosis; in his
concluding meditation he describes the suffering an unemployed person feels
is not a state of affairs or physical condition, but a change in that person's relationship (love affair) with the world and those in it; he compares the rat race
of life to a game of "chaises musicales" which is not a game at all (PR 196);
he makes connections between hyperactivity and unemployment, finds the
source of his *Angst*.

Apart from discovering the importance of the question and how it is for-
mulated, there is the remedy itself which he is determined to try out and that
lies in pursuing a new strategy in dialogue, a new approach to conversation.
In his hours of need he has summoned together his philosophical friends to
help him think his way through his fate—they have taught him that time is a
precious commodity and that he is not invulnerable; that passion can blind,
that illusion is the father of understanding and that his constant slaving for
recognition and praise cost him his personal freedom (cf. PR 225f). His unseen philosopher friends teach him a language with which he can tell his own
story, create a narrative about life's experiences: "I tell my story therefore I am"
(cf. PR 202).

The *remède* of philosophy brings about a cataclysmic inner change which at
first has gone unnoticed (cf. PR 197); step by step Cianni's *Weltbild*, is radically
altered: "What I had lost in life, I gained in being" (cf. PR 197). His capacity to
think, ability to pose questions, make unbiased judgments, powers of imagination and new conversational skills become his sources of epistemic resilience,

nourished by the basic capacities and principles of the same. The very last word in his book is: "reconciliation"—for which Cianni is grateful.

Cianni has mastered the art of reflection; he has built up an "inner social life" with interlocutors he can call upon and invite for conversations. He is able to "frame" his experiences differently in the light of the question about the point and meaning of life. This is a "home-building" exercise in times of displacement: reflecting on the bigger picture. To give two examples: Peter Geremia who worked as a missionary in the Philippines, was victim of a theft that made him lose his tape recorder and camera, a frustrating experience at the beginning of his work in South-East Asia. In his diary he muses:

> I suppose I have to become poor one way or the other. If the thief was a poor fellow without anything to eat, maybe he had a right to steal (...). If I sound rather philosophical it is because I know that there are so many poor people here and I also feel a bit guilty about it. The economy is exploited by American and European companies that get hold of the raw materials pretty much on their own terms.[14]

This is a constructive "philosophical" approach to a frustrating experience in a context of displacement. It provides a specific framework, a larger context. Leanne Olson (mentioned above) followed a similar approach when working in Liberia; she was clear about the meaning: "I was doing something good, and decent, and *right*. The insecurity, the illnesses, the exhaustion, were all part of the job."[15] She also reflects on the immense strength of the human spirit: "In every war, no matter how ugly or how cruel, there remains a part of the human spirit that will not be broken. A part that survives, grows strong, adapts and simply will not surrender."[16] This part of the human spirit can be strengthened by reflective processes that integrate one's experience, however confusing and challenging.

6.2   Thinking and the Inner Life

Difficult experiences need to be processed; reflection as vital part of that processing can be described as an intentional cognitive activity geared towards generating the capacity to learn from experience. Reflection is a process of

---

14   Peter Geremia, Dreams and Bloodstains. The Diary of a Missioner in the Philippines. Quezon City: Claretian Publications 1987, 38.

15   L. Olson, A Cruel Paradise, 58.

16   Ibd., 10.

gathering and ordering "mental" material. A reflective person sees beyond the surface, thinks things through and ponders upon implications and ramifications. A reflective person pursues a particular perspective and make experience the focus of reflective analysis. This was the experience of Jean-Louis Cianni, in philosophical reflection and analysis, he was able to put his experience into a wider context and actually find what he thought he had lost. A person engaged in reflective practices, i.e. practices of illuminating what I myself and others have experienced, can be described as "the practice of periodically stepping back to ponder the meaning of what has recently transpired to ourselves and to others in our immediate environment."[17] Reflective practices are deliberate and structured; they create "thought-ful" order and follow a "proper" process of thinking and cogitating. A good way of processing experiences is to keep a diary. Many missionaries follow this practice, for their own sake (coping with displacement), but also for the sake of the public. Arthur Tidman, for example, Foreign Secretary of the London Missionary Society, suggested to David Livingstone in 1852 "that you keep a regular journal (…) more likely to prove of permanent interest and value than the more vague and general impressions conveyed in a hastily written letter."[18] Processing experience means "placing" experience within an order; this is particularly helpful in contexts of displacement. My inner landscape is re-structured by reflective integration.

Thinking in solitude (as Hesychios might have described it) with or without specific inner interlocutors, is a means to creating an inner treasure trove. Thinking, very much part of reflection, is a fundamental epistemic exercise in building a culture of interiority. Thinking can bridge ideas, linking them and seeing one in relation to the other. Thinking gives interiority structure and texture. Some aspects of thinking are extremely complex and demanding, such as analyzing a tricky situation and stripping it down into its component parts. Thinking is also the ability to link up sentences into some logical order, equipping a coherent set of sentences with meaning and message; it is the ability to put problems into words and to ask the right questions at the right time in the right places and, most importantly for our discussion, thinking encapsulates the power to pass judgment and make major decisions.

Thinking presents us with untold possibilities to move around, to associate ourselves with a given occurrence or distancing ourselves from a particular situation. Abstract thinking helps us see beyond the single event, to set it in a wider, greater context, and to find common traits between ideas and notions

---

17   J. Raelin, "I Don't Have Time to Think!" versus the Art of Reflective Practice. *Reflections* 4,1 (2002) 66–79, at 66.

18   I. Schapera, Introduction to: I. Schapera, ed., Livingstone's Private Journals 1851–1853. Berkeley, Ca: University of California Press 1960, xii.

hopefully resulting in innovative perspectives. George Steiner collected arguments on the sadness of thought:

> Thinking makes us sad and fills us with heaviness of heart, because it
> never comes to an end, because there are no definitive answers, because
> there are so many thoughts already thought by others … well, the very
> same arguments could be used to show why and how thinking contrib-
> utes to the cultivation of a rich inner life![19]

Possibilities to distance self, to contextualize an occurrence and create something new out of it suggests that thinking heightens our senses, thus strengthening epistemic resilience. We have seen some of these dynamics in the "guarding
of thoughts" recommended in the *Philokalia*. During her seven years in captivity,
Ingrid Betancourt managed to create her own inner world of thinking, thus giving her a source of personal power. Thinking is a game of possibilities, it can be
a refuge or a place to boldly explore; thinking has its own built-in partners with
whom we can discuss whenever we are in the mood—night or day—and these
interlocutors contribute to boosting our inner levels of resistance.

Thinking does not leave us at the mercy of outside circumstance; thinking
makes us independent if we can create a rich inner sphere. In other words if we
can read or think, we have someone to exchange ideas with, we are never alone.
Inner discourse with self can contribute greatly to identity building because it
is the power of thinking which gives us human beings a perspective of a wider
universe and the knowledge that we too are part of that universe. In being part of
an oral community, a tradition of narrative, in being able to exchange ideas via
language and in being well acquainted with the structures of language, we can
access inner resources and inner maps to guide us along life's way.

According to Aristotle, thinking is that most fundamental of all human
acts.[20] If thinking can draw on powers of the imagination and the pictures
it draws in the mind, then thinking finds its own partner and purpose in the
same way as the eye needs an object *to see*. This faculty of the human mind to
think is referred to as the *nous*, that area of the mind through which the soul
sees, perceives and cogitates.[21] Thinking is a deeply rooted process, needing
an anchor point to cling to and, in the same way as an object seen is the cause
and reason of seeing, it is the conceivable, imaginable and feasible which is
the cause and source of thinking. We might say that anything can be pondered

---

19   G. Steiner, Ten (Possible) Reasons for the Sadness of Thought. *Salmagundi* 146/147 (2005)
      3–32.

20   Cf., Aristotle, De anima I,2, 405a8–11; De anima I,5,410a27–29; De anima III,3, 427a21–25.

21   Aristotle, De anima III,4, 429a22f.

over and dwelt upon long and hard, and because we might say and maintain this, the *nous* distinguishes itself from other levels of thinking by its flexibility and singularity of character. Thinking is malleable and as such can adjust to the object of concern.

The process of thinking is triggered by first being aware of one or the other object, in the same way as a transmitter will pick up or "receive" a signal, the signal depending on content (and language!) is then processed accordingly. This does seem to reduce the never-ending capacity of the mind to think in line with some logical classroom dictation exercise, which it is not, but the spirit of thinking can be compared to an empty board, a clean sheet of paper which is then filled out—never the same.[22] This blank piece of paper—to continue the metaphor—is an actual part of the thinking process and should not be left out. In contrast to what is seen by the naked eye, thinking is biased in a way the eye is not: what the mind perceives may be wrong, or may well be right, there is no clear picture at the outset.[23] Thinking is a longer process than seeing, takes more time, and the object of thought may not be physically presents and the thinking itself can change the nature of the object thought about, something the eye cannot do. It is the wider impact of this process which is important because thinking goes far beyond seeing and imagining.

Thinking can cultivate interiority if moulded and managed properly because of two main points: (i) Thinking cultivates a sense of possibilities; and (ii) thinking invites wisdom as the capability to distinguish the essential from the non-essential. Let us take a closer look:

i) Thinking frees us from the status quo, empowering us to reflect on alternatives. In Philosophy there are special situations ("proto-philosophical situations") which prompt thinking over and thus reliving the experience overlaid with a deep sense of doubt, depending on the process in motion. A sense of awe contributes significantly to the act of thinking since it voices an aspect of inner sense that things *are* as they are and *not* as the could be. Doubt, on the other hand, enables us to step back, look and think again. This stepping back provides a behind-the-scenes perspective of what we see taking place on our stage, so to speak. Philosophical reflection, nurtured by literature, considers these alternatives, the pros and cons and thrashes them out in inner discussion with utopian solutions weighed in the balance. It is a one-step-removed perspective of reality which encourages and endorses epistemic resilience

---

22   Aristotle, De anima III,4, 430a1f.
23   Aristotle, Metaphysics IV,5, 1010b1–3.

because the deep desire to consider alternatives nurtures a similar desire to act and the capacity to conceive alternative ways and means. Thinking empowers us to identify other solutions even in adverse circumstances, to find hope and vision in this possible *other*: thinking is the key needed to unlock the door of the suffocating tyranny of "now".

Thinking then promotes epistemic resilience because *this* moment in time as it is now can be perceived as *other*. The creative power to push the boundaries of this moment in time is vital for anyone who is unable to escape her circumstances, for someone held captive (see the examples of Havel, Bonhoeffer, Betancourt, Văn Thuân). Someone with a wealth of ideas is a *homo ludens*, who dares to try out new ingredients in new concoctions of ideas and notions. To continue the metaphor, ideas and visions like cooking ingredients are gifts; Max Weber talks about the power of the imagination (in his lecture on being an academic[24]), which provides the yarn with which we weave our stories and narratives (or 'sweaters' as Boris Cyrulnic proposed), inspired by any one moment in time. In "knitting" our threads together we are coping with and even finding answers to "life's little accidents." This persistent knitting and weaving of different threads into different textures, backgrounds and colors, trying out new ways and methods inspires us upwards and onwards in our desire to create and establish something new and unknown.[25]

In becoming acquainted with contingent possibilities, we are invariably expanding our inner powers. A master in this regard was Michel de Montaigne, who created the new literary genre of *les essais*. By going back over what he had just thought and just written in each sentence, he was able to perceive each idea expressed anew, from a different standpoint. He was thus able to wander and meander aimlessly through the most irrational of ideas and thoughts, and write them down. Montaigne works his way, question by question, through ways and means of dealing with the adversity he experienced after stepping down from his active political career. He was plagued by a deep sense of loss, fell ill and suffered mental torture and agony. He discovered that philosophising is learning to die, becoming acquainted with death, and only by treading that lonely path of isolation do we discover wisdom. Montaigne explores the world of thought in the same way an artist might try out new

---

24   M. Weber, Wissenschaft als Beruf. In: Ausgewählte Schriften 1894–1922. D Kaesler (ed). Stuttgart: Reclam 2002.

25   It is this tentative feeling-around-in-the-dark for something to hold onto, to break out and move on which Jean Louis Cianni discovers in his tentative approach to Philosophy: "Occupe-toi de toi, occupe-toi de ce grand vide qui est toi. Ne t'y abîme pas, au contraire prends tes distances avec lui (. . .). Joue avec lui. C'est cela que Socrates m'ensigne" (PR 29).

techniques in his art—he has a sketch book in his pocket ready to sketch down anything he might come across when out and about.[26] In other words, he cultivates the power of imagination, a sense of possibilities.

Imagination is crucial in cultivating interiority and strengthening epistemic resilience. Imagining is the capability to envisage alternatives to the status quo, to visually "tran-scribe" possible or impossible states and circumstances; this capability requires a sense of the real (as reference point for the construction of possible worlds) and a sense of the possible. Immanuel Kant introduced "imagination" as the bridging faculty between understanding and sensation, as that intuitive faculty to represent an object even without its being present.[27] Our sensory perception lacks intellectual content, understanding lacks sensual content—imagination connects the two. In this way imagination provides a particular way to appropriate reality, to guide perception and to shape agency.

Swiss philosopher Peter Bieri, for instance, suggests in his book on human dignity that the concept of human dignity opens up the possibility for a new way of perceiving, for a new form of life.[28] A new kind of imagination, a refined "sense of possibilities" opens up a new way of "being in the world". A moving example of dynamics such as these is the story of Shin Dong-hyuk who was born inside Camp 14, a huge political prison north of Pyongyang. As the son of two prisoners he was raised in the Camp but never given a sense of "context" or "alternatives"; only with the arrival of another inmate, who tells him about the outside world and the notion of escape, was his imagination ("sense of possibilities") triggered for the first time and a whole new way of being in the world opened up before him.[29] His imaginative capacity was moved by a deep understanding of the contingency of the world: Things could be different! This is an important element of the resilience-strengthening effect of thinking: Things could be different, there are possibilities, there are alternatives to the status quo.

The imagination can be inspired. A situation of displacement will invariably give rise to a widening out of one's imaginative horizons; Jean Donovan experienced this when she became a humanitarian volunteer in El Salvador after having worked as a management consultant; her experience in the Central American country as a lay missionary changed her sense of possibilities. Father Michael Crowley who knew her very well wrote: "Everything was

26   Cf., S. Bakewell, How to Live: Or A Life of Montaigne in One Question and Twenty Attempts at an Answer. London: Chatto and Windus 2011.
27   I. Kant, Critique of Pure Reason B 151.
28   P. Bieri, Eine Art zu leben. Über die Vielfalt menschlicher Würde. Munich: Hanser 2013.
29   B. Harden, Escape from Camp 14. London: Pan Books 2013.

thrown at her. She found herself challenged to be a giant, challenged to do bigger things than she ever dreamed she'd be asked to do. And she grew to meet that challenge … she went through a whole spiritual metamorphosis."[30] She committed herself to fighting for a different world since she was convinced that a different world was possible (and morally necessary).

ii) Thinking strengthens the inner life because it focuses our attention on what really matters and this helps us to re-assess adverse circumstances, setting them in a kind of framework which allows us to see events, encounters, and experiences in a context of meaning and structures of meaning. The above example, highlights the importance of framework in displacement experiences: a framework can be built on reflective practices. And if the sense of meaning gets lost, as vividly described by Timothy Morris in his account of failed development work in Yemen, the capacity to be displaced cannot be nurtured, cannot be considered and as a result one does not find one's own space in a new place.[31]

Thinking processes are possibilities to reflect on what really counts. This capacity to focus thought on what matters could perhaps be best described as wisdom. Wisdom gives us the power to make fair judgments and just assessment. Wisdom can only be seen as such when an individual leads her life according to certain "insight criteria" which build upon and add to the inner powers of judgment she already disposes of. However, a central epistemic tool is the capacity to collocate judgments reached and assessments made in the context of a wider canvas, to pick out the essential from the trivial and ability to differentiate between the two; and this is where thought and imagination are fused into wisdom. Wisdom differs from the capabilities of an "ideal chronicler" (who is able to record and remember everything) in that it sees and puts things in proportion in the contexts to which they are connected.[32]

Wisdom is knowledge learnt from life and internalized into personal identity. A wise woman will be guided by wisdom in all she thinks, says and does. Wisdom is not a discipline which can be taught or learned, it is a unique, personal trait, rooted in our character and way of life.[33] Wisdom is discreet and is

---

30   Quoted after: Anna Carrigan, Salvador Witness. The Life and Calling of Jean Donovan. Maryknoll, NY: Orbi 2005, 163 (in italics in the Original).

31   Cf., Timothy Morris, The Despairing Developer: Diary of an Aid Worker in the Middle East. London: I.B. Tauris 1991.

32   See A. Danto, Narration and knowledge. New York: Columbia University 1985; cf., D. Weberman, The Nonfixity of the Historical Past. The Review of Metaphysics 50 (1997) 749–768.

33   Ernst Bloch underlines true wisdom as follows: "there are no wise entomologists, this does not mean that entomologists may not be wise, they may be, but not on account of their professions, but there are wise doctors and judges because of what they do and

a way of life based on insight gained through judgments made. Those insights are often gained in suffering when realization suddenly dawns, truths revealed as the Book of Job illustrates. Only in his immense pain and loss does Job gain insight and wisdom into God's will and being. This newly attained wisdom in turn engenders a deep sense of humility which in itself is the knowledge that an individual human person is not the benchmark standard of the universe.

French philosopher Simone Weil who suffered perpetually from migraine and was afflicted by ill health during her short life time (she died from exhaustion in 1943, aged 34), found herself in a permanent situation of displacement because of her feeble health. Weil talks about "beauty" and "affliction" as two main sources of knowledge that teach us about the laws of the world. They offer, paradoxically, pathways into belonging even though these experiences constitute displacement: beauty and affliction are two primary routes to truth in Weil's thinking. The experience of affliction is an experience of the order and depth of the universe; affliction commands and dictates our attention, it leads us to knowledge.[34] Affliction exposes the individual to a world which exists but which this person would not have experienced without her condition, thus going through an exposure to the world the person would otherwise not have had. It takes wisdom to see this affliction thus and to reach alternative judgment on the experience.

There may be grounds to briefly reflect on the role of beauty in situations of displacement—it is a gift to both see and be grateful for all that is beautiful. Beauty, we can say, nourishes the soul; experiencing beauty builds up and strengthens the inner. Mother Mary Josephine, the founder of the Maryknoll Sisters, was quite clear about the role of beauty:

---

what they learn in the doing of it: they require both specialized knowledge but this is not enough, they require life experience and knowledge to be able to differentiate between what matters and what not: unlike the entomologist, this is a philosophical view of life" (translated from the German: E. Bloch, Über den Begriff der Weisheit. In: Philosophische Aufsätze zur objektiven Phantasie. Werke 10. Frankfurt/Main: Suhrkamp 1969, 355–395, here 386). Bloch characterizes a wise person as one who is mature, considerate, mindful and steadfast—this underlines the strong link between wisdom and epistemic resilience.

34   In her text "L'Amour de Dieu et le Malheur" (The Love of God and Affliction") written in 1942, one year before her death, Weil characterizes "malheur" ("affliction") as something overwhelming: "It takes possession of the soul and marks it through and through with its own particular mark, the mark of slavery.... There is not real affliction unless the event which has gripped and uprooted a life attacks it, directly or indirectly, in all its parts, social, psychological, and physical" (S. Weil, The Love of God and Affliction. In: The Simone Weil Reader. Ed. George A. Panichas. New York: David McKay 1977, 439–443, 439f).

How much more sensible to have comfortable, attractive things. Such things are really essential to our health. They are not a violation of poverty (...). At Maryknoll we try to have beautiful things even though these things are simple. There is no reason in the world why we should not be surrounded by beautiful things. God has filled the world with beautiful things.[35]

Poverty is an experience that sometimes goes hand in hand with deprivation of beauty; poverty routinely means having no access to beautiful places and spaces, no access to the beauties of nature and culture. Catherine O'Sullivan suffered from the lack of beauty while working in Peru. "Life was difficult during those early months. The first morning, when I went outside, I just couldn't take it. I went to my room and wept my eyes out. There wasn't a sign of vegetation anywhere. Huts of straw clung to the sides of rocky hills. Unfinished buildings made of concrete, with iron girders protruding from each corner, flanked the main road (...). The walls of house, like those of our neighbors, looked shabby and unsightly (...). In my first letter I wrote: 'I wonder how I will ever survive without a tree, flower or blade of grass.'"[36] And in another letter Catherine states: "there is no beauty in these cerros (hills)— devoid of vegetation, with rocks, sand, huts and ramshackle houses."[37] She confesses that the "bleakness of the desert surrounding," had the worst effect on her. She had to work hard on her inner balance. We see an additional aspect of "desert" at work here, an aspect of deprivation of beauty.

A conscious effort must be made to see beauty; the attitude to find beauty at second glance has been characterized by the Japanese concept *wabi-sabi* which alludes to the capacity to find beauty in the imperfect. The experience of beauty is not unrelated to the inner landscape; Pope Francis quotes Pope Benedict's observation "The external deserts in the world are growing, because the internal deserts have become so vast" (*Laudato Si* 217). The practice of thought control and ordered thinking, suggested in the *Philokalia*, can be recommended. Thinking and reflecting can be processes that make a person "see" in a different way, can make a person realize beauty. Thinking in all its facets strengthens resilience via interiority, since ideas take shape in our inner space, our inner world. The epistemic act of thinking in turn fortifies that interiority; in our knowing we always have an 'inner' partner with whom we can

---

35   Penny Lernoux, Hearts on Fire. The Story of the Maryknoll Sisters. Maryknoll, NY: 2012 (Centenary Edition), 128.

36   A. Clerkin, B. Clerkin, A Road Less Travelled, 65.

37   Ibd., 66.

consider never-ending possibilities and potential. Thinking helps distance us spatially from the immediate dilemma and context, and distance moderates and mitigates.

Gratitude is yet another aspect of resilience-strengthening, which is a matter of inner attitude and closely related to the way we think about life; Gratitude has to do with inner attitude and a proper control of thoughts. A person can develop a disciplined mind in cultivating a fundamental attitude of gratefulness. Dietrich Bonhoeffer and Francis Xaver Văn Thuân, as we have seen, each lived out of the sense of gratitude sustained during their terms of imprisonment. Gratitude is a major source of resilience; a source easily accessible from within—an important good in a situation of displacement. A convincing example of this cultivated sense of gratitude is Zenas Loftis (1881–1909): born in Gainesboro, Tennessee, he studied pharmacy and medicine, and was determined to work as a medical missionary in Batang, Tibet; he left Nashville, Tennessee for Tibet in August 1908 and recorded the dangers, challenges, obstacles, pains (and beauties and wonders) of his journey in a remarkable diary. He arrived in Batang, June 1909, after months of difficult travelling and died a mere two months later on 12 August having contracted smallpox and typhus.[38] His diary is full of a deep sense of gratitude.

On 10 October 1908 he met fellow Christians in Shanghai and was moved by the cordial reception: "Those few moments alone more than repaid me for many weary hours of trial I have had to reach this place. May God shower His blessings on this band of noble boys. It has been a glorious day, for which I am very thankful."[39] Expressions of gratitude such as this can be found throughout his diary; in November he had been able to give medical assistance to a Chinese man who would have otherwise died from an opium overdose; he experienced happiness via the gratitude shown by the man's wife and by the mother of the man: "I felt extremely thankful for this opportunity to do a little service for the Master."[40] Looking back at 1908 on the last day of the year he gives thanks to God for all the wonders he had been blessed with.[41] During his strenuous journey he is grateful for the beauty of nature he can experience;

---

38   An account of the final days of his life can be found in Albert L. Shelton, Pioneering in Tibet. A Personal Record of Life and Experience in Mission Fields. New York: Fleming H. Revell Company 1921, 73–75.

39   Z.S. Loftis, A Message from Batang, 29.

40   Ibd., 38.

41   Ibd., 39; gratitude also rings through on pp. 41, 47, 90, 93 etc.

arriving in Batang, being "so far from 'anywhere'," he is simply grateful to be
there, to have arrived.[42] We can safely assume that Loftin's sense of gratitude as
a "default position" in interpreting events and structuring experiences served
as a major internal source of resilience, as a source of epistemic resilience in
the uprooting transition from Tennessee to Tibet. Zenas Loftis was able to
endure hardships and displacement because of his fundamental attitude of
gratefulness. He "was a man who loved all the beauties of nature and was able
to see God on every hand."[43] The beauties of our inner landscape are and can
be shaped by reflection and watchfulness over thoughts.

6.3   Therapeutic Arguments

Cianni discovered that thinking, returning to and re-thinking Philosophy is
indeed therapeutic. It is a journey, it takes time, it takes effort, there has to be
a personalized way of finding the one appropriate therapy for one person.[44]
Ludwig Wittgenstein famously described language philosophy as therapeutic;
in his *Philosophical Investigations* he refers to philosophical problems as ailments in need of a good dose of thought and reflection. "Philosophy treats a
question like an illness."[45] Questions become pathological when they are the
result of language abuse: "Philosophy is a battle against the bewitchment of
our intelligence by means of our language."[46] In the same way as our body may
be "out of sorts" due to overeating or an unbalanced diet, leaving us weak and
sick, a one-sided diet of examples, can lead to pathologies.[47] With the proper
therapy, with a balanced diet, thinking can be both strong and of therapeutic
value.[48]

There is also a therapeutic reading of Ludwig Wittgenstein's early work, the
Tractatus Logico-Philosophicus. In one famous proposition (6.54) Wittgenstein
writes: "My propositions are elucidatory in this way: he who understands me
finally recognizes them as senseless, when he has climbed out through them,

---

42   Ibd., 143. "I'm very thankful for being here" (ibd., 144). And again in the entry on the fol-
      lowing day: "I am very thankful for being here, and would not exchange mission stations
      with any living man" (ibd., 145).
43   A.L. Shelton, Pioneering in Tibet, 73.
44   Cf., I. Yalom, The Gift of Therapy. New York: HarperCollins 2002.
45   L. Wittgenstein, Philosophical Investigations. Oxford: Blackwell 1967, 255.
46   Ibd., 109.
47   Ibd., 593.
48   Gordon Baker suggested a therapeutic interpretation of Wittgenstein's *Philosophical
      Investigations*—he read the text not as statements about grammar or language philoso-
      phy, but as offers of therapy (G. Baker, Wittgenstein's Method. Oxford: Blackwell 2004).

on them, over them. (He must so to speak throw away the ladder, after he has climbed up on it). He must surmount these propositions; then he sees the world rightly." This is the penultimate proposition in Wittgenstein's text and gave rise to a particular reading of the *Tractatus*. Philosophers such as James Conant, Cora Diamond, Juliet Floyd or Michael Kremer advocate a particular "resolute" or "therapeutic" reading of the *Tractatus* in the light of this key proposition.[49] According to this therapeutic reading, Wittgenstein does not set out to to present a "view" or "theory," but rather a *way* of speaking and looking. The *Tractatus* reminds us that philosophy is the practice of an activity and not the construction of theories: clarification is the aim of philosophy. Diamond and Conant ask the question: what does the *Tractatus* say about the status of its own propositions? They make the claim that the form of the *Tractatus* is connected with its philosophical ambition and with what it wants to express. The key term in a resolute reading of the *Tractatus* is "elucidate;" Wittgenstein's text is an exercise in elucidation. The most important image in the *Tractatus* is the image of the ladder.

> On this reading, first I grasp that there is something that *must* be; then I see that it cannot be said; then I grasp that if it cannot be said it cannot be thought (that the limits of language are the limits of thought); and then, finally, when I reach the top of the ladder, I grasp that there has been no 'it' in my grasp all along (that that which I cannot think I cannot 'grasp' either).[50]

Hence, the elucidatory strategy of the *Tractatus* consists in inviting the reader to engage in traditional philosophy up to a certain point. The results are not doctrines, but elucidations. "And the attainment of this recognition depends

---

49   This reading is distinguished from a "positivist" reading (Wittgenstein is seeking to construe a theory that would enable him to provide a method to expose metaphysical sentences as nonsensical and to demarcate the meaningful from the meaningless) and an "ineffability reading" (Wittgenstein distinguishes misleading from illuminating nonsense whereby the illuminating nonsense "shows" what cannot be said)—cf., J. Conant, C. Diamond, On Reading the Tractatus Resolutely. In: M. Kölbel, B. Weiss, eds., The Lasting Significance of Wittgenstein's Philosophy. London: Routledge, 2004, 46–99; J. Conant, The Method of the Tractatus. In E. Reck (ed.) From Frege to Wittgenstein: Perspectives in Early Analytic Philosophy, Oxford: Oxford University Press 2002, 374–462. D. Cora. 'Ethics, Imagination and the Method of the Tractatus', in A. Crary and R. Read (eds) The New Wittgenstein, London: Routledge, 2000; C. Diamond, Throwing Away the Ladder. *Philosophy* 63, 243 (1988) 5–27.

50   J. Conant, The Method of the Tractatus, 422.

upon the reader's actually undergoing a certain *experience*".[51] This experience is therapeutic, which is also a way of saying that the reading of thoughts and the thinking of thoughts can be both a cause for inner disease as well as a cure for it. Thinking is an important way of cultivating interiority and our senses of perception and judgment: in other words, a tap root of our epistemic resilience. Thinking can fortify our inner strength, an idea which is not as new as it might sound. The Stoics outlined therapeutic arguments such as thinking being able to heal a troubled or confused mind. The Christian Gospels also provide ample "therapeutic arguments;" In Mark's Gospel we find the dialogue between Jesus and the Gentile woman of Syrophoenician origin (Mk 7: 24–30). According to Mark, Jesus at first refuses to listen to the woman and then refuses to waste his healing powers on her since she is not of the tribe of Israel; he cannot fulfil her request. Dissonance, disappointment and disruption follow. The woman wisely employs a therapeutic argument based on *a minore ad maiorem* by arguing that even the dogs under the table get the crumbs and leftovers the children themselves do not eat. Her argument dissipates the tension: she surprises Jesus with her quick wit and reasoning. She introduces a new perspective to the "argument," a convincing argument; she knows the rules of the game being played which Jesus recognizes and can accept within the context of primary ministry. In this case, the argument solves the problem and enables therapeutic power to be granted. A similar example can be found in John's Gospel in the account of the adulterous woman who is to be stoned to death on account of her crime. Her accusers, who drag her before Jesus, eager to carry out her sentence are rather opinionated with their own-made wisdom: justice must be done and they will make sure it is done. However, the overriding feeling is one of jealousy; they hope to show Jesus up in front of his followers as being incapable of making a just decision and therefore a weak leader. They ask him what he would do according to the Law of Moses. Without looking up, Jesus begins to write in the sand in front of him. Nothing is said. There is silence. This is the first stage of therapy—he is obviously thinking.

The self-appointed judges are impatient and stubbornly goad him for an answer—without thinking. Then comes "that" answer, which has attained proverbial proportions: "Let anyone among you who is without sin be the first to throw a stone at her" (John 8:7). This simple argument sets the whole situation in a new framework and rather like Wittgenstein's *tractatus* "invites" the onlookers and would-be judges to take stock and reassess—re-think—the situation in a new context. They are shocked out of their limpid bias into action. Another therapeutic argument along the same lines is the account given by Matthew regarding the payment of taxes (Mt 22:15–22). Again Jesus is confronted by

---

51   Ibd.

hatred and scorn, falseness and scheming. The Pharisees are out to test him
once again and this time it has to do with whether or not it is allowed to pay
taxes to Caesar. Again Jesus does not reply immediately although in this account we are told that Jesus is "aware of their malice," in other words, he knows
what they do not say and knows too that the boundaries between what is "explicitly" said but "implicitly" suggested need re-thinking. Jesus thus introduces
this element of the unspoken into the argument which in turn opens up a new
perspective and creates a new context. Jesus unites the tangible with the intangible: "Show me the coin used for the tax." The therapy lies in Jesus' dropping
the ball back into the server's court, so to speak. His surprise answer wants his
listeners to think, he is inviting his counterparts to take part in a wider dialogue made explicit by the picture on the coin and implicitly suggesting that
paying taxes to the Romans is not to be condemned and is not a crime against
God: "Give therefore the things to the Emperor that are the Emperor's, and to
God the things that are God's." This reasoning sparks incredulity in those with
blinkered vision and ways of thinking. A therapeutic argument will be an invitation to look at things as they seemingly are from a different angle, to think
about them differently, too. It is therapeutic to change the game—to suggest a
sense of "things could be different," a sense of possibilities.

Again, we see "the power of framing"—a therapy of thinking can be a painful correction to habitual ways of perceiving and judging. Jerry Adriano Santos
de Jesus gave a speech in April 2000 during a Eucharist commemorating the
quincentenary of the first Mass on Brazilian soil, a mass celebrated by Cardinal
Sodano:

> You are in our house. You are in what is the heart of our people, the earth
> upon which you are all standing. This is our earth. Where you are now
> standing you must respect because this land belongs to us. You, when you
> arrived here, this land was already ours (...). More than 6 million Indians
> have been reduced to only 350,000 (...). Land for us is sacred. In it is the
> memory of our ancestors clamouring for justice.[52]

It is a painful therapy to be confronted with such framing of events. Obviously,
an experience of displacement can be therapeutic in this sense of re-framing
experience.

There is a tradition of therapeutic arguments in philosophy. Martha
Nussbaum, provided an in-depth study of the role and meaning of "therapeutic arguments" in both Greek and Roman philosophy, and developed the

---

52   Quoted after Thomas O'Reilly, An Acre Sown. St Patrick's Missionary Society in Brazil.
     Wicklow: Kiltegan Fathers 2001, 193 (in italics in the original).

ideas propounded there.[53] The Stoics frequently referred to the philosopher as a physician; in the same way as the practitioner's task is to treat and cure maladies and ailments of the body and perhaps mind, the philosopher has to cure diseases caused by false convictions. Unlike the Sophist application of argument as therapy whereby the argument as remedy can be construed to meet the needs of the individual patient, the Stoic stance is committed to pursuing truth in its endeavors to ease the suffering of the soul—*anima* (which in this context is seen as the source and abode of false convictions). The quest for a successful way of life—human flourishing—is the framework setting within which therapeutic arguments, "the larger picture," are considered. At the same time, however, the line of argumentation pursued does not adhere to a rigid set of principles independent of human requirements. Nussbaum takes this core idea and endeavors to iron out the rough edges of moral philosophy in non-scientific deliberations.[54] An approach founded on ethics, in contrast to one on physics, discovers and identifies structures *not* independent of human thought and action; it therefore becomes apparent that the ethics of such an approach cannot be applied as if ethical truths existed outside of the domain of human thinking and action.

Therapeutic arguments thus anchor the philosophical point of view in a conversation framework, rather like a tutorial between student and teacher, or exchange between therapist (doctor) and client (patient). This "setting", as it is commonly referred to nowadays in medical circles, is the framework within which mental "disorders" can be "analyzed"—not so very different from the medical concept underlying the idea of philosophy as therapy. Philosophy is the art of healing and the arguments it employs are the remedy. The ailments of major concern here are, as we have already mentioned, those caused by false convictions and jaded powers of judgment. Such symptoms require careful yet cautious treatment, but, it should be hastily added, treatment must be applied with a firm exacting hand if the root of the problem is to be remedied. Therapeutic arguments pursue a practical, tangible goal; they relate to the value systems on which they depend; they are concerned with the here and now of the case in question; they concentrate on the well-being of the individual; they apply ample portions of good common sense; and they universally work according to the asymmetrical question and answer pattern between

---

53   M. Nussbaum, Therapeutic Arguments. In: M. Nussbaum, The therapy of desire. Theory and Practice in Hellenistic Ethics. Princeton: Princeton UP 1994, 13–47.

54   M. Nussbaum, Non scientific deliberation. The vulnerability of the good human life. In: M. Nussbaum, The Fragility of Goodness. Luck and Ethics in Greek Tragedy and Philosophy. Cambridge: Cambridge UP 2001, 290–372.

teacher and pupil starting with clear and conclusive convictions; these stand in stark contrast to any culturally biased scepticism which does its best *not* to be nailed down to any fixed point on the compass of argumentation or, indeed, in solutions arrived at. Therapeutic arguments offer a different "framing" of a story, a technique which is key to resilience-building.

One particular therapeutic argument which Nussbaum touches upon and with which most of us have at least a passing acquaintance, is Epicure's famous argument about the sheer absurdity of fearing death: the main argument is broken down into five separate sub-arguments:[55] 1. An event can be good or bad for someone only if, at the time when the event is present, that person exists as a subject of at least possible experience, so that it is possible that the person experiences the event. 2. The time after a person dies is a time in which that person does not exist as a subject of possible experience. 3. The condition of being dead is not bad for that person. 4. It is irrational to fear a future event unless that event, when it comes, is bad for one. 5. It is irrational to fear death.

The argument starts with a general assumption which is then extended to include a general (human) fear of death following a down-to-earth approach that honors the human condition. The underlying idea of his therapeutic argument is that that the fear arising out of the individual's reflection on her own death can be eased, the mind put at rest and the equilibrium of the spirit restored.

A therapeutic argument is generally presented as to comprise three moments: a moment of aesthesia of sensibility, a cognitive moment of mindfulness and a moment of persuasion. In that initial moment of aesthesia it is essential that the "doctor" presenting the argument puts himself in the shoes of the afflicted "patient." A therapeutic argument needs to respond to a dire situation and can thus be regarded as *philosophie en situation*, which becomes involved in the condition given, or as an argument that works within a framework to generating a *vita contemplative*, providing a kind of "pastoral" context for the argument to take place. It is this moment of sensibility, embracing powers of observation and a keen sense of perception, which enables a diagnosis to be made. The cognitive moment of mindfulness incorporates claims to truth and knowledge and the conclusiveness of the argument. A therapeutic argument expresses a claim for understanding and on the basis of this is endorsed, becomes authentic. This cognitive moment relies to a large extent too on the

---

55   Nussbaum, The Therapy of Desire, 201f; cf., J.M. Fischer, Contribution to Martha
      Nussbaum's The Therapy of Desire. *Philosophy and Phenomenological Research* 59,3 (1999)
      787–792, esp. 788f.

analytical acridity and precision of the argument put forward. That third moment of persuasion is contingent on the ways and means, the style and tone in which the argument is presented; in other words, this is that decisive moment defining the "how" of the "what." A therapeutic argument must be presented in such a way as to facilitate the process of acceptance by the addressee. This means that there must be some recognizable drift in the argument inclining towards the addressee, with an element of affinity so that the listener in turn feels "inclined" to take on board and embrace the argument.

These three moments—together—embrace the unique character of therapeutic argument whereby the philosopher assumes the role of the therapist. It goes without saying that the sheer power and force of the therapeutic argument per se strengthens resilience which enables epistemic resilience to be engendered. Rather like physiotherapy which will loosen the muscles, ease tension and enable pain-free movement, therapeutic arguments will allow the mind to move more freely and more easily and without pain. Therapeutic arguments will break down the barriers of rigid, obdurate thought and assist thinking to maintain its role as epistemic resource. Yes, indeed, thinking can be a source for epistemic resilience as well as an important resource to cultivate a person's inner life. Meister Eckhart's thoughts on consolation based on the way we think about an experience explicitly spells out this self same point.

Even though thinking may lead to over-thinking, it is one of the most important resources for inner strength; it is connected to the imagination, to a sense of possibilities. Zenas Loftis, the brave American medical missionary described above, provides us with a diary entry, where he reflects on the power of the imagination. On that said journey to Middle China, in April 1909, they came up against all kinds of unforeseen obstacles, all kinds of not-anticipated hurdles which had to be mastered. He writes:

> This travelling on the Yangste (...) may be hard on the nerves, but it is decidedly harder on a fellow's imagination. He has to imagine all sorts of things. That he is not in a hurry at all, that he doesn't care if he does lose a day or two (...) He must imagine the captain is doing his level best to hurry on, and all delays and accidents are unavoidable. He must imagine that he has an unlimited supply of patience, and that he doesn't care a rap whether he gets to the end of his journey this year or next. All this is quite a strain, and unless his imagination is decidedly well developed, he is apt to have trouble.[56]

---

56   Loftis, A Message from Batang, 53–54.

The power of the imagination lies within the power of the person, even though the source of stimulation may be "unpleasant"; the imagination—if given enough scope and space—can master the impossible, can imagine and perhaps create a positive attitude or frame of mind. Even under extreme circumstances this power will survive—just like memory.

6.4   Memory and Remembering

Remembering, like thinking is an act of the imagination. The art of remembering is another important force in the project of cultivating interiority. Memory is a source of epistemic resilience as we have seen in the example of Ingrid Betancourt who remembered her family vividly and strongly in coming to terms with displacement. Let us explore that force of remembering in the final sections of this chapter on the imagination.

Memory, beautifully described in Augustine's *Confessions*, is a fascinating capacity: It is like a pantry full of tasty dishes, like an attic overflowing with old, dusty toys of a past childhood, like a dark cold cellar jam-packed with memories discarded, disposed of and forgotten. Some languages illustrate this idea of forgetting as "falling into oblivion" ("tomber dans l'oubli"). Forgetting is associated with the metaphor of nothingness, *lost-ness* undisturbed by the light of memory. Memory can be likened to a vast natural landscape with mountains, hills and valleys, lakes, seas and rivers, and prominent landmarks each representing important events to be recognized and remembered. The river of forgetfulness flows through this landscape, the river in which a memory with clear contours is suddenly washed away and lost forever. Without its reference point a memory's orientation is no longer stable, and without that resource of "sound" memories, resilience will become shaky. If we are unable to find familiar features in our mental map of memory, we will be unable to find our way in a world which requires such map-reading skills; if we are lost in life, how can we locate our place in the cosmos? This is the painful price people with Alzheimer's disease have to pay, vividly described in Alice Genova's novel *Still Alice*.[57]

Memory and identity are inextricably linked: Luigi Pirandello's novel *Il fu Mattis Pascal* describes the fateful life journey of a man who grabs an opportunity to cast off his identity and create a new one. All at once the world changes, it is another place, he no longer has a past; he can start a new life without financial debts, wife or mother-in-law. He is free to invent his own fictitious

---

57   Cf., L. Genova, Still Alice. Lincoln, NE: iUniverse 2007.

biography. But it all goes very wrong, he decides "to go back" but of course, he cannot. His wife has remarried and his old friends hardly remember him; it is '*come se non fossi mai esistito*' (as if he never existed). This novel reveals a great deal about the two most important functions of memory: Memories create identity and memories build community. And both identity and memory strengthen resilience.

The connection between orientation and memory is especially important for our context of epistemic resilience; a person with a clear sense of belonging and thus robust identity, is in a better position to develop epistemic resilience than a person without a clear and stable sense of orientation. Loss of memory undermines the idea of robust identity, a point also made in Nicole Krauss' novel *Man Walks Into a Room*.[58] Remembering gives us access to hidden inner treasures, things we "learn by heart," a phrase resounding with the very idea that contents that have been memorized cannot be taken away from us. Memory creates order and memory also relies on that same order as is apparent if we recall the images of the pantry, attic, cellar and landscape described at the outset.

Memory stores stories and stories provide access to sources of identity. The power of memory and the capacity to recall will cultivate resilience. As we have already seen with Ingrid Betancourt und Dietrich Bonhoeffer, it is those strong, colorful memories of their life "before" which gives them inner strength and contributes towards their developing epistemic resilience. Memories—like the pantry—can provide nourishing food which is energy-giving. This metaphor of spiritual food bringing energy is often found in the prayers of the Psalms, beautifully expressed in Psalm 103: "Bless the Lord, O my soul, and do not forget all his benefits," (Ps 103:2). Memories reminding us of our experience of God serve as a source of resilience. Remembering is an identity-building exercise, a life-saving exercise as Mattia Pascal's example underlines. Remembering cultivates a sense of one's inner wealth.

It has to be remembered, however, that the notion and meaning of "remembering" is not so clear cut as might seem at first glance. The actual "act" of remembering may be ambivalent. Remembering can be similar to a kind of sadness that does not allow a person to move on, arrive in the present because of an unhealthy commitment to an unrealistic image of the past; it is hampered by nostalgia. We have seen in Ellen Hilton Schneider's account that nostalgia can be weakening rather than a source of resilience and adaptation; her mother never adapted to the new environment and spent her final years

---

58   N. Krauss, Man Walks Into a Room. New York: Nan Talese 2003.

remembering the past and thinking of the countries and identities lost. Not only was she deceiving herself about the past, she was bathing in its nostalgia and preventing herself from arriving in the present, in affirming the here and now.

Nostalgia, a term coined by the Swiss physician Johannes Hofer in his dissertation in 1688, has been defined as a: "positively toned evocation of a lived past."[59] Notwithstanding, it is linked to pain, "a fleeting sadness and yearning to an overwhelming craving that persists and profoundly interferes with the individual's attempts to cope with his present circumstances."[60] There is "the wounding realization that some desirable aspect of one's past is irredeemably lost."[61] But even nostalgia, understood as sentimental longing for the past with its beauty and happiness and goodness and satisfaction, can have positive effects if connected to belongingness, meaning of life, and positive self-regard. Nostalgia can contribute effectively to building inner wealth and thus to growth.[62] Fred Davis argues that the negative experiences of the past "are filtered forgivingly through an 'it was all for the best' attitude."[63] The classic illustration of nostalgia can be found in Book v of Homer's *Odyssey* when Odysseus confides to the nymph Calypso: "Full well I acknowledge Prudent Penelope cannot compare with your stature of beauty, for she is only mortal, and you are immortal and ageless. Nevertheless it is she whom I daily desire and pine for. Therefore I long for my home and to see the day of returning."

Odysseus can resist the temptations of the nymph on the basis of nostalgic remembering. The cognitive process he engages makes him see his wife, and more importantly his attachment to her, as a real commitment in his displaced here and now. This inner awareness and sense of displacement is so strong as

---

59   Fred Davis, Yearning for yesterday: A sociology of nostalgia. New York: Free Press 1979, 18.

60   R. Peters, Reflections on the origin and aim of nostalgia. *Journal of Analytical Psychology* 30 (1985) 135–148, at 135.

61   Tim Wildschut et al., Nostalgia: Content, Triggers, Functions. *Journal of Personality and Social Psychology* 91,5 (2006) 975–993, at 977.

62   Matthew Baldwin, Mark Landau, Exploring Nostalgia's Influence on Psychological Growth. *Self and Identity* (2013) 1–16; for habitual worriers, however, may experience nostalgia as leading to even more distress because of the painful contrast between the allegedly worry-free past and the painful present: Bas Verplanken, When bittersweet turns sour: Adverse effects of nostalgia on habitual worriers. *European Journal of Social Psychology* 42 (2012) 285–289.

63   Fred Davis, Nostalgia, identity, and the current nostalgia wave. *Journal of Popular Culture* 11 (1977) 414–425, at 418.

to "dis-able" him from embracing the new place as "home." We can speculate whether being aware of "home" attachments and ties is part of a successful experience of displacement, whether it contributes towards the kind of robust identity required for dealing with strangeness.

Memories build bridges between present and past; these bridges can be unhealthy in the sense that they could prevent a person from moving into the present, by allowing painful memories to dominate; that is why a healthy bridge that strengthens resilience from within is a bridge sustained by healed and reconciled memories. A helpful element in the inner state that enables the capacity to be displaced is the art of dealing with the past in a reparative and forward-looking way; this art has been termed *kintsugi* in Japanese; *kintsugi* is a practice that gives new life to damaged ceramic objects, also acknowledging their frailty and history. The art consists in using lacquer mixed with powdered gold to restore broken pottery. It can be linked to the philosophy of *wabi-sabi*, embracing the imperfect, the aged, the flawed. It can also be linked to a spirit of detachment. *Kintsugi* is about "patching with gold," an art that can be translated into the art of dealing with displacement— displacement is an experience of brokenness, an experience of damage; the *gold* used for repairing the damage is taken from the inner center, is the inner strength.

Remembering is also a way of reassuring self of one's identity. A person's identity is shaped by her memories, meaning that personality is essentially dependent on the memories we have available to us. We gain identity in telling stories real and invented about persons or things and those stories appeal to a lesser or greater extent to our memory, making them (un)-worthy of being remembered. Memory is identity-building and strengthens epistemic resilience since it cannot be delegated or professionalized. Work on memory can only be authentically done in the form of 'personal discourses' that digest 'personal knowledge'. If our memories fall apart, our past disappears into the mist, identity becomes brittle; if memories lose their relationship to the present and the past becomes the reference point for orientation, one can no longer establish the continuity of one's own life. A person can be lost in memories unable to find the present. Identity through time is thereby at stake. This is true not only for the individual person but also for communities. And this is an interesting aspect to consider when thinking about epistemic resilience: There is not only an individual and personal aspect of remembering, there is also a social and collective aspect (which has been illustrated with the speech by Jerry Adriano Santos de Jesus in April 2000); this is also the case for epistemic resilience in general if we look at the social dimension of memory.

6.5   The Social Dimension of Remembering

Memories build communities: individual memory is a meta-contribution to tradition by not neglecting commitment, by not inventing another face, another name, another story to the one with which a person is linked through her face to face experiences. And personal memory puts us into a context that transcends both 'here and now' and my own, limited personal perspective. Working on memory is done within a context that transcends the first person horizon. A community of persons is a community of memories. In an important section, Wittgenstein points out that a linguistic community not only has to possess common linguistic institutions, but hold common convictions: "It is not only agreement in definitions but also (odd as it may sound) in judgments that is required."[64] Linguistic institutions can only be established on the ground of shared convictions. Shared convictions in turn presuppose a common framework for actions through which a view of the world can be developed; in other words, shared convictions presuppose a common framework for action. Experience, for its part, relies on the notion of memory.

It does, therefore, follow that linguistic institutions, convictions, and memories are interrelated in the way that convictions that may become the object of reflection and self-reflection cannot materialize without memories. The identity of a community is determined by linguistic institutions, convictions, a framework for actions, and memories. The identity of a community is essentially linked to its cultivated memories, those memories that have become part of its culture. We define ourselves by what we remember and forget collectively. The function of identity-building refers not only to the gathering of data about the past, but to the modality of how memories can be classified.

Culture is characterized by what it (as culture) remembers. A culture of memory interacts with the memory of a culture. Maurice Halbwachs famously stressed the function of memory as a social means for cohesion.[65] Collective memory can be reconstructed for a specific group and its spatial and temporal boundaries. The content of shared memories creates identity an identity expressed in common symbols that represent memories. And collectively acknowledged representations of memory constitute a shared sense of history and identity.

---

64   Wittgenstein, Philosophical Investigations, 242.

65   M. Halbwachs, On Collective Memory. Edited, translated, and with an Introduction by L.A. Coser. Chicago: University of Chicago Press 1992.

The ethics of memory has become an important part of the intellectual landscape since WW II. The debates around the Holocaust Memorial in Berlin show some of the issues surrounding that debate. The history of the impressive site was not without difficulties—first suggested in 1988, the property near the Brandenburg Tor was dedicated in 1992, a competition launched in 1994, winning design vetoed by the Federal Chancellor in 1996, a second call for proposals issued in 1997 with a final opening in 2005. There were a number of ethical aspects involved in the debate, key questions discussed included: Should there be memorials? Who decides? What is the budget? Who is (not) represented? Who are the addressees? What is the message?

Within our global political discourse on collective memory, Auschwitz is a major cornerstone. Auschwitz is a wound that must never heal and must never be forgotten by Europe. It is a wound that shall inflict new wounds, above all, the wounds of knowledge. The wound of knowledge arises out of injury to the illusion of one's own integrity. It brings about the pain of the tragic. Knowledge about Auschwitz is tragic knowledge, remembering Auschwitz is tragic remembering: the tragic can be defined as a situation ('a situation is tragic, if…') that meets at least four necessary conditions:[66] a) we are faced with a feeling of seriousness and importance caused by the *irreversibility* of events, events that we can no longer influence. In a tragic situation we are confronted with events and things that are beyond human control. The irreversibility of this situation is usually accompanied by a sense of loss that cannot be remedied by rhetorical or euphemistic means—for this very reason, I.A. Richards refers to 'tragedy' as "proof against irony and irrelevance."; b) We are faced with a tragic situation if this situation causes human *suffering*. Human suffering can be defined as an undesirable, pervasive and adverse condition, characterized by fragmentation and alienation, restriction, passiveness, by the inability to predict the future, and by pain.[67] In human suffering, an individual's life is perceived in terms of social debt and dependence. A tragic situation is always accompanied by suffering, by a feeling of restrictedness, loss and pain. c) A situation can be referred to as tragic if we are faced with the experience

---

66   There is no doubt about this: the tragic forces one to look at life in its entirety and to ask questions of fundamental importance; cf., E.W. Schipper, The Wisdom of Tragedy. *The Journal of Aesthetics and Art Criticism* 24,4 (1966) 533–537 (examines the tragic as a source of wisdom as it induces to look at the whole); G. Steiner, The Death of Tragedy. London 1961 (examines the tragic as a provocation for reason and as a reminder of the limits of the rational).

67   G. Pitcher, The Awfulness of Pain. *The Journal of Philosophy* 67,14 (1970) 481–492; N. Newton, On Viewing Pain as a Secondary Quality. *Nous* 23,5 (1989) 569–598.

of *violent change*, with a disruptive and unusual experience that reaches the limits of what we can understand and control. The tragic forces us to change direction and to plan our lives anew. An experience perceived as destructive makes us feel like an 'unwelcome guest.' According to Karl Jaspers, tragedy occurs wherever the powers that collide are truly independent of each other.[68] Finally, d) a tragic situation arises if we are faced with a sense of *frustration*, the feeling of unnecessary loss—a loss that increases the experience of contingency. Christoph Menke has coined the term 'tragic knowledge,' which consists of knowing both too much and too little, and of a feeling of frustration in the face of this impotence.[69]

When we know a little bit about the atrocities in Auschwitz, then we know too much to believe in the innocence of human beings, in the innocence of the history of Europe. We know too much to be able to go back to normal. And at the same time, we know too little: too little, to know what right action in this situation means, too little, to know what to do with the little knowledge we have, and too little to undo what has happened. We know too much to be able to bask in complacent innocence, but we do not know enough to have a clear idea about how we should go about coming to terms with this tragedy. This kind of knowledge can be described as 'tragic.' It is the knowledge of Oedipus, who knew too much and too little at the same time to live a proper life again. Tragic knowledge is the knowledge of those who survived atrocities and our knowledge of those who did *not* survive: it is the knowledge of those who know about the past and need to live in the present.

Tragic knowledge as a fruit of remembering can lead to a sense of limitedness which again can serve as a basis for moral integrity. Remembering Auschwitz is a central moral resource for Europe and our planet as a whole, a source for moral orientation and moral motivation. This kind of moral resource is not weakened by the fact that the knowledge about Auschwitz is tragic—accepting the non-exhaustibility of this knowledge makes it a constant source of disruption. What confronts us when we look at Auschwitz—a place and abbreviation for inhumanity—is the authority of the inextricable, the finality of the open wound. We are confronted with a finality, behind which we cannot go back, which cannot be abolished and, conversely, cannot be undone, and likewise cannot be ignored.

---

68   K. Jaspers, Tragedy Is Not Enough. Transl. H.A.T. Reiche et al. Boston: Beacon Press 1952, 57.

69   Chr. Menke, Die Gegenwart der Tragödie. Frankfurt/Main: Suhrkamp 2005, 18.

But this normative implication gives rise to a call for resilience. I would at this point like to introduce the term "*anamnetic resilience.*" It is an attitude that ensures remembering remains a contribution to resilience and resistance: evil shatters our trust in the world, evil leaves us with a sense of helplessness. We have a moral need to "name evil", so we need to make moral judgments. Some of the ethical questions concerning remembering have been raised by Israeli philosopher Avishai Margalit in his Horkheimer Lectures in Frankfurt.[70] He pondered the question about the importance of remembering names, about the importance of not forgetting the radical evil—radical evil as the kind of evil that undermines humanity.

On the one hand, the importance of memories for a community rests in the permanent obligations that result from the knowledge of past events and things suffered. These obligations must be clarified in terms of a theory of corrective justice. On the other hand, the value of memory results from the power to give orientation that reconnects present to past events. Both moments can be summed up in the expression of *anamnetic resilience:* the power of resistance resulting from the knowledge of past things. If no hope existed that the effort of remembering the holocaust is productive—who would undertake the effort involved?

Anamnetic resilience, therewith, refuses to accept the 'acedia of memory,' the feeling of weariness in questions of remembrance; it resists the 'atrophy of memory' and its burnout. Anamnetic burnout is present when looking at the past turns lacklustre, and becomes faint. Anamnetic 'acrasia' characterizes the lack of will to deal with history and memory. These states of exhaustion, as they are described in the spiritual tradition through the aforementioned notion of acedia, can also emerge within the realm of epistemology and a culture of remembrance. Acedia, as we have seen in chapter 3, is the experience of the conviction that one's own doing is in vain and meaningless; a form of mental weariness or lethargy: this is also a trap memory work can fall into.

The atrophy of memory advances through the loss of perception through the senses ('why remember?'). Pascal Bruckner, for example, warns us in no uncertain terms about the hypertrophy of memory, i.e. an 'excess' of remembrance. Buckner links inferior self-esteem and exaggerated reminiscence work. His remarks recall the so-called Walser-Bubis debate, involving the 'dosing of reminiscence work and memory content.'[71] *Anamnetic resilience* becomes

70   A. Margalit, The Ethics of Memory. Harvard UP 2002.

71   Cf., A. Fuchs, Towards an Ethics of Remembering: The Walser-Bubis Debate and the Other of Discourse. *The German Quarterly* 75, 3 (2002) 235–246.

controversial wherever a community is split over its views on its origin. How should the communal view of the past be shaped? How can looking back, look forward at the same time? The way the past is viewed is decisive for that past, the present and the future—we are touching upon the foundations of an intangible infrastructure here. "Memory" is part of this underlying structure that informs our tangible structures, and "anamnetic resilience" is the readiness and capability to resist fatal forgetfulness.

Anamnetic resilience—like other forms of resilience—benefits from mainly three factors. First, social interest and social anchorage facilitate the power of memory, understood as the framing of remembrance, translated into social and cultural memory.[72] Social memory is the discursively maintained exchange of individual memory contents; cultural memory is social memory as objectified in historical monuments and commemorative places. A group of people considering itself to be—or have—a 'community of memories' can gain special stability through common and shared access to past events. Second, *anamnetic resilience* is nourished by a sense of control and the conviction that essential issues of the social world fall under the auspices of human agency. This sense of control can likewise be understood as rejection of historical victimization. Historical victimization, for example, can be detected in the message: 'Nothing could be done,' 'it could not have been prevented,'—or in the apologetic gesture: 'things were simply like that then.' It can affect those who were victims of atrocities, and others who participated in those atrocities, either by way of condoning, or fellow-travelling.

An overly rigid codification of the roles of victim and offender contribute to resilient-weakening forms of fatalism, making us believe that there was no alternative. This message is occasionally uttered in present-day Europe and must be treated with great caution if it is based on the a priori assumption that the room to manoeuvre is radically restricted. Third, *anamnetic resilience* is conveyed by a sense of direction, and a sense of orientation. If a community of memories knows which directions it wants to go (like: *'Nunca mas!'*), then this goal provides the power for remembrance. The realization of truth and searching for truth oppose the atrophy of the power of memory. Reminiscence work turns here into an unforgiving sting that defies integration; an epistemic wilderness beyond the possibility for domestication.

---

72   For the role of social and cultural memory, cf., A. Assmann, Der lange Schatten der Vergangenheit. Munich: Beck 2006, ch. 1 and 2.

This sting, however, prevents anamnetic acedia and invites us to view the past not as an irrelevant and closed moment.[73] Whoever touches on atrocities becomes aware of this sting. The American Philosopher Robert Nozick describes the Holocaust as 'so momentous an event that we cannot yet grasp its full significance.'[74] Reminiscence work is equally hindered by not finding a single event that would be able to encompass all that has happened. For a heuristic purpose, Nozick compares the Holocaust in its significance for humanity with the distinct importance of the 'Fall' for Christianity. Nozick reaches the conclusion that after the Holocaust it would not have been an exceptional tragedy if humanity had ceased to exist: 'Humanity has lost its claim to continue.'[75] This confronts us with a caesura that once more closed the door that was open as answer to the Fall of Man through the incarnation. The Holocaust has accorded a new status upon the human family that hereby entered into a new context. In this context suffering has a new and incomprehensible meaning.[76]

This incomprehensibility seems to be of exceptional significance and a delicate balancing act between mystification and respect for the incomprehensibility of this atrocity. Dealing with irreversibility is one of the great burdens that historicity places on the shoulders of humanity. The necessity to deal with what can never find closure, marks the limits of what can be manipulated and restored: the 'unfinished.' Here events of the past cannot be put to death by a thousand analytical steps or clarifying qualifications without forfeiting their essence. Resilience is broken when people stop living in a larger context and start to exist solely for themselves. Resilience is undercut where reference points are missing that allow experiences to be embedded in a larger horizon.

In her epic study of totalitarianism, Hannah Arendt, maintains that a concentration camp cannot by its nature create martyrs by the simple fact of life that if everyone is exterminated, there is no one left to tell the tale, recount the horror lived through by individuals. The murder of the moral human being was thus made possible for the first time in human history and those who did indeed manage to survive had effectively been cut off from life as such, more

---

73 Against this background, Rolf Zimmermann enunciates his plea for moral contemporariness in the light of Auschwitz. Cf., R. Zimmermann, Philosophie nach Auschwitz. Reinbeck: Rowohlt 2005, 92ff.

74 R. Nozick, The Holocaust. In: R. Nozick., Examined Life. New York: Simon & Schuster 1989, 236–242.

75 Ibd., 238.

76 A difficult point: 'Perhaps it is only by suffering ourselves when any suffering is inflicted, or even when any is felt, that we can redeem the human species. Before, perhaps, we could be more isolated; now that no longer suffices" (Nozick, ibd., 241).

so than if they had been killed, because the weight of memory, the burden of not being able to forget was too immense. Refusal to listen, to believe in what these survivors told, the denial of fact and truth was almost as bad—if not worse—than what they had been through during WWII. The lack of "interest," the refusal to believe, triggered victimization of those who bore witness to the tragic events they had "lived" through. Knowing this, experiencing rejection and denial drains any dregs of identity that might remain; this loss of identity is synonymous with a loss of resilience. May this be a lesson for future generations!

The historian Emanuel Ringelblum sensed the enormity of this denial and universal loss of memory and went about putting together an archive, an "oral history," code named *Oyneh Shabes* of life in the Warsaw Ghetto, by collecting letters, poems, photographs, official documents and much more besides amounting to 35 000 testimonies. He was determined to let the victims have their say and write their story, our history.[77] In his above-mentioned Horkheimer Lectures in Frankfurt, Avishai Margalit raised the question of our collective obligation not to forget radical evil of the kind that undermines humanity and its potential to be human. Memories are deemed a source of knowledge. They are subject-oriented and perspective-laden, embedded and intermeshed, isolable and fragmentary, unreliable, dynamic and fleeting. But as fragile as they are, memories are sources for resilience. The Bible is full of testimonies to the power of remembering, of reminding the people of God of His Divine promises and the experience of blessings and grace in the past. The people in exile remembered their home and made this an element of an ethics of remembering, an act of anamnetic resilience: "If I forget you, Jerusalem, may my right hand forget. May my tongue stick to my palate—if I do not remember you," (Psalm 137:5).

Memory of what has gone before is a source of power, a resource to combat present adversity. The power of memory has a long tradition in Jewish culture with festivals primarily celebrated so that the people, God's people, do not forget that God is there by their side as companion, he guides and leads, and is faithful. The role of memory comes to the fore in chapter 29 of the Book of Deuteronomy, when Moses takes his leave; he reminds the people in great detail of their history and what God has done for them. It is this collective memory which provides orientation and a good foothold in those liminal stages and events in life. Moses is able to set his own "short" human life in the greater context of world history (as we might call it today) and in God's wider

---

77   Cf., S.D. Kassow, Who Will Write Our History? Rediscovering a hidden archive from the
        Warsaw Ghetto. London 2009.

framework of the cosmos. And it is this message that strengthens his people's sense of power even facing the adversity of losing a leader and entering an unknown land.

Anamnetic resilience has a social-ethical dimension: an ethics of memory is an obligation, a duty to truth and a duty to those who suffered. The work of memory takes place within a normative context of duties and rights. Victims have a right to be remembered, and survivors, perpetrators and succeeding generations have a duty to remember. The work of memory cannot be separated from truth claims, truth obligations, and commitments to the truth. And truth is recognized by many as the major epistemic good, thus a key point of reference in finding sources of epistemic resilience.

CHAPTER 7

Resources of Epistemic Resilience: Existential Commitments

Displacement can be experienced as outright cruel or "crazy"—Ita Ford, on her way to Chile, writes to Jeanne Evans: "Of course, this is a crazy life. Just when you get somewhat settled and comfortable in a situation—know your way around, make some friends and sort of feel at home—you uproot and start all over again (...)."[1] Life loses predictability, order, a clear idea of "what to expect next." Because of the fragility of assumptions about the future, the person herself becomes more vulnerable, exposed to threats to her identity. Peter Geremia, serving as a missionary in the Philippines, felt a deep sense of being "out of place" during his first Good Friday procession when he found himself in the middle of many poor parishioners: "I am a stranger among them. I understand very little of their life (...) I am just a stranger still searching for some meaning in life (...). All kinds of thoughts passed through my mind during that procession (...). At the end I felt physically exhausted and also emotionally drained."[2] Displacement is tiring and draining, just like grief: perhaps displacement is a kind of grief.

Displacement can be prepared and intentional, but it can also be sudden and unexpected; writing from her experience in Liberia in 1993, Leanne Olson witnesses this second kind of displacement in all its cruelty: "People have been displaced with nothing but the clothes on their backs. They can lose everything in an instant: homes, family, money, jobs, security."[3] If "things fall apart" and structures collapse, there are only social and especially inner sources of resilience available.

Thought and memory have been identified as key elements in cultivating the inner; these acts create and provide access to inner treasures which external circumstances cannot easily divest us of. These treasures allow a person to cultivate a sense of possibilities, a sense of how things could be different; a person with a cornucopia of memories and thoughts awakens with the realization that the imagination is a major source of inner wealth and a major force of epistemic resilience. Further to these sources for the cultivation of an

---

1   Jeanne Evans, The Letters and Writings of Ita Ford, 75.
2   Peter Geremia, Dreams and Bloodstains, 42.
3   L. Olson, A Cruel Paradise, 23.

© KONINKLIJKE BRILL NV, LEIDEN, 2017 | DOI 10.1163/9789004342453_009

interior life, I would like to look at the role of existential commitments as resources for epistemic resilience. We have seen that meaning-making serves as an important source of resilience from within. Meaning-making is linked to inner orientations. Existential commitments are strong beliefs constituting a person's moral and spiritual orientation. They can be seen to build the intangible infrastructure of a person's life. Let us take a closer look at this kind of infrastructure, after that I would like to explore the concept of meaning and religious faith as resources for epistemic resilience.

7.1   Existential Commitments and Spiritual Infrastructures

We are all well acquainted with the tangible infrastructures of railroads and airports, streets and traffic lights, and waste water disposal systems. But next to the hard factors of tangible infrastructure the soft factors of intangible infrastructure have to be considered, too. In his homily at Manger's Square, Bethlehem, during his pilgrimage to the Holy Land in May 2009, Pope Benedict exhorted the assembly to cultivate a new spiritual infrastructure: "Your homeland needs not only new economic and community structures, but most importantly, we might say, a new 'spiritual' infrastructure; capable of galvanizing the energies of all men and women of good will in the service of education, development and the promotion of the common good."[4]

This spiritual infrastructure is brought about by the good will and commitment of persons who have identified priorities in their lives and who have cultivated a rich tapestry of values. Pope Benedict's 2009 visit to the Holy Land was altogether a call for a renewed spiritual infrastructure. His speeches during his pilgrimage reflect his intention of motivating a sense of this urgency for such an infrastructure. The Pope did not go to the Holy Land in order to make politics. He did not go as a politician, but as a pilgrim—and his message was not about tangible and visible infrastructure, but about intangible and spiritual ones referred to the 'invisible,' 'the moral,' and 'the religious' dimension of human existence. In his address during the welcoming ceremony, Pope Benedict mentioned the fact that the Holy See and the State of Israel have many shared values and commitments. He mentioned the shared commitment to memory, the special status of Jerusalem, and the need to honor victims of past atrocities. In his address to the President during the courtesy visit to the Presidential Palace, Benedict mentioned trust as a key element of

---

4 See C. Sedmak, Spiritual infrastructure: Memory and moral resources. *Israel Affairs* 16,4
   (2010) 510–533.

this spiritual infrastructure ("A deeper understanding of trust can be gained by looking into the Hebrew term *'batah.'* It is not just the absence of threat, but also the sentiment of calmness and confidence."). In short, he was alluding to the spiritual infrastructure that Israel and the Church share. This spiritual infrastructure has a human and cultural dimension: values which have to be lived.

The spiritual infrastructure cannot be separated from the tangible infrastructure; human beings need bread, but they do not live from bread alone. This has been the experience of Liberal Studies professors Clark Power and Stephen Fallon from the University of Notre Dame; they hold a course for clients of the Center for the Homeless in South Bend, Indiana. Within the framework of this course they read classical texts, "big books," Antigone, Plato, Shakespeare; one participant very clearly justified this engagement when a curious journalist quizzed them about the course being a waste of time: "not by bread alone!" was the answer.[5] This is a reminder of the intellectual and spiritual dimension of the human person, a reminder of the spiritual infrastructure.

Recognizing the importance of spiritual infrastructure is also a key to mission and development work. People need hope and grounds for hope, which is also a matter of the spiritual infrastructure. People need access to a meaning-making larger dimension. Passionist priest Father Celestine Roddan (1887–1947), who led the pioneering mission of his order in China (leaving for China in 1921) describes an early experience:

> The cry of the beggar at the gate seeking a bowl of rice or a penny (...)
> A woman clad in rags and tatters is begging for food and a little medicine.
> Two tiny tots are bundled in a basket strapped to her back. One of the tots
> is evidently dying. No doubt about that. It is probably starving. We give
> the woman a little rice in a bowl. Then Leopoldino tells her, 'I will now
> give the medicine to the baby, the only possible medicine that will do this
> child any good. I baptize you Mary Joseph.'[6]

Obviously, one could comment on the structural violence involved and the imposed sacramental ministry; but I would like to focus on a universal human concern that transcends the tangible; the concern with building a spiritual infrastructure. Indeed, it is almost impossible to credibly celebrate the Eucharist

5 F. Clark Power & Stephen M. Fallon Teaching and Transformation: Liberal Arts and the Homeless." In D. Groody & G Gutierrez, eds., The Preferential Option for The Poor Beyond Theology: An Interdisciplinary Reader. Notre Dame IN: University of Notre Dame Press 2013.

6 Quoted after Caspar Caulfield, Only A Beginning. The Passionists in China, 1921–1931. Union City, NJ: Passionist Press 1990, 23.

in the midst of famine, but sometimes this is the only focus left; and what the Eucharist expresses is always an appeal to our human core, our human "heart". The scene described by Father Celestine might bring to mind a scene described in Acts 3: Peter and John are asked by a crippled beggar to give him money; Peter's response: he "looked intently at him, as did John, and said: 'Look at us.' And he fixed his attention on them, expecting to receive something. Peter said: 'I have neither silver nor gold, but what I do have I give you: in the name of Jesus Christ, the Nazorean, [rise and] walk." (Acts 3:4–6). Peter first and foremost focuses on "attention" and "companionship," and then speaks a spiritual message; both attention and spiritual commitment are translated into tangible healing; the spiritual infrastructure has formed and informed the tangible one. There are good reasons to argue that the spiritual dimension must not be overlooked in an understanding of resilience or "development."

Values as much as knowledge constitute what can be called the intangible infrastructure of a community or a person. A useful analysis of the concept of 'intangible infrastructure' has been provided by the Credit Suisse Research Institute.[7] Whereas tangible infrastructures refer to aspects of roads, water supply, energy utilities or airports as already mentioned, intangible infrastructure deal with knowledge driven contexts such as education, technology, and healthcare. Developments towards knowledge-based economies make it quite probable that elements of the intangible infrastructure will be the key to future socio-economic prosperity. The above-mentioned study identified five related pillars of intangible infrastructure: education, healthcare, financial development, technological investment and the penetration of business services.[8] It is education that emerges as the key element. Intangible infrastructure is hereby defined as 'the set of factors that develop human capability and permit the easy and efficient growth of business activity.'

The intangible infrastructure is key for the resilience of an institution or a business; inner life plays an important role in business: Czech Economist Tomas Sedláček has stimulated the discourse on the foundations of economics with his widely discussed book The Economics of Good and Evil.[9] Sedláček presents us with a vision of the inner lives of human beings as the basis of any economic dynamics—he draws a picture of untamed desires and "the wild

---

7 Cf., St. Natella et al., *Intangible Infrastructure: Building on the foundation*. Credit Suisse Research Institute 2008.

8 Ibd., 7.

9 Tomas Sedláček, Economics of Good and Evil. The Quest for Economic Meaning From Gilgamesh to Wall Street. Oxford: OUP 2011 [I will use "EGE" as an abbreviation]; see the review by Roger D. Johnson in *Faith and Economics* 59 (Spring 2012) 86–90; see also: Clemens Sedmak, Utility and Identity: A Catholic Social Teaching Perspective on the Economics of Good and Evil. *Studies in Christian Ethics* 28,4 (November 2015) 461–477.

things in us" when describing human interiority. He reflects upon the role of "dreams" and heroes" in economics: "Let us … note that the first 'macroeconomic forecast' appears in a *dream*," writes Sedláček alluding to the Pharao's dream as told in the book of Genesis (Gen 41). "A dream—that irrational, pictorial, and difficult to understand phenomenon which has long caused serious people to shake their heads and which has only recently been rehabilitated by psychology—becomes the bearer of the economic future," (EGE 65). Dreams are important windows into our inner lives. They are powerful. Dreams are still with us, they still influence us (EGE 283). And it is especially in times of crisis that we see what we have stored in our unconscious (EGE 213). Sedláček describes the dynamics driving Economics by wild desires and by greed. "We are naturally discontented," (EGE 223). Human beings are constantly "driven," "the more we have, the more we want (…). The more we have, the more additional things we need," (EGE 227). We are driven by cravings and yearnings: "The reason why we have grown so much (in GDP) in the recent past is that we *wanted it very, very much*," (EGE 239); strong desires, embedded in a framework of comparison-driven greed, are the engines of economic dynamics.

We are facing the challenge to resist these dynamics in the very same way as has been described by John Cassian in his reflections on greed. An interesting experiment in resisting the temptation to buy was carried out by Judith Levine who decided to buy only what is strictly necessary for the period of an entire year. She found out that you have to be deeply rooted in your commitments and your commitments in turn have to be expressions of your identity, of who you want to be, if you want to resist the permanent temptations of goods yelling at you "Buy me!"[10] This is an example of epistemic resilience—the same point is made by Sedláček. Saving the planet and creating economics as if people mattered, all depends on the domestication of our inner lives.

Wild things, Sedláček reminds us, are within us, since our inner lives are untamed: "Wild things are not in the past, in heroic stories and movies, or in distant jungles. They are within us," (EGE 324). That is why a solution to the contemporary economic crisis must be found in human interiority, i.e. in controlling desires:

> There seem to be two ways to minimize the discrepancy between demand and supply. One is to increase the supply of goods (in personal lives as well as in permanent GDP increases) until it satisfies our demands—to have, so to speak, all that we want to have (…). The other reply (…) is an opposite one, and it can be found in the ideas of the Stoics: If there is a mismatch, a gap between demand and supply, then *decrease demand* to meet your existing *supply* … In this view, a truly 'rich' man is someone who wants nothing (more) while the needs of the poor man are many" (EGE 221f).

10   J. Levine, Not Buying It. New York: Free Press 2006.

Many of the authors cited from the Christian tradition would concur with these thoughts. Greed is an expression of a particular intangible infrastructure underlying and shaping our tangible infrastructures. Changing a tangible infrastructure requires a change in basic commitments, a conversion of manners, and a transformation of the spiritual and moral infrastructure. An influential example of a business culture clearly dedicated to the idea of "the intangible takes priority over the tangible," is the Benedictine tradition. It is a tradition and structure which puts the spiritual before and above material needs and demands. Swiss economists Bruno Frey and Emil Inauen have explored Benedictine monasteries from an economic perspective. They were impressed by the economic success (and resilience!) of monasteries that survived difficult centuries. The single most important factor for the economic success they identified was "good governance." A clear, shared and internalized value basis (the "rule" as something to be lived, not to be followed), careful recruiting on this value basis, proper division of labor on this value basis, proper decision making processes on this value basis.[11] The Benedictine tradition with its clear commitment to a primacy of the intangible over the tangible turns out to be economically successful even under adverse circumstances. How does such an intangible economy work? By adopting and applying absolute trust in God—any action taken by the Abbot should be born of absolute trust in God: "do not worry about any lack of monetary profit," (*Regula Benedicti* 2, 35). A Benedictine monastery will have business structures and infrastructures at its disposal, which are not a means in themselves, or the means to monetary gain. In other words, a monastic business is unlike any other company in that first and foremost it is a spiritual 'business' with the intangibility of spirituality its overriding principle and concern; additionally it engages in 'tangible trade' to supply the monks it has to feed with their 'daily bread', so to speak. Chapter 57 of the *Regula* provides guidance for 'Artisans in the monastery', i.e., those men who have learnt and practiced a trade before entering the monastery. They may be allowed to continue their trade, *but*: "(…) if any one of them becomes conceited over his skill in his craft, because he seems to be conferring a benefit on the monastery, let him be taken from his craft," (*Regula Benedicti* 57:2).

---

11   E. Inauen et al., Benedictine Tradition and Good Governance. In: L. Bruni, B. Sena, eds., The Charismatic Principle in Social Life. London: Routledge 2012; B. Frey et al., The Corporate Governance of Benedictine Abbeys. *Journal of Management Studies* 16,1 (2010) 90–115; E. Inauen et al., Monastic Governance: Forgotten Prospects for Public Institutions. *The American Review of Public Administration* 40,6 (2010) 631–653.

Business success, profit and gain in cash terms are subordinate to the overall spiritual good of the community. The maximization of profit and yield is incommensurate with Benedictine spiritual values and traditions. Similarly in the sale of crafted goods, craftsmen must be careful: "(. . .) And in the prices let not the sin of avarice creep in, but let the goods always be sold a little cheaper than they can be sold by people in the world". (*Regula Benedicti* 57:7–8): "that in all things God may be glorified" (1 Peter 4:11. Ibid.). The Benedictine 'business' is governed by a principle which is not making a maximum cash profit: workers should be given the chance to lay aside their tools at regular intervals during the day for inner spiritual reflection: "(. . .) then let all labor at the work assigned them until None. At the first signal for the Hour of None let everyone break off from his work" (*Regula Benedicti* 48:12); work in itself is not the point or overall aim, it is intangible infrastructures which guide, lead and govern any work carried out.

Epistemic resilience, and this is the point I want to make, is enabled and expressed by a proper intangible (spiritual and moral) infrastructure, both on an individual and communal and institutional level. It is first and foremost a value basis, a set of value commitments that allows an intangible infrastructure to flourish; it builds the foundations for robust identity. Here again we see epistemic resilience at work on both an individual and a collective level.

The intangible infrastructure is a matter of 'second order resources'. Second order resources are those that determine the way we handle those resources we have available to us. Second order resources make us decide what to do with those resources. There are spiritual resources (spiritual values), epistemic resources (knowledge), and moral resources (moral values) as an expression of such second order resources. Let us briefly turn to moral resources; these are resources for moral orientation and moral motivation, sources for commitments and sources for the power to build commitments. Moral resources have at least three dimensions: a cognitive dimension, which is connected to convictions and beliefs; an affective dimension, which is related to an emotional coloring of these ties; and a volitive dimension, which transforms these ties into the result as well as the engine of wilful decisions. Because of these three dimensions moral resources are forceful, they instil a sense of urgency, and direct human imagination towards action. Moral resources provide coordinates for normative orientation.

Moral resources are indispensable in a situation of displacement. In the 1960s, US American soldiers found themselves in utter displacement in the jungles of Vietnam: On March 16, 1968 five hundred Vietnamese villagers (men, women, children, babies) were slaughtered by 120 American soldiers within four hours, in an outbreak of unbelievable cruelty and unnecessary and unsolicited violence. Jonathan Glover tried to grapple with the question "Why?" and provided thoughts on the loss of a sense of normality, loss of a moral frame of reference and pressure to conform, a moral gap between "inside" and "outside," the erosion of moral resources, loss of empathy and undermining of character with its moral commitments. Glover makes the point that the US Army soldiers lacked a strong inner moral compass, had no robust moral identity and were morally vulnerable in a situation of displacement with no visible reminders of moral expectations (so-say "traffic signs").[12] You have to be very strong in order to resist moral temptation; you have to have a robust moral identity, firm and identity-conferring existential commitments.

Existential commitments are tested and revealed in moments of crisis; a displacement situation is in many cases, an experience of crisis. In his autobiographical novel *A Secret*, the story of his Jewish family in Paris during the war years, Philippe Grimbert writes a story of displacement. This story may resemble some of the many stories of families that were pressed into new constellations by the confusion of the Second World War in Europe. However, this story becomes a moral resource for him and is decisive for the life decisions he later makes. Accessing the story of his family, which included entanglements, diversions, and a deported brother, serves as a moral resource in a displacement experience of identity-giving. The story constitutes a moral space within which the protagonist can position himself. The self-location in a moral space, finding identity by way of positioning oneself within a context of relevant questions is an important element in the construction of Self. The question "Who do you want to be?" is as important as the question "Where do you stand on topics X and Y?"

Moral resources can be identified in times of crises, especially in times that call for resilience. It is precisely in difficult situations that the moral resources from which we draw become manifest. To take yet another example from France: Irène Némirovsky, who was murdered in Auschwitz in 1942, depicted in her novel *Suite Française* (which was left undiscovered for decades), the events of summer 1940 in Paris. The mass exodus of people was beginning, and here as in most times of catastrophe the moral faculty and character of men reveal themselves. She describes the well-off Madame Péricand, who though at first distributed alms with great gestures, then visibly recognizes the extent of the drama and the shortage of food and strictly forbids her children

---

12   Jonathan Glover, Humanity. A Moral History of the Twentieth Century. London: Pimlico 2001, 58–63.

to distribute further supplies. Némirovsky describes how the Christian love of neighbor, 'the benevolence of centuries of civilization' fell like vain ornaments from her and revealed her 'parched, naked soul'. They were alone in a hostile world, she and her children. And she must feed and protect her young ones. The rest no longer counted. The rest no longer counted in the face of crippling fear, of the narrowness of uncertain exit and through it the growing denial of solidarity. Available moral resources show themselves precisely in crisis situations.

Hence, there is a need to reflect upon the question of what really counts, what really matters. A good way to think about existential commitments and basic values is to think about the question: What kind of life would I want a newborn person who is dear to my heart to live? This question has been tackled by two important yet not immediately recognizable aspirants, namely Dietrich Bonhoeffer and Alfred Delp. Both men were imprisoned for what they believed in and in the face of imminent execution both wrote letters to newly-born God-children they would never see. Both letters voice the hopes and wishes to accompany each tiny child on its way through life, in growing up and finding their way in the world. Both men recognize their role in guardianship even after their own untimely deaths, and in what can only be described as hope and a commitment to hope, feel it is their duty and responsibility to assist and accompany the child on its way through life.

May 1944, Dietrich Bonhoeffer writes a letter to his four-month old god-child Dietrich Wilhelm Rüdiger Bethge on the day of his christening.[13] Bonhoeffer is in a situation of displacement, in prison. But he has access to inner moral resources which he can share and confirm through letters. Bonhoeffer underlines the dimension of new beginning in birth and feels in some way a close bond with this new arrival to life as he is about to take his leave. Bonhoeffer tells this new-born baby that its life now and to come will bridge an outgoing *old* generation and an incoming *new* generation. In his letter to the child's mother Bonhoeffer reminds her of her duty to remember their cultural heritage of values. He gives a detailed description of a good home—the vital background for a child to grow and develop; the home should be both nursery and refuge, a source of both intellectual and spiritual motivation. In the letter to his Godson he tells him to trust in his parents and their caring, guiding hands and that the virtuous goodwill of his mother and father for those around them will

---

13   D. Bonhoeffer, Letters and Papers from Prison, Enlarged Edition, London: SCM Press, 1971, 294–300.

bring him many friends and helpers. Bonhoeffer then concedes that we cannot plan everything in life, some things are beyond the realm of learning but this perspective begs to be learnt. We must take care not to lose ourselves and our lives in too much "thinking," such as starting the day by considering various possibilities and ensuring that none of them go wrong, or at least without mishap. We realize too late that thinking alone is not enough, what really matters is are willingness and readiness to take on responsibilities which come our way in the course of the day—in the course of life.

This willingness to assume responsibility is the main message of his letter, since Bonhoeffer concludes that the undeniable trait of his generation is its failure to do just that. Alfred Delp writes a similar letter to his own Godson Alfred Sebastian beginning: "You've chosen a difficult time to begin your life,"[14] and wishes him a life shared with family, friends and community both at home and at work. Delp hopes Alfred will develop practical skills so that he is not a burden to others and hopes too that he will seek that humility which is the foundation stone of a fulfilled inner life. Specifically, Delp reminds him of the legacy of the 'obligation' which lies in his name: 'Alfred Sebastian,' going on to emphasize how vital is to stay steadfast. He wishes his Godson to have sharp eyes so as to be able to distinguish good from evil, a rare ability in the 1940s, and a good head for heights so as not to slip and fall at the slightest obstacle on life's path. Both letters underpin life's bare essentials; holding on to certain values and moral resources.

Here again we see that moral resources will show themselves in crisis situations. Displacement, as in experiencing imprisonment on death row, is one type of a crisis situation. And this is when epistemic resilience is required (and put to the test). Firm commitments are deeply rooted a person's sense of self. One key source for identity are processes of meaning-making and questions to do with purpose and "point of life."

7.2   Point and Purpose

Situations of displacement can be hard, especially if there are security issues involved—a major factor in the work and lives of humanitarian workers.[15] A list of intrapersonal resources required for resilience among aid workers includes

---

14   A. Delp, Prison Writings. Maryknoll. NY: Orbis 2004.

15   Valeska P. Korff et al., The impact of humanitarian context conditions and individual characteristics on aid worker retention. *Disasters* 39,3 (2015) 522–545, at 527.

adaptability, problem-solving skills, emotional regulation, self-awareness, but also a sense of meaning and purpose.[16] A "sense of purpose" is a source for identity as well as a prominent resource of epistemic resilience: knowing that the *point* of an event can be found in the adverse circumstances we experience and in which we can draw on our knowledge of purpose and point in doing or not doing something. The Maryknoll Sisters in Hong Kong found their strength in difficult times during the Japanese occupation in the attitude: "ad maiorem Dei gloriam." They went on a retreat in the middle of the war to find reassurance in a deepened sense of mission.[17]

Point and purpose ask the *whys* and *wherefores* of life's challenges; it seeks reasons and orientation. Friedrich Nietzsche famously wrote: "He who has a why to live for can bear almost any how."[18] This is a powerful statement about the connection I am interested in, the connection between epistemic resilience and a sense of meaning. In the light of a highest good or an ultimate goal, or in the light of a perspective that looks at life as such and the world as a whole adversities can be dealt with.

The American theologian and newspaper photographer Mev Puleo, died of cancer on 12th January 1996 at the age of 32. Since being at college, she had lived a life in the service of and in solidarity with the poor, working in Haiti, Brazil and El Salvador. During her studies she had memorably remarked on how she would lead her life which she did then go on to do: "I'd rather die young, having lived a life crammed with meaning, than to die old, even in security, but without meaning."[19] She found her mission in life in serving and making sacrifices. Her point and purpose of life helped her overcome adverse circumstances including that of a terminal disease and to reach out to help others worse off than herself. The general observation: "Life's purpose is to serve others" may well be lived out by some and rejected by others, but it does transmit a sense of placing your life in a bigger framework. Studies in poverty alleviation have shown that the two most important internal factors in overcoming poverty are

16   Lisa McKay, Resilience. Building Resilient Managers in Humanitarian Organizations: Strengthening Key Organizational Structures and Personal Skills that Promote Resilience in Challenging Environments, London: People in Aid 2011; Alice Gritti, Building aid workers' resilience: why a gendered approach is needed. *Gender & Development* 23,3 (2015) 449–462, at 452.

17   Cindy Yik-yi Chu, The Diaries of the Maryknoll Sisters in Hong Kong 1921–1966. Basingstoke: Palgrave Macmillan 2007, 84.

18   F. Nietzsche, The Twilight of the Idols. Maxims and Arrows, para 12.

19   Robert Ellsberg paid tribute to Mev Puleo in his book All Saints (New York: Crossroads 1997); Mev Puleo's husband Mark Chmiel paid a similar tribute (M. Chmiel, The Book of Mev. Bloomington, IN 2005).

a "sense of identity" and a "concept of future". People who know who they are and who know who they want to be, have higher chances of getting out of poverty.[20] It helps to see oneself as part of something bigger, this gives meaning and significance to a person's life.

Questions of point and purpose can arise on an everyday basis. As the Polish paediatrician and director of an orphanage, Janusz Korczak asked himself in 1942: "What is the point in clearing away the dirty dishes from the breakfast table every day?" Korczak wanted to lead a challenging life, one that served some purpose, one that had a point. In doing so, he chose a hard road rather than an easy one but one that was full of dignity, was useful *and* beneficial, and beautiful, one that pursued the obligation of duty willingly and happily. "I exist not to be loved and admired, but myself to act and love. It is not the duty of those around to help me but I am duty-bound to look after the world, after man," he writes in his Warsaw ghetto diary.[21] Korczak is given opportunities to escape, more than one; instead of relief or joy, he is astonished that anyone could conceive of him leaving his children to be murdered. The children are murdered, but he accompanies them into the gas chamber and does not abandon them when they need him most. The point in doing it? Janusz Korczak *made* a point, his point, by wrestling with life, his own personal life and life in general by serving the wards in his guardianship, under his protection, children who had no voice and were shown no respect; children who were never considered or the cause of concern for anyone but Korczak. He found meaning in his life because he cared about something, he cared about persons. He found meaning because he had entered strong commitments, had expressed "robust concern" in his life.

Rachel Corrie, a US activist working in the Gaza Strip in Rafah to improve the lives of the Palestinian families living there, well knew that living there meant living with the real daily threat of being killed which is what happened to her on 16th March 2003; she was hit outside the house of the family she was living with by a passing tank and killed.[22] She was convinced that what she was doing served some purpose, had a point and it was this conviction which gave Rachel Corrie the energy and power to take the risk and to face

---

20   C. Sedmak, Armutsbekämpfung. Wien: Böhlau 2013, ch. 5.

21   J. Korczak, ghetto diary. New Haven, CT: Yale UP 2003, 69.

22   Rachel Corrie's family compiled a collection of Rachel's sketches and notes and had them published; the book is a testimony of Corrie's quest for point and purpose, a testimony of her conviction to do what was right and being prepared for this genuine purpose to make the sacrifices which would have to be made. The Corrie Family (ed.), Let Me Stand Alone. The Journal of Rachel Corrie. New York 2008.

those everyday lethal situations. She had someone to care for, she had a clear sense of robust concerns and commitments. Finding meaning is the challenge in defining a wider context beyond the boundaries of one's own interpretation of point and purpose; commitment to a cause empowers a person to see her life as part of wider whole. The absence of this sense of care, concern, and commitment, can rightly be called: "hell."

In the ca. 4th century *Apophthegmata Patrum*, (The Alphabetic Collection of the Sayings of the Desert Fathers), Abbas Macarios the Great is quoted as giving an account of his encounter with the skull of a dead man describing the torments of hell: "We are ourselves standing in the midst of the fire, from the feet to the head. It is not possible to see anyone face to face, but the face of one is fixed to the back of another. Yet when you pray for us, each of us can see the other's face a little. Such is our respite."[23] The key sentence to be noted here is the second statement ("It is not possible to see anyone face to face"). Hell is a situation without eye contact, a situation where the "face" (prosopon) of the one is not made visible to the other. Emmanuel Levinas uses the category "face" to describe the living presence of the other as a way of being open to that other—those others—as an undeniable reality. Loss of face is loss of disruptive force but also loss of responsibility-evoking force. The experience of the nakedness and defencelessness of the face leads to a resistance to possess and control.[24] Hell is a situation of "facelessness". It is a situation where there is no person to care for and about; C.S. Lewis' description of hell in *The Great Divorce*, describes a place where we are unable to love.[25]

That is why even if you are in the midst of hell, in a war zone, in a concentration camp, in a post-disaster setting, it is not the circumstances that determine "hell," but your attitude. As long as there are areas of robust concern, it is not "hell within." Images of hell are deep since they express conceptions of the undesirable. Whereas "values" could be understood as "conceptions of the

---

23   The Sayings of the Desert Fathers. Transl. B. Ward. Revised Edition. Kalamazoo, MI: Cistercian Publications 1984, 136f; cf., B. Müller, Der Weg des Weinens. Die Tradition des 'Penthos' in den Apophthegmata Patrum. Göttingen: Vandenhoeck und Ruprecht 2000, 203f. Müller points out that there is a rich tradition in monastic wisdom talking about hell as a place of darkness ("skotus")—a darkness that precludes the possibility of seeing the glory of God (The Sayings of the Desert Fathers, ed. cit., 82—Theophilus, Archbishop of Alexandria).

24   E. Levinas, Totalility and Infinity. Dordrecht: Kluwer 1991, esp. 194–201, 212–216; on "face" and "vulnerability" in Levinas see R. Burggraeve, Violence and the Vulnerable Face of Others. *Journal of Social Philosophy* 30,1 (1999) 29–45.

25   C.S. Lewis, The Great Divorce. New York: HarperCollins 2015.

desirable,"[26] concepts of hell characterize conceptions of the undesirable with a similar normative force as values, values "ex negativo". That is why it is telling which images we find for hell in different cultures. They describe "loss of meaning." Both images of the spiritual tradition as well as works of literature provide helpful insights into meaning and its loss. Let us think of Simone de Beauvoir's famous novel *Tous les hommes sont mortel*, for instance. Simone de Beauvoir presents a key figure, Fosca, who takes an elixir promising everlasting life whereupon he falls into a stupor of languid insensibility which teaches him that one single action no longer had any meaning considering he now had all the time in the world. This reflects Thomas Nagel's point that any human act can be rendered meaningless and absurd if placed in in an immense depersonalized context; so, if you think about the fact that you are a small piece of dust on a planet which is a small piece of dust in a galaxy which is a small piece of dust . . . asking the question whether you should brush your teeth tonight will seem simply absurd.[27] The anonymous macro-context makes our life lose both weight and relevance.

A concrete life context provides a sense of depth, weight, and meaning. One of the interviewees in Christina Montaiuti's PhD dissertation on resilience and meaning-making among Aid Workers expressed his clear sense of purpose and mission as strengthening his resiliencve: "Well, probably the biggest button for me is doing mission work. Why did I come to a mission such as this one? I came at the request of a colleague who had a need that wasn't filled within the mission and who knew the skills and tools that I had could meet that need. As part of what I do within those skills, focuses me more and what the need of overall group is and to try and meet that need. In this case it's medicine, emergency medicine."[28]

Point and purpose within the realm of service, context and rules set out above, was the thread running through Viktor Frankl's thought and reflections on the same. Viktor Frankl assumes that "purpose" is not simply there for the taking, not some ready-made product which is served up to us as individuals.[29] No, each and every human being is called upon to seek and discover the point and purpose of his and her own life. There is no guide book, no flat-pack structures needing to be put together with the right tools; it cannot be sussed out by

---

26   Cf., J.W. Van Deth, E. Scarbrough, The Concept of Values. In: Van Deth / Scarbrough, eds., The Impact of Values. Oxford: OUP 1998, 21–47, 27.

27   Cf., Th. Nagel, The Absurd. *The Journal of Philosophy* 68,20 (1971) 716–727.

28   Monaiuti, The Effect of Meaning-Making on Resilience Among Aid Workers, 153.

29   V. Frankl, The Will to Meaning. Cleveland, OH: The World Publishing Company 1969, 50–79.

observing the world around us, yet, at the same time, the world is rather like a book of life which we need to endorse with our own signature by being open to what happens around us and to us, we are called to respond to the questions of life we are presented with.

The "treasure hunt" for purpose is an invitation for each individual to seek context and live up to the demands it makes but at the same time look over the rim of that—*my*—life into a wider universe of purpose. The purpose of this is that each human being goes about it in a different way—no two ways are the same; this is a fundamental law of life which demands a basic sense of responsibility for self: a concrete purpose is discovered in a concrete situation and time, and addressed to a concrete individual, and just like every situation is inherently unique, each and every human being is also unique. The challenge of point and purpose is inextricably linked with irreversibility and future hope which in Frankl's view cannot be divorced from the point and purpose of the past—our past life. We enter commitments, we make choices, we live with irreversible decisions. There is permanency in our lives, that cannot be removed. But we are still free to choose an attitude towards what is happening to us, we find dignity in the fact that nobody can remove the freedom to choose inner dispositions, to position ourselves vis-à-vis our experiences and the events in our lives. This includes pain and suffering as well. Frankl survived the concentration camp based on his inner sources for strength, his sources for inner strength; He survived on the basis of his imagination, his hope, his goal to be able to talk about his experience while going through this experience, thus placing his experience in a wider context.

Finding one's position with regard to suffering is key in the search for meaning; Viktor Frankl turns to the parable to explain this disparity; he compares suffering to an ether-like gas which will flow into and fill the hollow space it is pumped into no matter how wide or deep the space may be, but it will distribute itself evenly throughout the space given. Pain and suffering work along similar lines: if allowed suffering will fill the human soul whether the suffering be great or small.[30] However, unlike gas, suffering is not a phenomenon which can be merely observed detached from point and purpose and it is this which enables us as humans to seek our own individual point and purpose in life even in extreme adverse circumstances; thus, a key question together with "what can I know?" is "What can I hope for?" and the question so often asked: "What can I do?" is in fact "what must I suffer?" The situation cannot change and cannot be changed but attitude and perception can.

---

30   V. Frankl, Psychotherapy and Existentialism. NY: Washington Square Press 1967, 87–94; V. Frankl, The Doctor and the Soul. NY: Alfred Knopf 1968, 105–116.

Frankl cites the Holocaust, which caused him extreme personal suffering, and the example of Yehuda Bacon who wonders about the point of all those years spent in Auschwitz; in his youth he had been determined to tell the world what he had experienced there, in the hope the world would change. But the world did not change, and the world did not want to hear about Auschwitz either. It was only many years later that he realized what the point of all that suffering had been: suffering serves some purpose if *you* yourself change as a result. Suffering can thus be described as being the acid test of our quest for meaning. Someone who is convinced of the purpose of his life will not sink into despair because despair is suffering without purpose; at the same time, happiness is not the purpose of life, but having a reason to be happy is. Frankl distinguishes between "meaning" and "happiness", a differentiation Julian Barnes focused on some 50 years later in his "novel" *The History of the World in 10 ½ Chapters*: a collection of perspectives of love, purpose and suffering against differing historical backgrounds of crisis. In each case there is one circumstance embedded in the infinity of history and time itself; this endless loop of life and love is expressed most poignantly in the last chapter which takes place in heaven with the inexplicit question of the sense and purpose of love and whether it could or should last forever.

In pondering on point and purpose we are too pondering on the world per se and life as an inherent part of that world. Frankl firmly believes that all life situations and occurrences have a point, which is not an in-built aspect like the solution to a cross word puzzle, but a creative quest. The creative power engendered in the search, and the freedom to structure that search according to our needs and the context given can never be taken away from us. Frankl remembers Camus' myth of Sisyphus condemned to rolling a boulder uphill only to see it crash down again: the struggle itself must fill a man's heart with gladness, Sisyphus must be happy. Even in hopeless, pointless situations we are free to make purpose out of it creatively. And if we were to name one essential element of meaning, purpose, and the point of life, it would be love. Love is essential; we will dedicate a good part of the final chapter of the book to love. Frankl talks about the truth of love being the highest and ultimate good attainable and worthy of being sought by any human being.[31] Love is the embodiment and driving power of point and purpose; love is the source of inner power; love alone can create that depth of life we as humans seek and it is love which provides us with the orientation we need: love is resource of epistemic resilience and a source in the quest for meaning.

---

31   V. Frankl, The Doctor and the Soul, 132–175.

In a nutshell: purpose, as we have seen, provides access to inner resources and these enable us to tackle the adverse circumstances we find ourselves in, by equipping us with the power to tolerate and endure suffering—which does not mean that we avoid it as best and as much as we can; it is a capacity to develop certain attitudes and aspects of mind to certain situations. There is a primacy of "Why" over "What", and a connection between "Why" and "How."

7.3   Existential Commitments: Faith as Resource for Epistemic Resilience

A major resource of epistemic resilience is faith; we have seen that both Ingrid Betancourt and Francis Văn Thuân drank from this well in their efforts to tap resources of epistemic resilience. Faith is powerful, it serves as a source of identity. Faith and religions serve as moral resources that give both motivation and orientation to act. They provide an inner home in the midst of displacement. They express existential commitments that people have entered. People with a religious sense of identity can be remarkably strong—for the better or the worse. They can cope with difficult situations. Faith and religion are sources of resistance and resilience.

Displacement and deprivation can be endured on the basis of spiritual and religious resources. We have seen that Francis Xavier Nguyen Văn Thuân spent thirteen years in prison, nine of which were in solitary confinement. He recalled and recited the sentences of the Bible he could remember, he confirmed his belief that he was not alone, but in God's presence, he found himself in the presence of the Communion of Saints. We can also think of Jesuit Father Walter Ciszek who spent twenty-three years of his life in Russian prisons and in Siberia. He describes the faith sources of his strength.[32] We could mention Pastor Richard Wurmbrand who suffered torture and imprisonment because of his Christian faith in Romania.[33] We could reflect upon Albert Schweitzer's decision to sacrifice his brilliant academic career to become "jungle doctor" or upon Mother Teresa's stepping out of a secure monastery to live with the poorest of the poor in the slums. There are many stories that can be told about faith informed decisions and religiously motivated ways of enduring hardships and making sacrifices.[34] There is something remarkable about the strength

32   W Cziszek, He Leadeth Me. Garden City, NY: Doubleday 1973.
33   R. Wurmbrand, Tortured for Christ. London: Hodder&Stoughton 2004.
34   Cf., the collection by R. Ellsberg, All Saints. New York: Crossroad 1999 (3rd printing).

that can sometimes be found in religious people; a strength of commitment that expresses itself in endurance and a sense of direction. It is this sense of direction and this experience of not losing the knowledge of one's place in the universe even in moments of crises that indicate that people of faith can draw on special sources for their identity.

Religions have been rediscovered as an important resource in development work, in social change work.[35] Faith is a resource for epistemic resilience because it is powerful—let me mention three reasons why:

Firstly, religions are powerful because they provide material for human identities. They provide both a cosmology and a concept of Self in relation to that cosmology. According to William James all religions include two fundamental statements in their cosmologies—the statement that the world is not perfect and needs to be redeemed, and the statement that there is a way towards that redemption.[36] Religions provide a space for existential and moral questions (Where do I come from? Where am I going to?) and enable people to position themselves in this space of existential questions. This position is a position with a soteriological promise and a position of moral importance. It places an individual life within the framework of a bigger picture that gives significance to a person's otherwise rather insignificant existence. As someone with a part to play in a bigger plan, a religious person's life also becomes instilled with a sense of "having a mission." Thus, religions provide a resource that endows, sustains and restores human identity.

Secondly, religions are also powerful because they cannot be finally negotiated. It is not possible to assign a definite place to a religion, a position in the space of moral and epistemic commitments. More importantly, religion does not allow itself to be domesticated in a safe intellectual or political home. Religion makes claims as to the non-finality of the natural. All religions assert that the way things appear to us as they do does not mean that this is the last word about the universe. All religions claim that there is an order beyond the visible and tangible. In this sense, religions open up a space for

---

35   Cf., Severine Deneulin with Masooda Bano, Religion in Development: Rewriting the secular script. London: Zed Books 2009; Jenny Lunn, The Role of Religion, Spirituality and Faith in Development: A critical theory approach. *Third World Quarterly*, 30,5 (2009) 937–951; Lea Selinger, The Forgotten Factor: The uneasy relationship between religion and development. *Social Compass* 51,4 (2004) 523–543; Gerrie Ter Haar, ed., Religions and Development: Ways of transforming the world. Hurst and Co., London 2011.

36   W. James, The Varieties of Religious Experience. New York: MacMillan ⁵1970, ch. 2.

a "Beyond", a "Magis", a "More". By opening this space beyond the sphere of human manipulation and control, religions cannot be negotiated in the same way as a political programme or a philosophical theory. This creates new entry points for power and also new entry points for challenging established power. At the same time we have to face a paradox, namely the paradox that on the one hand religions cannot be definitively contextualized and on the other that each religion with its claim of enabling access to some kind of supernatural or the absolute sets a finality against which all history has to be measured. It is because of this finality that Rowan Williams identified the temptation to take God's perspective as the ultimate challenge for a religion in its efforts towards integrity.[37] Religions are powerful because they cannot be definitely negotiated.[38]

Thirdly, religions are powerful because they make statements about the human condition, about human cognition as such and our access to epistemic objects. Religions say something about the limits of human reason. If we accept a power that delineates human reason—how should we talk about this power, let alone control it? In this sense, religion introduces a sense of wilderness, of rawness into the processed world of human reasoning with its acceptable arguments (and arguments that can be recognized as such) and a common ground for discursive interaction. Religions make claims about the cognition of the absolute and by doing so they make claims about the limits of human cognition in general. Religions are powerful because they make statements and provide tools in order to make statement about the human epistemic and moral condition.

Religions are powerful because they provide sources for robust identity. A religious person is a person whose identity depends on his or her particular convictions concerning the world as a whole and life as such; religions provide resources to be someone in particular with a special mission and a unique position in the universe and at the same time they express an invitation to

---

37   R. Williams, Theological Integrity. In: Idem, On Christian Theology. Oxford: Blackwell 2000, 3–15, 6.

38   This was the experience of C.S. Lewis after he had lost his beloved wife. He was wrestling with God, trying to make sense of God's ways and the rationale behind this death. But ultimately he had to accede: "My idea of God is not a divine idea. It has to be shattered time after time. He shatters it Himself. He is the great iconoclast. Could we not almost say that this shattering is one of the marks of His presence?" (C.S. Lewis, A Grief Observed. London: Faber and Faber 1966 [1961], 55–56). Religions are powerful because they cannot be brought to final terms.

minimize one's ego. This is one of the deep paradoxes of being a religious person—knowing that there is a meaning in (and to) life, that it makes a difference what we do and how we do it, who we are and who we are struggling to become; and yet at the same time knowing that life is not an ego trip but about a universe that centers around me. Religions, we could say, grant *heterocentric views of the universe*, views that tell us that the center of the universe is not the individual human being who is in search of his or her identity. William James has described the saint as the person who moved from Ego-centeredness to World-Centeredness, who shifted focus of attention and effort, extended boundaries of Self, and accepted a heterocentric reading of the world.[39]

7.3.1   *What does it Mean to be a Believer? Three Insights*

There is a sense of forcefulness in committed religious life, a sense of concentrating one's energies. Committed religious life allows a person to be a citizen of the world, precisely because her citizenship is "not from this world." This is the message that we can learn even more poignantly from the testimony of the life of Mahatma Gandhi as he gave it in his famous autobiography.[40] Mahatma Gandhi teaches us basically three things: (i) A religious person has a clear sense of direction; (ii) a religious person has a deep sense of humility; (iii) a religious person is engaged in a constant spiritual struggle if she takes her religiosity seriously:

(i) A clear *sense of direction* stems from the orientation to a good that has been recognized as the highest: "What I want to achieve,—what I have been striving and pining to achieve these thirty years,—is self-realization, to see God face to face, to attain *Moksha*," (GA x). Gandhi testifies to worshipping God as truth only and to searching the Truth in all aspects of his life. "I am prepared to sacrifice the things dearest to me in pursuit of this quest," (GA xi). This clear sense of direction of the committed religious person is identity-giving since it enables us to recognize ourselves as dependent creatures, and yet it is identity-taking since the clear focus on the divine intensifies our sense of separateness from God and our sense of limitedness. Human identity then becomes at the same time a gift with clarity and undeniability, and a promise with hiddenness and non-controllability.

Following Gandhi, searching the truth is the essence of religion: "The term 'religion' I am using in its broadest sense, meaning thereby self-realization or

---

39   W. James, The Varieties of Religious Experience, lectures 11–13.

40   M. Gandhi, An Autobiography or The Story of My Experiments with Truth. Ahmedabad: Navajivan Publishing House 1966 (1927) [GA].

knowledge of self," (GA 22). Knowledge of self cannot be separated from knowledge of God and knowledge of life, knowledge of fellow-beings and knowledge of the universe. It is a clear statement that a religious person has to be characterized by a special way of receiving and guarding identity. For a religious person identity is a gift and a task, not a construction and a choice. The search for self-realization can precisely *not* be found in self-centeredness. "If I found myself entirely absorbed in the service of the community, the reason behind it was my desire for self-realization. I had made the religion of service my own, as I felt that God could be realized only through service," (GA 118). This is an important aspect we have identified in Bonhoeffer's work as well. The religious person sees her life as an invitation to serve, to go beyond the boundaries of one's self. Gandhi became used to following the inner voice, his sense of God's presence in his life (GA 100). Following God gives human life a clear sense of priorities and a clear sense of direction. This sense for truth needs to be nourished, it is geared towards growth. "Truth is like a vast tree, which yields more and more fruit, the more you nurture it. The deeper the search in the mine of truth, the richer the discovery of the gems buried there, in the shape of openings for an ever greater variety of service," (GA 164).

(ii) A deep *sense of humility* is the result of self-knowledge and awareness of the greatness of God. Gandhi was convinced that deeper insight into self led to a deeper sense of humbleness. There is no room for self-praise in spiritual experiments (GA x). This humility may be linked with the pain of separateness of God: "It is an unbroken torture to me that I am still so far from Him Who, as I fully know, governs every breath of my life, and Whose offspring I am," (GA xii). Prayer is a necessary expression of human devotion to God, it is a means of purification, but needs to be done with an attitude of deep humility (GA 54). Humility is an attitude of understanding, of understanding the proportions of the human and the Divine, of accepting God's guidance and providence. Many a time Gandhi referred to his strong sense of being guided by God (e.g., GA 16; 34; 131). It is a humbling experience to accept the loss of control and choice. "It may be said that God has never allowed any of my own plans to stand. He has disposed them in His own way," (GA 188).

Gandhi teaches us that the religious person is not the one who maximizes her choices, but the one who ultimately has no choice but to do God's will. This sense of humility is, as we have seen, nurtured by a distinct renunciation of autonomy. Gandhi's sense of a divine order would not allow a distinction between "public" and "private." This can perhaps be seen most clearly in Gandhi's approach to sexual morality: "I think it is the height of ignorance to believe that the sexual act is an independent function necessary like sleeping or eating. The world depends for its existence on the act of generation, and as the

world is the play-ground of God and a reflection of His glory, the act of generation should be controlled for the ordered growth of the world. He who realizes
this will control his lust at any cost, equip himself with the knowledge necessary for the physical, mental, and spiritual well-being of his progeny, and give
the benefit of that knowledge to posterity," (GA 153). One is tempted to think
about this position as a more general approach to being a religious person: is
it characteristic for a religious point of view which conceives of the world in
terms of creation that a clear distinction between "private" and "public," between "individual ethics" and "social ethics," between a "sphere of autonomy"
and a "sphere of relational dependence," cannot be made? Gandhi's view of
things would certainly point in that direction.

(iii) The commitment to a constant *spiritual struggle* is a commitment to
ongoing spiritual growth, to self-discipline and self-restraint. Human life is
about attaining perfection, walking on the road to perfection. The spiritual
struggle of self-purification is not one's own unaided battle: "The existence of
God within makes even control of the mind possible," (GA 158). The commitment to God's presence in every aspect of one's life serves both as the motivation, the engine and the aim of the spiritual struggle. Perfection can only be
made a human category with humble reference to God. Gandhi was committed to removing all obstacles from this road to perfection, including exclusive
intimacies.[41] The religious person lives among others with a sense of detachment (GA 210). A commitment to growth is the presupposition to conceive of
situations as "lessons." The overall image for human life is the image of the
school. It is in the school of life that we are invited to learn our lessons. Even
(and especially) one's own limits become sources of lessons to be learned.

Gandhi mentions his constitutional shyness, his hesitancy in speech:
"its greatest benefit has been that is has taught me the economy of words,"
(GA 46). It seems that this offers grounds for being in harmony with one self, of
accepting one's very being. The lessons of life are lessons about self-perfection
and self-purification and ultimately lessons in the art of loving. "I know that
nothing is impossible for pure love," (GA 9; cf. GA 135). The spiritual struggle is a
Hindu ideal that Gandhi embraced thoroughly: "*Brahmacharya* means control
of the senses in thought, word and deed," (GA 158). The spiritual struggle is not
an additional element in religion, but the essence of being a religious person:
Gandhi uttered his conviction "that religion and morality were synonymous,"
(GA 125). The spiritual struggle is not a luxury for the "spiritually gifted and

---

41   "He who would be friends with God must remain alone, or make the whole world his
       friend" (GA 13). In 1906 Gandhi took a vow of chastity to pursue this commitment to per-
       fection even more radically and "officially".

talented" but a necessary part of the human condition: "Man is man because he is capable of, and only in so far as he exercises, self-restraint," (GA 238). Self-restraint did not remain a vague concept for Gandhi. The extent of one's capabilities of self-restraint manifests itself primarily in one's ability to control lust and in one's ability to control the palate (GA 157), i.e. in one's capacity to fast (GA 249). "Passion in man is generally co-existent with a hankering after the pleasures of the palate," (GA 240). Self-restraint—another indication that the distinction between "private" and "communal" does not hold—can be enhanced and consolidated by public ceremonies and commitments.[42] But the attainment of perfection does not lie in human hands: "Perfection or freedom from error only comes from grace," (GA 238). The clear direction of one's life and the constant struggle for spiritual growth cannot be separated. Gandhi refers to an understanding of life that is seen as a constant invitation to grow.

We could translate this message into the simple words: Life is not supposed to be easy: the religiously committed person does not look for comfort to travel the road of least resistance. The religious person is committed to self-renewal and self-perfection; she is prepared to travel the road less travelled and to walk the path less known. By reading Gandhi one could, in my opinion, gain some important intuitions about what is meant in the frequently mentioned Muslim term "jidhad" (moral struggle)—a commitment to self-discipline and self-perfection even against the surface of one's nature and desires.

Summing up, we could say that a religious person lives in a religious universe that provides a wider context for the individual human life. This context gives depth and meaning as well as a mission and challenge to human life. Let us look at a powerful testimony of faith-based epistemic resilience.

7.4   Strong Faith in Adversity: Corrie ten Boom

If we were to pick an example, a "role model" of resilience through faith, "how God can use weakness" (HP vi), we need look no further than the Dutch lady, Cornelia (Corrie) ten Boom, who during the German occupation of the Netherlands in WWII was imprisoned together with her father and sister Betsie, for having assisted fellow countrymen, Dutch Jews, by hiding them in

---

42   After unsuccessful attempts to live a private desire for chastity, Gandhi made a public vow: "I realized that in refusing to take a vow man was drawn into temptation, and that to be bound by a vow was like a passage from libertinism to a real monogamous marriage," (GA 155).

their own home and helping them to escape Holland. She provided a "home" for the persecuted and found herself in displacement in a concentration camp for doing so, and in serving as a citizen of the world and as missionary after the War.

In her book *The Hiding Place*, Corrie gives a first person witness account of remaining strong in adversity.[43] Religious faith provides "security in the midst of insecurity." Strong faith empowers Corrie's father to remain steadfast in what he believes during interrogation—he held on to his commitment to open the door to anybody in need of help. He is able to make such a strong statement because his life is based on a personal relationship with God, nourished by reading God's words. Corrie is brought up in this tradition, her faith is rooted in the Holy Bible. She describes her joy when she manages to smuggle the Gospels into the camp; it is a precious treasure to be guarded and protected. She finds the experience of solitary confinement unbearable, but is able to find solace and strength in the scriptures—she sat on her bunk, opened the Gospels at St. John and began to read and read . . . Corrie reads the Gospel as a letter written to her personally. Feeling she is the addressee fortifies her sense of being close to God, of being on first name terms so to speak. Corrie's sister Betsie, equally strong in her convictions and love of God, shows her inner resources in other ways; she becomes a source of strength for the women squeezed into the cattle wagons taking them all to Ravensbruck, even in this hell-on-earth she finds good reason to be grateful: for God (Do you know what I'm thankful for? (. . .) I'm thankful that father is in heaven today, HP 174). Her heartfelt gratitude is her only means of survival in Ravensbruck, a lice-infested flea pit which they are forced to live in. It is exactly because their barracks are so infested with vermin and the toilets emit such an obnoxious stench that the guards avoid going near it—for fear of contamination—ironically, perhaps, giving the multi-national female prisoners ample opportunity to meet and pray to their heart's content.

Corrie and Betsie experience the world differently; perhaps the best way of describing it would be that they experience the world, life, as a parable. Someone who can "live" his or her faith in everyday circumstances perceives the external world as impacting their own inner being and faith; they are able to understand that everything is for a purpose, is part of a much wider, intangible framework. While Corrie gains inner strength through her "letters from God," Betsie is able to convey this parable perspective to others. While Corrie sees a monster of a woman in a grey uniform, wearing a cap and carrying an umbrella, Betsie sees something else, she sees that woman's inner being and

---

43   Corrie ten Boom, the Hiding Place, London [25]2004. Abbreviated throughout as "HP".

sees a human being destroyed. Corrie is outraged and distressed beyond measure when she discovers who it was betrayed her family, a man they had trusted
and whom her father had befriended. Betsie, on the other hand, remains calm
and collected; on being asked if she is not bothered that this man has betrayed
his country, she promptly replies: "Oh yes, terribly! I've felt for him ever since I
knew—and pray for him whenever his name comes into my mind. How dread-
ful he must be suffering!" (HP 169).

    As a citizen living in two *parallel* worlds, Betsie *sees* the external world of
appearances and actions, she *sees* even more clearly underneath those appearances, that inner world of being hidden to the human eye and it is this world
which for her is decisive in her perception. This ability to see underneath and
in-between is basically a parable-like take on life which has its own language
and special ways of expressing things: a religious language. Corrie tries to share
this language and "view" with her counterpart in "dialogue" during interrogation, to impart this vital aspect of a world in which things are not always as
they appear to be: God's viewpoint is often quite different to our own, and unless he had given us the Book which tells us about it, we could not even hazard
a guess (HP 151). This is not a *lingua franca* invented by Corrie and Betsie for
prisoner purposes; it existed, it was the language used before Ravensbruck by
the ten Boom family at home, every day to express both worlds: "This was evil's
hour: we could not run away from it. Perhaps only when human effort had
done its best and failed, would God's power alone be free to work," (HP 119).
This is an interpretation of how the family sees it, an interpretation in religious
language ("It was evil's hour") to express that what is seen is linked with what
cannot be seen, yet both are inextricably part of a higher order (in both senses
of the word) which is not chaotic but "ordered" and "orderly".

    It is this close tie (*re-ligio*) with an order—a higher order—which provides
a safe haven via faith in that order regardless of the atrocities being carried out
by human hands and which without faith one might despair about. It is this
rock of faith which enables Corrie and Betsie to realize they have a role to play
in this (dis)order. They trust in God's Divine timetable of things implicitly. This
trust of faith helps them make it through those Dark Nights of existence, such
as when Betsie is brutally whipped; Betsie's key concern is for her sister's pain
in seeing the bloody whip marks: "Don't look at it Corrie, look at Jesus only,"
(HP 191). Betsie knows in whom she can trust, she knows her life is on solid
ground, ground which will never shift and never let her down; she is able to
interpret her bloody, brutal beating as a parable of life—lives.

    The power of the parable lies in that moment of transformation, that mo-
ment which takes external circumstances and raises them to a higher and at
the same time deeper level: faith has the power to transform, to transform what

is seen to the inner unseen. Betsie knows this power of transformation and sets about transforming their flea-infested barracks, into a place God would want to reside in: her tools? Prayer: "Lord Jesus, (...) send your peace into this room. There has been too little praying here," (HP 186). Services are held regularly in the barracks in the conviction that it is in absolute darkness such as here that God's light of Truth will shine brightest. So it is that in the midst of the God-created fleas that his word is spoken and heard. "We sat by deathbeds that became doorways of heaven. We watched women who had lost everything grow rich in hope. The knitters of Barracks 28 became the praying heart of the vast diseased body that was Ravensbruck," (HP 197).

Prayer creates light both outside and in; prayer brings its supplicants closer to each other in sharing their second person perspective of God. They pray that the world be healed of its wounds in the knowledge that their faith and trust in that wider vision transcends the immense and immediate suffering in the here and now. Their physical surroundings are unbearable, but deep inside they are filled with the light and glory of God.

> The blacker the night around us grew, the brighter and truer and more beautiful burned the word of God (...). Life in Ravensbruck took place on two separate levels, mutually impossible. One, the observable, external life grew every day more horrible. The other, the life we lived with God, grew daily better, truth upon truth, glory upon glory, (HP 182).

Betsie moves increasingly towards this glory; the weaker her body becomes the "bolder" her faith (HP 191); she withdraws into the world of her diseased body in which the boundaries between life and pure prayer blur and merge. When she dies, Corrie is afraid to look and see the dead face of her sister disfigured by suffering, but what she sees is something else entirely: a face transformed, a face radiating peace, beauty and hope: "Now what tied me to Betsie was the hope of heaven," (HP 204) und: "The beauty of Betsie's face sustained me over the next few days" (HP 205).

It is the beauty of service—Betsie refused to give in to the pervading selfishness in the Camp—in which the ten Boom sisters discovered that there is a "special temptation" in "concentration-camp life," the temptation for the individual to think of self and self alone, with no regard for other or neighbor (HP198), if during roll call there is a chance to stand out of the way of the bitterly cold wind, then "you" do: "Selfishness had a life of its own," "and even if it wasn't right, it wasn't so *very* wrong. Was it?" (HP 199). The second rampant disease Corrie highlights is: "(...) stony indifference to others that was the most fatal disease of the concentration camp. I felt it spread to myself: how could one survive if one kept on feeling?" (HP 207). Corrie is filled with shame and despair; she stumbles in her own attempts to do what is right. In overcoming her own revulsion of the grime and stench, forced to do so by an encounter with two gypsies, Corrie comes out much stronger, having overcome not revulsion but her cold indifference to the needs of others. (HP 207).

It is this tremendous power of faith to endure which enables a true believer to forgive, and Corrie ten Boom manages to do this—though unwillingly at first—after a church service in Munich when she unexpectedly comes face to face with a former S.S officer from Ravensbruck. At first she feels she is paralyzed to the core, all the old, terrible memories rise up before her eyes; she cannot raise her hand to shake hands, she feels no warmth or charity towards this man; how can she forgive him, this officer who caused so much physical pain and mental anguish. Yet, at the same time, she knows that ill will achieves nothing and breathes a silent prayer: "Jesus, I cannot forgive him. Give me Your forgiveness", (HP 222); and the ability to forgive is a powerful tool that strengthens resilience since the inability to do so weakens the soul.

William Blake's famous poem *A Poison Tree* describes the dynamics of the inability to forgive as an act of planting a poisonous tree in the depth of your heart.[44] If one cannot forgive a person, this attitude is like a tree that grows and grows, but this tree is poisonous and spreads this poison, sowing embitterment and frustration that will affect the inner situation, the way people perceive, judge, desire, and remember. A poison tree, to use this image again, can infiltrate every memory, every thought, every emotion, and every desire. "As Blake says, it is concealed anger that plants the poison tree (...) It may exclude all other concerns from our attention so that we can't work or play or love as we would wish."[45] That is why there are good reasons in the spiritual tradition to call for a cleansing of will and thought. Betsie and Corrie were both intent on casting out bitterness and thoughts of revenge from their hearts.

Religious faith is a source of inner energy and power even in the face of atrocities. In the midst of such cruelty, "too much to grasp and too much to bear," Corrie can only pray "Heavenly Father carry it for me," (HP 164). In the Camp she manages to recall the words of her father, his teaching and his faith in God (the resilience strengthening power of remembering!) and in doing so is able to put herself and her unbearable burden into God's trustworthy hands. Faith is trust, even when all else fails, it is this habit of trust built up with regular prayer that impacts and pervades body and spirit; such trust is an

---

44   Cf., J. Brenkman, The Concrete Utopia of Poetry: Blake's 'A Poison Tree.' In: Ch. Hošek, P. Parker, Lyric Poetry. Beyond Criticism. Ithaca, NY: Cornell UP 1985, 182–193.

45   L.W. Countryman, Forgiven and Forgiving. Harrisburg, PA: Morehouse Publishing 1998, 99.

exceptional gift made possible only via a second person perspective; via the realization that heterocentric identity is more than just some kind of internal machine manufacturing interiority: it is a gift which is the source of that interiority.

7.4.1   Two Key Traits of Religion

Religion evokes identity-conferring existential commitments. These commitments are constitutive for robust identity that can resist the pressures of situations of displacement. We have seen this strength in Dietrich Bonhoeffer and in Archbishop Francis Xavier Văn Thuân; they lived in a wider context, saw themselves accompanied, transcended the tangible layers of reality by offering a connection to the invisible. Having looked at the exemplary life of Corrie ten Boom I would now like to characterize one particular strength religious faith can provide, I will look at two key traits of religions that foster epistemic resilience: (i) Religion offers a sacramental view of the world; (ii) religion offers a second-person perspective.

Religious faith can be characterized as fostering a *sacramental view of the universe*; this is to say that a believer thinks and speaks in parables, she accepts a religious interpretation of the universe, thus offering a "symbolic interpretation" of experience. A symbol connects the visible to the invisible. An event is not only "an event", but lends a deeper dimension to any historical event or any experience, telling us something about the non-observable and deep structure of the universe. In his encounter with the rich young man, Jesus sees not *only* a man of wealth but a man with a soul to be saved (Mark 10:17–25). It can be shown, against this background, that believers work with a *sense of ultimate questions* about the "Why" and the "Where to" accepting the gravity of those questions as well as the mystery surrounding them.

A religion is an attitude towards the world as a whole and towards life per se. A religion provides a framework for interpretation within which events "in the world" can be interpreted as signs for "another world". A religion invites us to interpret events in the visible world as signs for the invisible world. A religion equips us with a framework for interpretation within which any event—and especially borderline situations and experiences—may be embedded. Such a framework may be called symbolic cosmos, an interpretation of the world on the basis of an attitude towards the world as a whole. In a symbolic cosmos every visible occurrence is given its definite place and a definite importance. An event "in the world" may be interpreted in a very specific way within the framework of the symbolic cosmos. Each religion constitutes a symbolic cosmos and in this way provides a framework for interpretation of human experience.

A symbolic cosmos hence is a framework for interpretation that (i) sets obligations to certain ontological responsibilities, (ii) includes the acceptance of certain propositions, and (iii) implicates obligation to action. The construction of a symbolic cosmos is the crucial point and purpose of cultures and religions. In the search for identity, meaning and security, people avoid chaos, disorder and insecurity and find their answers in their needs for orientation in cultural systems that provide symbols, myths and rituals. A symbolic cosmos is a symbol system that interprets fact as accessible symbol for something invisible, something hidden. Crises will demand and incite recourse to this symbolic cosmos. Religion offers a system to cope with border situations in which the knowledge of living everyday life does not suffer because a non-standardized type of situation is at hand. A symbolic cosmos assumes that the facts of the world do not suffice. Within the frame of a symbolic cosmos every fact is considered a signifier that refers to a signified. A symbolic cosmos allows a "reading" of the world as a whole, like a book. Hence, it is not surprising that the metaphor of the world as a book is often picked up in the Christian tradition. To be able to read the world as a whole means that the world as a whole is part of an order that exceeds the world. It is inherently linked to the concept of a symbolic cosmos that it is not present as such and may not be derived directly from the events "in the world." Because of its independence from sources "in the world," faith can become a source of epistemic resilience.

A second aspect of religious belief is the idea that faith makes you live in a second person perspective: "We are always being addressed. That is to say, our time can be apprehended by us as a question, or a challenge, as something to be filled. To sense my future as being a question to me is to sense that what I can receive, digest and react is not yet settled or finished."[46] A religious person living a life in the theistic tradition lives that life in a second person singular relationship with God, or to put it another way, that person lives a life in prayer to God. Psalm 139 reminds us that we cannot flee from God (vv 7–10). This perspective as we have seen above in Corrie's experience, is rooted in "knowledge by acquaintance" and not second-hand accounts. Betsie knows she is in the presence of God and this knowledge of a living counterpart, unseen with the naked eye, but seen with that inner eye enables her to live a life of truth and trust. God is not "he" for Betsie or Corrie, but "you"; he is both Father and father who empower them to be who they are and remain true to their own identity—which is God-given. We have seen the same dynamics in the diaries of Zenas Loftis.

---

46   R. Williams, Interiority and Epiphany. In: R. Williams., On Christian Theology. Oxford: Blackwell 2000, 239–264, at 249.

A believer lives in a second person perspective. First person accounts are direct accounts of experiences made by the speaker, whereas third person accounts are distanced in time and space and experience and make "objective" claims. Second person accounts differ from their counterparts in that they require a partner, a listener who is present and not imagined. Genuine discourse enables corrective strategies to be utilized and allows the "other" to have his or her say too, to take a turn in the telling. A second person perspective constitutes a situation, a special kind of situation rooted in dialogue which in our present enquiry is of ethical importance in that certain claims gain validity via that perspective of other and in defending that perspective. This is an attitude which Stephen Darwall has investigated in his study of the ethics of second person accounts.[47] Gerald Cohen sought the source of normative claims in a similar vein calling for an "interpersonal test" or the acid test of the justification of claims: Are you willing to tell people to their face what you said about them?[48] The presence of a person changes the language game. When someone is present, we make different claims, use different language than if they are absent. Thus, a second person perspective arises when two subjects share and acknowledge the same normative origins: "Call the second-person standpoint the perspective you and I take up when we make and acknowledge claims on one another's conduct and will."[49]

A second person perspective creates new obligations and commitments. Eleonor Stump reviewed Frank Cameron Jackson's well-known experiment "What Mary Didn't Know,"[50] and considered it from this second person perspective, i.e., the affect it would have on the narrative of the situation.[51] If we

47   Stephen Darwall, The Second-Person Standpoint: Morality, Respect and Accountability. Cambridge, Mass: Harvard UP 2006.

48   "The test asks whether the argument could serve as a justification of a mooted policy when uttered by any member of society to any other member" (G. Cohen, Rescuing Justice and Equality. Cambridge, Mass 2008, 42).

49   Stephen Darwall, The Second Person Standpoint, 3. Darwall outlines the role of the second person perspective in the first two chapters of the book.

50   Frank Cameron Jackson, Epiphenomenal Qualia. In: *Philosophical Quarterly* 32 (1982) 127–136; idem, What Mary Didn't Know. In: *Journal of Philosophy* 83 (1986) 291–295. Jackson asked what would happen if someone were given all the information there was to be had pertaining to colors, but had never seen or experienced an actual color, what that person—here Mary—would learn for the first time if she were to then actually see colors for the first time. What would be the difference? In other words is experience knowledge?

51   Eleonor Stump, Second-Person Accounts and the Problem of Evil. In: E. Yandell. ed., *Faith and Narrative*. New York: Oxford University Press 2001, Stump, The Problem of Evil: Analytic Philosophy and Narrative. In: Oliver Crisp., Michael C. Rea, eds., Analytic

imagine that there is a girl called Mary who knows everything there is to know about people but has never met her own mother. Then one day she meets her mother and in the encounter learns something new: "Mary will know things she did not know before even if she knew everything about her mother that could be made available to her in expository prose, including her mother's psychological states."[52] A second person perspective within the framework of interaction is an involved perspective requiring and creating knowledge hitherto unknown and outside of what is knowable through learning.

Eleonor Stump attempts to show that such knowledge is not what we would normally term propositional knowledge (knowledge that) but it does abound in stories: in other words stories express the distinct character of the second person perspective since a story always needs a listener or reader even if only an imagined reader. At the same time, new boundaries of verification and validation arise which Stephen Darwall calls "second personal reasons" that is reasons verified by relevant structures which in turn are validated by an acknowledged authority which in turn introduces the factor of accountability. If, in an interaction, I list the reasons for the claims I am making, those reasons are the natural result—evolve—out a known context, e.g., a reference to a promise made in the past or obligations agreed upon. A second person perspective affords a new form of knowledge and awareness which again evolves organically when subject A is perceived by subject B. This knowledge is beautifully characterized in Martin Buber's Philosophy of Dialogue.

A believer lives in a second person perspective because she lives in the face of God; she has a "Thou" in God. John Henry Newman differentiated between "a notion" and "a real image of God": "The proposition that there is One Personal and Present God may be held in either way, either as a theological truth, or as a religious fact or reality. The notion and the reality assented-to are represented by one and the same proposition, but serve as distinct interpretations of it."[53] This distinction between an existential and an affective notion of God can be illustrated through the Hebrew Bible book of Job, as suggested by Stump: Job is "comforted" by his friends Elifas, Bildad und Zofar. They remind him of God's greatness and how lowly humankind is in comparison: they seem to be reciting

---

Theology: New Essays in the Philosophy of Theology. New York: Oxford University Press 2009; Stump, Wandering in Darkness: Narrative and the Problem of Suffering. Oxford: Oxford University Press 2010.

52   E. Stump, Second Person Accounts, 88.

53   J.H. Newman, An Essay in Aid of a Grammar of Assent. Notre Dame, IN: University of Notre Dame Press 1979, 108.

phrases and words of wisdom learnt by rote. In chapter 38 God, on hearing Job in his plight, answers him, speaks to Job personally. It is interesting to note that God has nothing new to say, in fact there is very little difference between what he says and what Job's comforters have been telling him. But then comes that moment of surprise: Job is reluctantly forced to admit that although his friends had said the same, he was not convinced by what they said (42,1–6); and, somewhat unexpectedly, God tells Job that in fact he is not convinced by Job's comforters either (42,7–8) and that Job should in fact intercede for them. How should we interpret such statements? The situation would seem to suggest that the second person perspective together with Newman's distinction does offer an explanation: Job has a "real image of God", an emotional relationship linked with an existential understanding of God as being and it is this which moves him to eat humble pie because something decisive has taken place: there have been no theological revelations but Job is unable to take on board what his friends tell him because they only have a "notion of God" gleaned from books and hearsay, in other words "knowledge by description." It was only Job who truly lived in and with a second person perspective.

A sacramental view of the universe and second person perspective as the main pillars of a person's religious identity are interlinked. The relationship with God is the main point of the epistemic resilience of believers. A second person perspective transforms our perception of self. God, for a believer, transforms everything. If we consider the life and work of George Muller who built an orphanage in Bristol, England, founded purely on prayer, trust in Divine Providence and physical hard work, this along with Betsie and Corrie will serve as an example of a life perspective anchored in a second person perspective.[54] After his conversion to Christianity, George Muller judged every aspect of his life through the eyes of God and his second person relationship to God. He endured adversities and showed remarkable resilience, knowing that he lived his life under the eyes of the Almighty. This is the inner strength nourished by faith. It helps to build an inner "home," even in the midst of displacement.

---

54   C. Langmead, Robber of the Cruel Streets. The Prayerful Life of George Muller. Farnham 2006.

CHAPTER 8

Hope and Love: Epistemic Resilience and "Magis"

We have explored some of the sources of epistemic resilience including thought, memory and existential commitments. The most significant goods in the hierarchy of sources of epistemic resilience are probably hope and love. Mission work is inspired by the hope of fruitfulness, as is humanitarian, aid and development work. Helplessness and hopelessness drain a person; Leanne Olson who worked to assist the Serbian population in Sarajevo in 1995 was there during the time of the siege and wrote about the experience of looking out over the city: "the sense of horror, the shame. I wanted nothing more than to sob my heart out for all those people below me, who were helpless and forgotten, at the mercy of the same people I struggled every day to assist."[1] She almost collapsed.

Hope and love are "dilatory goods", they widen horizons, open up our life-world towards *magis*, that sense of "more of life". They offer deeper perspectives and wider frameworks of life. They give us reasons to act and reasons to live; life without hope is hell, and so is life without love. This chapter will explore hope and love as two major sources of epistemic resilience. We have discussed thought and memory as well as moral and spiritual infrastructures, meaning and purpose, faith and belief as vital commitments to cultivating interiority and significant sources for epistemic resilience. The most important factor of all those discussed this far, is "love"—as something that fills us with a sense of commitment and concern. But what does that really mean? Let us have a look at both, first hope, then love.

8.1 Hope as Epistemic Resource

Tiziano Terzani whom we encountered in chapter 3, pinpoints hope as something we express more than anything else: hope is in big demand. If you are fighting cancer, hope will be your source of strength; hope becomes a decisive factor in developing epistemic resilience. When someone loses all hope, they lose a main source of life. Those haunting pictures of prisoners, of *muselmänner*, found in Buchenwald and other concentration camps at the end of WWII, have made this term a byword to express people who lost *all*

---

1   L. Olson, A Cruel Paradise, 124.

© KONINKLIJKE BRILL NV, LEIDEN, 2017 | DOI 10.1163/9789004342453_010

hope and as such lost their reason and will to live: no will, no life. When someone is no longer capable of constructing and configuring a life, their life, they
plunge into a resigned state of drifting and drowning; any remains of what
might have been resistance have been drained completely; those last sparks
of life-energy consumed. The US journalist William Vollman investigated
the state and condition of people living in extreme poverty and summed it
up as an overriding sense of "numbness."[2] There is a preponderant sense of
resignation. People in poverty live in the confined space of bleak hopelessness; they make no demands on life and expect nothing in return. Many have
given up all hope. German journalist Guenter Wallraff met a homeless man in
Cologne who told him that he had nothing left to live for; he was just waiting
to die.[3]

But hope is stubborn, it hangs on for dear life and does not simply seep
away into nothingness. Even empty hope is some form of hope as Ruth Kluger
describes in her memories of giving hope a tough time while she was growing
up: "They all say that hope keeps you alive, but that isn't true, hope is only the
flip side of fear, and fear might manage to convince you that she is keeping you
alive, somehow because you do tangibly feel fear—your mouth feels as dry as
the desert and fear courses cold through your veins like a shot of some drug."[4]
Kluger cites Tadeusz Borowksi to defend her argument; he firmly believed that
despair empowered boldness and courage, but hope—hope was a coward, a
quitter. Hope was the key culprit in making people no longer take the present
seriously and instead treat it lackadaisically.

What does become clear against such vivid illustrations is that hope is
not a category which can be easily pinned down and does therefore need a
framework of ethics to function "properly". Hope can "do well" in adverse circumstances because it has that additional dimension of future which other
attitudes of mind and perspective do not have. Hope is an attitude of expectation of change in situation and life, hope makes demands on a future which
as yet is still fiction; it depends on that fiction becoming reality in something
new; hope does therefore solicit change and is not merely a continuation of the
status quo. In *Expecting Adam*, Martha Beck the author and protagonist knows

---

2   W. Vollman, Poor People. New York: HarperCollins 2007.

3   G. Wallraff, Aus der schönen neuen Welt. Expeditionen ins Landesinnere. Cologne:
    Kiepenheuer&Witsch 2009, ch. 2.

4   See R. Kluger, Still Alive. A Holocaust Girlhood Remembered. New York: Feminist Press at
    the City University of New York. 4th Printing 2009 (an earlier version published in German:
    weiterleben. Goettingen: Wallstein 1992).

that her baby-about-to-be will be fine even though from the medical and social point of view there is every reason to suppose this will *not* be the case:

> How did I know this? I just did. I have always liked Albert Einstein's comment the "people like us who believe in physics, know that the distinction between past, present, and future is only a stubbornly persistent illusion." (…) I have experienced this kind of foreknowledge half a dozen times since Adam was born. (…). So, far this sense of knowing which feels a lot like "remembering" something that is NOT past but future (…). If we pay attention we all bump into our own futures.[5]

In the same way as thought can create inner depth if mind, hope can create a vastness of inner scope. Hope turns its sights to a specific object and a specific horizon: both transcendental since neither are as yet visible or tangible. This vastness of inner scope can, if left unbridled, becomes destructive and deadly when left to descend into escapism. The art of proper hope is to find an inner attitude which is capable of transcending the present moment without losing sight of the present or feeling it only "numbly" as William Vollman describes it. Again, Martha Beck transcends the exceptional of the present moment and basks in the relieving reality of normality and all it encompasses:

> I knew this was the foot of baby a with Down Syndrome. I loved that foot as much as I have loved anything in my life (…), but I was not without resources. I loved my baby. My love for him was normal, limited, mortal. Nothing any other mother doesn't feel. But it would do for me, because as soon as I felt it, I recognized it for what it was. It was the way home.[6]

Hope is a *dilatory asset* and as such a core resource of epistemic resilience, it is comparable in some ways to thought, as already mentioned, in that it can transcend the here and now. Hope is dilatory in that it can identify possibilities beyond those that might be immediately obvious to the eye and the mind. Hope is dilatory in that it extends to the future; it is actually remarkable that we can do that. Let us stop here one moment to consider what this actually means: we can articulate sentences about something which as yet has not come about even though our tools of expression are the everyday tools we would use for any other statement or utterance but with one key difference:

5   M. Beck, Expecting Adam. New York: Three Rivers Press 2011, 297f.
6   Ibd., 306.

statements made about the future are related to an occurrence which according to the natural order of things is neither absolute not irrevocable. We
say, "Tomorrow is Saturday," or "Next summer I will be going to Italy again,"
or "In a week or two, I will have forgotten this lecture,". It is remarkable that
we can build sentences like this about the future, and even past in the future,
the sense of time and tense is nowhere felt more strongly than in expression
of the future; it is certainly different from the sentences about the past or
the present. The future cannot be determined in the same way or with the
same rules as the past. Although we may be able to contribute even creatively to a future event, we cannot pre-empt it in the way we can consider past
possibility.

References to the past have to do with things that lie beyond what we can
manipulate. The framework of time does not allow me to access or intervene
in past occurrence. I cannot rewrite history according to my own will or deny
historical facts. What happened in the past did so according to events and circumstances which irrevocably took place. It is this element of irrevocability
which contrasts sharply with possible future context; we can actively design
the future, contribute in some way towards it, but we cannot interpretively
anticipate it in the same way as we frame the past. The past can be re-perceived
(but not changed) through interpretation.

An important element in the way we interpret the past is the framing
of memories. Memories can be always re-arranged—this makes them important sources for epistemic resilience as we have seen. Memories can be
moulded and fashioned to highlight some aspects and disregard others.
Epistemic resilience is also about having a sense of realism, to know about
the doors "closed" because we walked (or did not walk) through them. The
past has irrevocable points of reference, "historical facts" that cannot be
changed. In contrast, our vision of the future is "open," can be shaped by interpretation, but—and herein lies the key and subtle difference to the past—
also by planning, by action.

The possibility to operate creatively for and towards a future and, at the
same time, be kept at a distance from that as yet unknown and non-existent
context, yields a peculiar ambivalence of our relationship with the future. I
would like to characterize this relationship with the future through two factors:
Uncertainty and Decidability:

On the one hand we have to do with a moment of uncertainty. Sentences
about the future have something unique and special in them: they are jug-
gling with uncertainty and with factors over which they—we—can have no
command in the here and now. In the ninth chapter of his *On Interpretation*

Aristotle discussed the truth value of the sentence: "There will be a sea-battle tomorrow." He seems to have decided that the truth value of this statement was neither true nor false, but undecidable.[7] We cannot say today with certitude whether a sea battle will take place tomorrow. Likewise we cannot say with certainty today that this time next year we will be alive, or tomorrow we will be able to catch the bus or reach the office. A vision of the future relates to something that is "in abeyance", which can end up in one or the other way. We call events and things that are possible, but not necessary, "contingent." Contingent things are not predictable because they do not proceed with the rules of necessity. Verdicts on the future have to do with uncertainty of vulnerable things. That is why an attitude regarding the future is hope, but also fear. This is one reason why Gabriel Marcel has expressed the thought, that hope can only be there, where the temptation of despair appears.[8] Hope opens a situation, despair closes it: "The man who despairs is the one whose situation appears to be without exit."[9]

On the other hand there is a moment of decidability when talking about the future; the future is not arbitrary. We do not live in a universe that would continuously change itself. There are trends, developments that can be anticipated, processes that have begun. The newness of the future is based on familiar material, "new worlds" are built on the basis of "established worlds."[10] The new requires a connection to the familiar, in order to be understood. We cannot frame, or even authentically process, any notion of "radically new." Ernst Bloch worked on the ontology of "the as-yet non-existent". Our vision of the future deals with kinds of possibilities. These possibilities can be realistic to a greater or lesser degree. This notion holds true both for the term "potential" (subject-based and agency-bound prospects expressed in statements like "For X it is possible to," "X can,") and for the term "possibility" (possible developments of situations and states of affairs), expressed in propositions of the form "It is possible, that p." These types of possibilities structure our view of the future and our epistemic position to judge probabilities. Decidability is helped by distinguishing between relevant

---

7 There is a debate about that—see an important contribution by D. Burrell, Aristotle and 'Future Contingencies.' *Philosophical Studies* 13 (1964) 37–52.

8 G. Marcel, Homo viator: Introduction to a metaphysics of hope. New York, NY: Harper Torchbooks 1962.

9 G. Marcel, Desire and hope. In N. Lawrence and D. O'Connor, eds., Readings in Existential Phenomenology. Upper Saddle River, NJ: Prentice-Hall Inc. 1967, 277–285, at 281.

10 Cf., N. Goodman, Ways of Worldmaking. Indianapolis: Hackett 1978.

and irrelevant possibilities. John Austin had a wonderful example of an irrelevant possibility, i.e. writing about a goldfinch that "does something outrageous (explodes, quotes Mrs. Woolf, or what not)."[11] Indeed, it would not only surprise us if the goldfinch started spouting Woolf, we would gobsmacked, instantly and literally rendered speechless to describe the "hitherto-non-existent", we would not be linguistically prepared. This shows that indeed we are operating with a distinction of relevant and irrelevant possibilities.

That characteristic element of ambivalence between what we know in the here and now of we have before us, and what we do not know in the distance of the future and are not able to calculate, could perhaps be conveyed as *hope* characterized by "determinable indetermination." This ambivalence of the vision of future is important, it allows us to preempt certain actions, prepare plans and make decisions, but it does not enable us to anticipate with certitude what is going to happen. And it is this absence of certitude which makes our lives "open," instilling a sense of vulnerability but also a sense of a wide horizon full of possibilities.

Basel missionaries Fritz and Rosa Ramseyer were held hostage for four years (1869–1872) in Kumase, today's southern Ghana; they had lost their child in captivity, were dragged from place to place into ever new situations of displacement; they sustained their mental health in the hope they cultivated, the hope to be able to do mission work. The account of these years *Vier Jahre in Asanti* recounts the struggle to sustain hope.[12] Their future was open, but in the mode of "determinable indetermination," since they knew about the volatility of the political situation and they never gave up hope; they placed their hope in God, in God alone.[13] Based on this hope Fritz Ramseyer went to serve as missionary as summarized by Paul Steiner: "Mr. Ramseyer, who, after his liberation, had again resumed his missionary labors on the Gold Coast, was fired by the intense desire to enter Kumassi at some future time with the message of salvation. He did not give up the hope, that that hour would one day come. For twenty long years he hoped and prayed for it, and from the boundary station of Abetifi, established in the former province in Ashanti, in Okwawu, with a view to the evangelising of that state, he watched with eager gaze, for the time

---

11   John Austin, Philosophical Papers. Ed. J.O. Urmson, G.J. Warnock. Oxford: Clarendon 1961, 88.

12   Gundert, H., ed., Vier Jahre in Asante: Tagebücher der Missionare Ramseyer und Kühne. Basel: Missionskomptoir 1875.

13   Ibd., 161: "Wir aber (...) dürfen nichts von Menschen hoffen; unsere Hilfe kommt von ihm allein."

when the closed gates of Kumassi should be opened. And he did not hope in vain."[14] So his hope also guided his actions, which is a major building block of an ethics of hope.

8.2   Towards an Ethics of Hope

Ruth Klueger points out that hope can be counter-productive, a void or empty husk. It can serve as a source of escapism, rather than genuine resilience. That is why we need an *ethics* of hope. Hope may be as ambiguous as nostalgia. Hope involves a moment of trust that cannot be reduced to accepting a set of propositions.[15] Hope is rooted in trust of the unknown ahead and has something to do with implicitly trusting in what is good even though a high degree of risk is involved. Foolhardy though this might sound, it can perhaps be explained by stressing that hope lies between what we can reasonably plan or envisage for the future based on our faculties of human reason and experience, and yet, at the same time, it comprises an existential component based between emotional and existential trust.

Hope links what we can forecast, what we desire deep down inside, and what we think we know with certainty. But this does not mean that hope is blind; similar to "well justified trust," *docta spes* indicates grounded hope, justified hope, hope based on reasons. In the long run, epistemic resilience will be strengthened by well-reasoned hope founded in reality. Furthermore, hope has implications if I hope my way of life as well as particular actions will be shaped by this hope. Hope requires energy and effort to be exerted: hope as complex process is an ethical issue raising ethical questions to do with allowing our actions to be shaped by the normative implications of hope.

Reflections in an ethics of hope are key for the capacity to be displaced, since the proper sense of hope nurtures resilience whereas misplaced hope can lead to escapism and illusions. Both mission and development work are based on the hope they bring to people, a grounded hope. There is another ethical aspect, namely the *object* of hope. Aquinas describes the object of

---

14   Paul Steiner, ed., Dark and stormy days at Kumassi, 1900; or, Missionary experience in Ashanti, according to the diary of Rev. Frits Ramseyer. Translated into English by Miss Meyer. With a pref. by Thomas Nichol. London: S.W. Partridge 1901, 24.

15   See H.H. Price 'Belief "In" and Belief "that" ' *Religious Studies* 1,1 (1965) 5–27.

hope *as bonum futurum arduum possibile*.[16] Hope focuses on what is good or in Aquinas' language: as long as hope pursues the subject hoped for, it will be assisted by love.[17] Hope is directed at something good, at a *bonum*, a claim of immense ethical relevance since according to this line of thought, you cannot hope that your neighbor will have a painful accident. It would also weaken inner strength, as we have seen, if there was a sense of poisonous bitterness. The *bonum* of hope is *arduum*, in that hope is directed at a goal which is not the easiest of goals to reach; hope, as has been said, implies effort and commitment. This is also a point where hope differs from mere desire or wishful thinking; true hope empowers its subject to act. This decisive difference also testifies that hope requires obligations which have to be met and that cannot be fulfilled without effort and action. Thus, hope differs considerably from passive expectation which sits back to see what happens no matter how outrageous that expectation might be, and here too we find another major difference: hope needs a degree of yearning and longing but will and can only work within the limits of what is possible. The object of hope is *possibile*, attainable. Hoping for the impossible has a similar effect as living in hopeless poverty: it numbs all senses and motivation, and this triggers despair—at the opposite end of the scale to hope; despair reckons with and is resigned to the worst that can happen, hope does not, and as such remains alert and active in her endeavors. Finally, the object of hope is *futurum*, it is "not yet" there. Hope as a resource which is focused on the future in some way or other gains power from this perspective; our view of the future shapes the way we act in the Here and Now.

An ethics of hope would look into the *object* of hope in the light of these attributes, but also into the *foundations* and *connections* between different kinds of hope. An ethics of hope is based on its insistence that hopes of all kinds (both the small hopes and the big Hope[18]) must be in harmony with each other. Small hopes, not surprisingly, are about those small things in life and the big Hope, that final Hope, which for Christians, is that salvation is real. An ethics of hope insists, too, on consistency in compatibility and conviction. I cannot hope in life after death if I am at the same time convinced that that there is no afterlife of any kind. An ethics of hope insists on consistency in our way of life, the way we live every day and in the way we hope; hope must ring and hold true in the reality of life. Again and again we come back to this point: Epistemic resilience is not served by escapism and illusions nor is it

---

16   Aquinas, Summa Theologica I/II, 40, 1.

17   Aquinas, Summa Theologica I/II, 40, 7, resp.

18   Cf., Benedict XVI, Spe Salvi, 31.

served by hope that is not deeply rooted; epistemic resilience is inspired and built on hope that is uplifting.

Hope needs to be taken seriously and the obligations it brings similarly; this means living in a way that justifies that hope, living in a way that is meaningful, in a way that will engender power and strength in structuring resources. Eli Wiesel notes this close connection between the serious nature of hope and the conviction that it is meaningful—there is a point to hope—it serves some purpose; in 1986 his Nobel Peace Prize lecture, entitled "Hope, Despair and Memory," Wiesel spoke about the power of memory and the power of hope.[19] "Without memory, our existence would be barren and opaque, like a prison cell into which no light penetrates; like a tomb which rejects the living;" without hope, a person cannot live. The opposite of the future "is not the past but the absence of the past." That is why *docta spes* is hope grounded in memory, and memory without hope is not a source of epistemic resilience but of despair. Eli Wiesel talks about the invitation to forget, an invitation he had received frequently. But remembering is truly *re-membering*, putting the members of memory back together, gaining and regaining identity, doing justice to what has been and to those who have been part of this story and history. With the hope that something good can come out of atrocities, the memory of the past is hopeful and hope-filled.

Memory and hope are connected via the imagination; it is a connection which can be life-saving as it was for Amanda Lindhout who was kidnapped in Somalia for more than a year. She built up epistemic resilience through the sheer force of her imagination, imagining "a house in the sky," far away from her ordeals, a house in which she could hide, a house that she could inhabit, a house where she could wander through the rooms. She developed resilience from within by imagining the past, remembering her mother: "My mother. I could build her in my imagination, head to toe, from the dark shine of her hair to the worn brown cowboy boots she liked to wear ... In my mind, I talked and talked to my mother. I imagined thoughts strung between us, spider threads floating over the ocean;"[20] she built up epistemic resilience in her displacement by imagining the present, following in her mind the kidnappers who had left her alone in a room: "In my mind, I could picture them all. I imagined them being warm and open, as people who wouldn't betray me. In my mind, I was

19   E. Wiesel, Hope, Despair and Memory. In: I. Abrams, ed., Peace 1981–1990. Singapore: World Scientific Publishing 1997.

20   Amanda Lindhout & Sara Corbett, A House in the Sky. A Memoir of a Kidnapping That Changed Everything. London: Penguin 2013, 215–216.

going to follow them right through the back door and to their dinner table,";[21] she built up epistemic resilience by imagining the future: "I imagined Somalia as a story I would tell my friends. Not a happy story, clearly, but a story with an ending. Walking circles in my room, I awarded myself a future."[22] At the same time Amanda Lindhout was aware of her duty to remember this past at some time in the future.

An ethics of memory and an ethics of hope are interlinked. When someone is unable to hope that on the basis of her knowledge, experience and suffering, something good can come of it, she may well be engulfed by her own solitude and loneliness; hope can ease the burden of tragic knowledge about the past by calling for resolute action, this calling is strengthened by the point and purpose of *doing*: this is that moment when hope becomes a resource of epistemic resilience which cannot be undermined by the vagaries of memory and recall or in the face of "numbness".

An ethics of hope would also imply the commitment to building a culture of hope and to cultivating the art of hope. One learns an art best through examples. The skill of hope orients itself to people, who through their life-examples have showed what hope can be, what a life of hope means. One need not search for such examples in epochs of the distant past or in remote lands. In November 1960, a London lawyer, by the name of Peter Benenson was sitting on the Underground on his way to work and reading a newspaper article about two Portuguese students who had been arrested because they had made a toast to freedom in a restaurant. Since it was by no means a single case of a politically motivated curtailment of the freedom of expression, Benenson decided to act: on 28th May 1961 he started on an article "The forgotten Prisoners," which appeared in *The Observer*: the "Appeal for Amnesty 1961." Those now famous introductory words to the article, pointed out that while individual human beings were often powerless to take a stand for what they thought to be right or to defend themselves in the face of attack, if they could be brought together as a group, all those like-minded individuals had a tremendous potential to act and achieve something:

> Open your newspaper any day of the week and you will find a report from somewhere in the world of someone being imprisoned, tortured or executed because his opinions or religion are unacceptable to his government. There are several million such people in prison—by no means all of them behind the Iron and Bamboo curtains—and their numbers are

21   Ibd., 206.
22   Ibd., 212.

growing. The newspaper reader feels a sickening sense of impotence. Yet if these feelings of disgust all over the world could be united into common action, something effective could be done.[23]

Amnesty International had been born. It was to give inducement to hope, and reason for optimism that profound and re-experienced powerlessness can be overcome—a single life can make a significant difference. Trust in the possibility to contribute to a better world need not be naive and unfounded. Dom Helder Camara, the long-serving archbishop of the Brazilian diocese of Recife, never gave up the hope for change and trusted in the "minorities of Abraham"—those minorities who are eager for change, who are found in every social group and background, minorities who like Abraham are prepared to undertake an adventure for a new-beginning. Dom Helder Camara had steadfastly nurtured his optimism on trust in God. He devoted his life to prayer, not during the day when he was confronted with the seeming impossible, but during the night hours. He was blessed with a gift to manage with only a few hours' sleep. This commitment to prayer gave him the energy he required for difficult projects, and the energy to persevere and to withstand all kinds of adversities.

Hope nurtured can become a vital virtue; a virtue which provides orientation—an on-board navigation system—that not only finds the direction and guides you on your way but (unlike that car version) provides purpose in the pursuit of that direction and goal. Hope as virtue shapes life in a particular way; an individual is enabled to source a specific goal and, based on habits cultivated with the aid of this virtue can aim to achieve that goal, of a truly human *telos*. The Christian tradition encourages the creation of a culture of hope. It is fainthearted not to trust in the possibility of transformation and the power of the Spirit to transform everything to good. A lack of hope is a lack of trust in God; a life without hope is not a life, it is anti-life; it is not immaterial that Dante's hell requires: *All hope abandon, ye who enter here.* Virgil tells Dante that "we are come, where I have told thee we shall see the souls to misery doom'd, who intellectual good have lost" and "These of death no hope may entertain: and their blind life so meanly passes, that all other lots they envy,"(line 45).

Epistemic resilience is ultimately nourished by a spirituality of hope. A spirituality of hope demands an equilibrium of both the human and the Divine in its attitude. Augustine juxtaposes profane hope which focuses on human

23   P. Benenson, "The Forgotten Prisoners." *The Observer* 28 May 1961.

beings with hope in God.[24] Putting your hope in human beings is absurd, while hope in God for its part is not something which can be brought about by human agency but is a gift of God's mercy.[25] In his first letter to the Thessalonians, Paul characterizes pagans as people who "have no hope" (1 Thess 4:13; cf., Eph 2:12). The baptized are in contrast re-born "to living hope" (1 Peter 1:3) and should be always ready "to justify their hope" (1 Peter 3:15; cf., 1 Peter 1:21). Those who are in Christ can say: "In hope we are saved" (Rom 8:24). And this is a source of inner strength that external circumstances cannot "undo."

8.3   Characteristics of Hope in a Tradition of Wisdom

The Judeo-Christian tradition has a famous *hi-story* of wisdom, which tells us a lot about hope. In the first book of the Pentateuch we find the famous story of the deluge, Noah's construction of the Ark and life after the Flood. In the few verses of Genesis 8: 5–12, a whole philosophy of hope unfurls. I would like to focus on eight points within these events to underpin the nature of real hope.

(1) The story of Noah's Ark is a narration about hope, which soars up after a catastrophe of unknown proportions, after a crisis. Hope blossoms from the midst of this natural calamity. Hope is the child of crisis. The Flood represents a critical time in which life arrives at a major crossroad. Hope emerges out of this crossroad, a place or space where changes are essential. Hope emerges at a place and time in which the world as a known quantity no longer exists; a life of fullness as previously experienced is not possible. Hope recognizes that the "now" and "here" is not good, at the same time realizes this status quo need not be, need not remain so. Hope develops in and out of crisis and it is this which makes hope so important as resource for epistemic resilience. Hence, hope-lessness may be called a "luxury" which we cannot afford in a crisis.[26] Hope is not the private property of a satisfied life; hope lives in loss, hunger and thirst. Hope originates in crisis—needs crisis to come into being.

(2) Verse 5 tells us that the floodwaters recede and for the first time in ten months land is visible, a mountain peak can be made out above the waters. The sudden appearance of the peak sparks a surge of hope that the Flood is at

---

24   "Nunc iam audiamus ista duo genera hominum: (…) unum sperantium de terrenis, quibus pollet hic mundus: alterum praesumentium de caelestibus, quae promisit non mendax Deus" (In Ps 51, 6 [PL 36, 603]).

25   Cf., Augustine, In Ps 61, 2 (PL 36, 730).

26   Cf., D. Soelle, F. Stefensky, Wider den Luxus der Hoffnungslosigkeit. Freiburg/Br: Herder 1995.

and end, the crisis is over; light at the end of the proverbial tunnel. It is a hope which is not based on the vast emptiness of an endless ocean; it is a hope based on a sign at a given time. It is a hope which knows the basis of what it can see, it is rooted in a known aspect, an experienced reality and logically marks the receding of the flood: the mountain peak is a *docta spes*. The story does not narrate a blind hope, but tells of a hope which relies on firm grounds of reason, grounds and reasons that can be explicated. There are reasons to hope, there is well-justified, illuminated, learned hope.

(3) After 40 days, we read in verse 6, Noah opens the window of the Ark. The time period of 40 days is symbolic; it expresses wholeness, completeness and fullness of time. The time is mature. Hope has its *Kairos*, its right moment. 40 days are a long time; again and again therefore hope will be connected with the virtue of patience—hope is patient. And patience is an attitude that accepts that there may be rhythms and forces bigger than myself; in this sense, hope is realistic, connected to humility.

(4) Noah opens the window of the Ark after 40 days; hope has to do with opening up, being faced with the vast unknown, which inherently suggests taking risks and experiencing vulnerability. An open window is a sign of hope as well as a sign of someone taking a risk. An open window allows light and air to enter, but also wind, rain, noise and debris. Hope originates in closed spaces, narrow confines which, though unpleasant, proffer security; but hope cannot stay there. Hope cannot flourish without openness. Hope, in this sense, is an opposite of fear and *angst* (from *angus* meaning narrow); fear and *angst* paralyze, reducing space and capability to act, hope opens it up.[27] Hope needs a readiness for and to change, it requires the will of transition. A beautiful picture for hope is a beam of sunlight, falling into a dark room from some source high up, out of sight. The beam of light must be allowed to break into the space; take up residence inside this space since a room engulfed in complete darkness cannot nurture hope.

(5) Noah opens the window and sends out a raven; it does not return and then Noah sends out a dove "to see if the waters had subsided," but the dove finds no land and Noah is forced to take the dove back on board, but hope is persistent; hope will not be discouraged; hope is audacious and must be so to empower action. Noah waits seven more days before sending out the same

---

27   The same can be said about love—we see clearly in the first letter of John that the opposite of love need not necessarily be hate, but fear: "There is no fear in love, but perfect love casts out fear; for fear has to do with punishment, and whoever fears has not reached perfection in love." (1 John 4, 18). Love broadens and liberates, emboldens to live and to act, paralyzes and constricts fear.

dove again a second time; hope waits persistently and patiently. Not by chance Charles Péguy describes hope in his *Mystery of hope* as the little girl, who walks beside the elder sisters of Faith and Love; a little girl who amazes God himself. It astonishes God, how time and again this little girl makes her presence known, in spite of all requests to remain silent. It is amazing that this power of hope, the flowers which are breakable through the blankets and shields, time and again voices itself. Hope is persistent. Hope nourishes epistemic resilience.

(6) This second time, the dove does eventually return to the Ark towards the evening of the seventh day, with a fresh olive branch in its beak; it is *this* olive branch that has come to symbolize hope against hope down through the ages. It is a small dove that brings a small sign of life. Hope commits itself to and accepts "small beginnings;" hope hears those small, soft voices, and sees those small, not so obvious signs and it is hope's attention to those small, not so obvious, weak details that makes it strong.

(7) The olive branch which the dove carries back is a symbol of life, that life goes on, that life on earth is possible; it is a promise of growth and blossoming, emergence and maturity: the subject matter of hope is life, of the possibility of life to sprout, bud, blossom and flourish. Hope widens our horizons and heightens our sense of being alive. Hope creates "Magis," a "More of Life".

(8) In verse 12 we read that Noah sends the dove out again and like the first time does not return. Noah now knows the dove has not drowned but has settled, found a new home and started its own new life on solid ground. Hoping means being able to let go, hope accomplished has no more need for hope, hope undergoes change as the life it hopes for undergoes change, too. Hope makes way, makes room for change and transformation, it makes way for life.

We should remind ourselves what the message of the dove is; we should hold on to what we can learn from the hope in the story of the Ark: Hope originates out of crisis, it is resilient and strengthens resilience from within; hope is not blind, but can state grounds; hope needs patience and has its "Kairos;" hope means vastness and openness, implies risk and a readiness to change; hope is both persistent and consistent; hope confesses itself to small beginnings; the subject matter of hope is life, the possibility of life, the promise of life in full.

8.4   Love and the "More" of Strength

Life in full, to take up this word, cannot happen without love; love as concern, commitment, care, is the ultimate source of epistemic resilience, connected to memory and hope, existential commitments and faith, meaning and purpose.

Love is not only a force that establishes and structures social relationships, it is also the most important factor in structuring our inner landscape, our structure of commitments. Let us explore love insofar as it is a resource for epistemic resilience; we have seen that the experience of displacement was endured and able to be turned into growth on the basis of love, on the basis of staying committed to what really matters. Love may make displacement even more difficult; it is hard to be a missionary, separated from family, friends, home and roots. But then it is love that is home-building, creating bonds, establishing and nurturing commitments. Leanna Olson had returned from a challenging time in Liberia and yet wanted to return there as soon as possible; when sharing her feelings with former classmates she met up with at the ten-year nursing reunion, "they kept asking me why I wanted to do this. What could I say? That in spite of the disease, the heat, the struggle, the harassment, the unending problems, I loved it. I loved the work, the staff, my colleagues, the country, I loved it all. I wanted to go back."[28] Love is the driving force that shapes the structure of commitments.

Love can be approached from many different angles, it has many aspects, is multifarious and cannot be wedged into a round or a square hole: Love is like art, even a craft, one needs role models to grow into a loving person, one needs a lot of practice as well as patience to grow in the art of love; fifty years ago, Erich Fromm observed that love can be understood as an art that requires discipline, concentration, patience and practice.[29] Love is a capacity, a competence such as being capable of supporting someone both literally and metaphorically so they don't slip and lose their foothold; love is the capacity to bring out the best in someone, make them smile, help them shine. Love is also a discipline since it depends on and demands an unwritten code of conduct; it needs rules, rules similar to the *Regula* of an Order, a monastic order. Love is willingness and disposition, an attitude of mind and heart, expressed in outer behavior, conduct and habits including those of perception.

Love is a source of emotions: Reinhold Niebuhr has distinguished four moments that have their roots in love.[30] Love is a form of joy in being and being-there of the other: love is a form of gratitude for the being of the other; love is a form of respect oscillating between nearness and distance, holding on to something and letting go; love is a form of loyalty accompanied by the readiness to put aside self in a critical moment. Love is also order that structures our lives: love structures our moral space and allows to distinguish

---

28   Olson, A Cruel Paradise, 75.

29   E. Fromm, The Art of Loving. New York: HarperCollins 2006 (reprint).

30   R. Niebuhr, The Purpose of the Church and Its Ministry. New York 1956, 35.

between that which is important and that which is not. Let us recall an image
of hell suggested by C.S. Lewis: hell is a place without colors, a grey misty place
where nothing can be found to embrace with robust concern. Love adds nuances and colors to our lives. Love is finally a force of "inner productivity;" love
has identity-forming power and the power to make a person enter identity-
conferring commitments. Because of its identity-power love requires purification and maturation.[31] Working on oneself means in a very real sense working
on the purity and maturity of one's love. Mature love makes a person enter
deep commitments. This is the basis for what we have called "robust identity,"
identity based on strong concerns and commitments. Mature love changes the
person.

Amélie Rorty reminds us that love is "dynamically permeable" to the effect
that lovers alter one another by loving. This transformation has the tendency
to affect the whole character of loving persons.[32] The historical dimension of
love is its historical narrative: Others become truly "precious" (carus) and we
are willing to pay love's high price because love makes a person vulnerable—
she opens up to another person, embarks on an identity altering journey and
can be left fragmented in the event of a relationship breakdown or a loss of the
beloved. To love a person means to see a value in the person that others do not
see. The American philosopher Velleman understands love primarily as a form
of recognition of, and answer to the value of the other. This recognition causes
vulnerability—"love disarms our emotional defences: it renders us vulnerable
to others."[33] The love for another person makes that person irreplaceable. This
increases the vulnerability that loves brings since the loss of the beloved is a
fragmentation of one's identity, constitutes a wound that will leave a scar. Love
is a risk as its narrative shapes one's own identity—loss of love can result in
the loss of identity[34]—precisely because love has identiy-conferring power. So,
paradoxically, the fragile good of love is the most stable basis for robust identity. And robust identity has been identified as a key to epistemic resilience.

Love has many facets and can be characterized in many different ways.
I have suggested looking at love as an art, a capacity, a source of emotions and

---

31   Cf., Benedict XVI, Deus Caritas Est, 17.
32   A.O. Rorty "The Historicity of Psychological Attitudes: Love is Not Love Which Alters Not
      When It Alteration Finds." In: N.K: Badhwar, Friendship: A Philosophical Reader. Ithaca,
      NY 1993, 73–88, at 77.
33   J.D. Velleman, Love as Moral Emotion. *Ethics* 109 (1999) 338–374, at 361.
34   Cf., M. Nussbaum, "Love and the Individual: Romantic Rightness and Platonic Aspiration."
      In: M. Nussbaum, Love's Knowledge: Essays on Philosophy and Literature. Oxford 1990,
      314–334.

structures, a discipline. I now want to suggest a major aspect that plays a main role in establishing love as a source of epistemic resilience: In a special way love can be seen as the capacity to make commitments. The act of love as power of commitment shares structural features similar to the act of pledging. In rendering a promise we structure the life of another person. "When I make a commitment to another person, I will dwell in the other by means of my word."[35] Like a pledge, love is designed for the future; a promise generates self-chosen and morally relevant structures of dependence creating "structures of the self" through which I define myself and which defines me. A pledge or the promise to give a talk tomorrow places me in relationships with people and structures extending beyond me, hereby expanding what I recognize as belonging to me. In a similar way love extends the boundaries of things that constitute my life.

Love as commitment engenders dependability and reliability established through a promise. The commitment of love is a promise bestowing identity upon the person rendering the promise as well as upon the person receiving the promise. To understand love as a form of commitment shows that love is directed toward permanency. This idea can be found in the writings of Plato.[36] Love makes us enter deep commitments that are like anchors in the sea of life, giving stability and something to hold on to in times of crises. Love is a fundamental stance before life and the world. Love anchors identity and lets the inner being of a person enter into the outside world by way of commitments. Commitments are like tent pegs that stabilize the tent of one's life so that it will even resist storms. Every commitment entered is like a resilience-conveying tent peg. That is why the exploration of love as a source of epistemic resilience cannot be separated from the question of what it means to love a person.

8.4.1   *To Love a Person*

A person who loves another person has a source for inner strength; we have seen that Ingrid Betancourt found strength in the loving relationships with her family, her children and her mother. Judith Tebutt made this experience, when she was held as a hostage of Somali kidnappers for six months. She lost a lot of strength, her life world broke down when she found out that her husband had been killed, but the love of her son Ollie kept her going.[37] This was the experience of Lev Mishchenko and Svetlana Ivanova who were separated for many years after Lev's deportation to a labor camp in Pechora in the far north of the

---

35   M. Farley, Personal Commitments. Maryknoll, NY: Orbis 2013.

36   Symposium 206A.

37   J. Tebutt, A Long Walk Home. London: Faber&Faber 2013.

Soviet Union. They exchanged more than 1200 letters over a period of eight and a half years. They affirmed their love for and commitment to each other, and this love was the source of strength for Lev during all those years. They built their respective future in the other. The endurance of their love was also the stability of concerns and commitments for both of them.[38]

Now, what does it mean to love a person? Let me propose five different approaches to this question:

(i)   To love someone means the desire to provide someone with a home. A wedding is the event in which two people publicly declare that they have found a true home in one another. Home becomes an important image for a bond formed in love, striking roots, and step by step creating something lasting. Home is a place for growth, where we can blossom and mature, and where trials and mistakes are permissible. Home is likewise a place that offers the security to undertake travels without getting lost in restlessness. Home is also a place to abide, a place where a person does not have to justify her existence all the time. A home is likewise a place that we take with us, in our luggage, no matter where we might finally go or settle. One cannot deny one's origin and home. A home is a place to which one truly wants to return to and to which one looks forward to being in again. It is a place of warmth when it is cold outside; a dot on the landscape instantly spotted from afar. A commitment to another person can establish a home. If it is a sign of a full and happy life to know about one's place in life, then a full and happy life is a life that answers the question: "where do you live?" by saying: "Come and see."[39] It goes without saying that the image of the home is one built on love and with love

(ii)   To love someone means spending—be willing to spend—time with that someone. Love is both willingness and capacity to devote oneself (and one's time) to that other; this in itself suggests self-discipline is required. Time spent with other is time in which something takes seed and grows, steadily, imperceptibly, both forming and being formed. Jean Vanier's life is testimony of life shared willingly to other, devoting one's time and self to other. When we spend time with another human being, their inner being and value of self is revealed twofold: to themselves and ourselves alike. The time spent with the person we love may be time wasted, wasted together doing something which may have nothing to do with some particular life-changing goal. Love is less about acting and operating

---

38   O. Figes, Just Send Me Word. London: Allen Lane 2012.
39   Cf., John 1:39.

than just being there, with and for the one you love. The fruit harvested is joy and gratitude of being—experiencing and sensing own self anew. Jean Vanier underlines the healing powers and properties of *time-spent*: "People with disabilities, who have been rejected or abandoned, rise up with new energy and creativity when they feel loved and respected (…). The presence of someone who loves them reveals to them their value and importance."[40] This presence—willingly being present—has a singular effect which works through the recognition and acceptance of our own vulnerability and fragility.[41] Being present in mind and body means meeting other face to face on equal terms; being present is willingness to transform and be transformed.

(iii)   To love another person is capacity, discipline and willingness to be pierced to the heart by the one we love. Love "makes everything new", empowers action and deeds, encounters and often overcomes resistance, may be hit by adversity. On the death of his beloved wife, C.S. Lewis found it was not so much the sudden loss of another being which hit him most but the loss of: "the most precious gift that marriage gave me was this constant impact of something very close and intimate yet all the time unmistakably other, resistant—in a word, real."[42] He describes this disruption to life as he knew and loved it as the most painful to bear. Mourning and grieving for his "most precious gift" leaves him feeling paralyzed, overcome by asthenia; losing someone you love means realizing the unique power and energy the other person exerts by her mere presence and which marks the boundaries of one's own action and self; the inexhaustible resource embodied in that other, who affects and impacts every decision taken, every conviction clung to; love means not allowing self to fall into those

---

40   J. Vanier, Drawn into the Mystery of Jesus through the Gospel of John. Mahwah, NJ 2004, 128.

41   John Swinton expressed this idea beautifully: "To love requires fragility and vulnerability. It requires an opening up to the other in a way that inevitably makes the lover vulnerable and open to being either loved or broken. […] Genuine love means opening oneself up to the possibility of rejection" (J. Swinton, Raging with Compassion: Pastoral Responses to the Problem of Evil. Grand Rapids, MI 2007, 65f).

42   C.S. Lewis, A Grief Observed. London 1966, 17. Love is experiencing resistance and disruption, when we lose the one we love, we experience so much more than "loss", we feel, "when reality is no longer there to check me (…)", the loss of that "constant impact of that something very close and intimate (…) resistant", "the insidious beginning of a process (…)" of memory and "composition" of the one remembered "becoming more and more my own", realizing that certain important things gradually "fade out of the mental picture" we have of someone.

cul-de-sac patterns of habit. Love breaches walls built around self, love shatters those preconceived notions we may have and enables us to be humbly aware of and accept other as authority; in other words love makes us live in a second person perspective. Love willingly accepts disruption and this demands obedience to the imperatives of the moment.

(iv) To love a person means having the capability, self-discipline and willingness, to enter relationships of and with robust concern. Love can be understood as active concern for the life and growth of those we love. To love a person means to care and be concerned about the welfare and well-being (in the truest sense) of that person, in other words develop deep commitments which will withstand adversity. Love builds structures of concern and commitments that permit forms of partiality. Love does not know "a view from nowhere," an impersonal standpoint, or a neutral perspective. Love generates reasons for actions that are recognized as grounds for this love.[43] Because of this partiality, love makes us occupy a particular space, provides access to a particular perspective. This perspective fills us with a sense of urgency and stewardship. The attitude of care is an expression of love whose power appears in the readiness to assume responsibility. The word "concern" is ambiguous and oscillates between "care" (cura) and "worry" (sollicitudo). To love a person implies "worrying about this person." Care is an attitude that one can paraphrase with the words: to mind, to protect, to regard, to save. The care for someone is an attitude that expresses an absence of indifference. The English word "caring" expresses this attitude, an attitude of interest, of respect, of esteem. Lack of love constitutes carelessness; a specific fruit of unkindness is apathy, leading to unhappiness.[44] That is why a life without love is hell. Harry Frankfurt expands upon the idea of love as caring about, as being governed and guided by human will linked with a strong sense of responsibility. Love empowers us to "be" concerned about other; concern shown, shows in

---

43   Impartiality is indeed important, but foremost in situations that do not primarily include friendship structures: "Thus it is mortally appropriate or us to favor our friends with our beneficence, simply because they are our friends (and outside of any moral obligation to do so); and this is not to be explained through appeal to some higher-oder principle of impartiality. The good we do for our friends cannot be expressed within Kantian categories" (L. Blum, Friendship, Altruism and Morality. New York 1980, 5).

44   Aquinas, Summa Theologica II–II, 35.

our own character and impacts the value of our own life.[45] The things we care about are important to us: "it is by caring about things that we infuse the world with importance."[46] Love, as we have seen, structures the world through the commitments that we enter. That is why we take ourselves seriously if we know what we care about.[47]

(v)   To love a person means having the capability, self-discipline, and willing-ness to push through one's own boundaries of self and "embrace" the one loved making her part of self, part of my own awareness of being; she becomes part of my own life narrative. To love a person means feeling you belong together with that person, but with no sense of ownership, in other words a close relationship with someone who in absolute terms does not belong to me. The relationship which develops is more akin to that sense of identity described in the third chapter, a loving relation-ship with other generates and deepens one's sense of own identity. We are who we are on the basis of relationships entered upon and experi-enced with other, and love creates a perspective through which the one loved is seen as part of self.[48] When we talk about self-esteem and self-awareness, this assumes new dimensions through love felt and experi-enced. We could say that love does in fact create a whole new framework of identity; when a couple become parents then those boundaries of self are broken through yet again and a new aspect of *belonging* and *belong-ing to* comes into being; care takes on new dimensions, too, and so does the understanding of vulnerability: birth and death bring with them new understandings and perceptions of "myself".

8.4.2   *Love and Epistemic Resilience*

If we now consider those aspects of love against the core issue of our discus-sion—epistemic resilience—then it is the empowering nature of love in which we are most interested and concerned. Love empowers capacity, discipline and perspective. Love endows life with new contours, a new sense of orien-tation and direction, lends it real weight. The contours love endows us with become so clear, so manifest that individual moments and objects are bound to forfeit their aura of complacent half-heartedness; objects which may have

---

45   H. Frankfurt, The Reasons of Love. Princeton 2004, 10–17; similar fundamental reasoning can be found in G. Taylor, Love. *Proceedings of the Aristotelian Society* 76 (1976) 147–64.

46   H. Frankfurt, The Reasons of Love, 23.

47   H. Frankfurt, The Importance of what we care about. Cambridge 1998, 159–176.

48   Robert Solomon investigated the meaning of love along similar lines. Cf., R. Solomon, About Love: Reinventing Romance for Our Times. New York 1988.

been of importance before fade into insignificance seen in the light of love; there is a shift in our sense of priorities. Love provides life with new orientation and direction; points and purpose of doing change, shift in significance; we are suddenly motivated to do "other" things we would not have done without this love. When asked why we do A or B, or what the point of doing A or B is, we answer simply: "because I love X". X becomes a prominent landmark on our map of life and this landmark is both destination and the orientation I need to get there. An experience of displacement within a missionary experience can become a source of joy and fulfilment because of love of neighbor, love of community. Love in itself is the point and the purpose, any other reason in comparison to that would be superficial and superfluous.[49] And because the dynamics of loving involves "resting on itself," providing a place of "bedrock," that does not require further justification, love is a powerful source of epistemic resilience.[50] Love exerts force, love can stir us to actions we would not have deemed possible before; this new-found energy emerges out of that sense of care and concern for other and actively striving for it. When I love someone, I am willing to make sacrifices, I am willing to do things which might cause me pain and which might limit my own space and personal freedoms, I am able to endure hardships.

In the last analysis, love becomes a source of epistemic resilience if a person can respond to many different challenges in the language of love if a person has mastered the art of polyglotty in languages of love. In her *Sovereignty of Good* Murdoch compares loving—learning to love another—to learning a foreign language:

> If I am learning, for instance, Russian, I am confronted by an authoritative structure which commands my respect. The task is difficult and the goal is distant and perhaps never entirely attainable. My work is a progressive revelation of something which exists independently of me. Attention is rewarded by a knowledge of reality. Love of Russian leads me away from myself towards something alien to me, something which my consciousness cannot take over, swallow up, deny or make unreal.[51]

---

49   Cf., H. Frankfurt, The Reasons of Love, 33ff.

50   Cf., Wittgenstein, Philosophical Investigations 217 (on the limits of justification: "If I have exhausted the justifications I have reached bedrock, and my spade is turned. Then I am inclined to say: 'This is simply what I do'").

51   I. Murdoch, Essentialists and Mystics. Philosophical Writings. Ed. P. Conradi. New York: Penguin 1999, 373.

Learning to love a person is comparable to learning a language. A polyglot person speaks many different languages. This may refer to English, French, and German, but it can also refer to the languages of encounter. There are different languages of love. Different people want to be loved in different ways. There are different "styles" of being with a person, there are different ways of expressing closeness and distance, concern and commitment. In other words: different people want to be loved and need to be loved in different ways.

This was an experience of Sheila Barton, mother to a boy who was diagnosed as being on the autism spectrum. In her memoirs about what it meant to raise a special child like her son Jonathan, she talks about that she had to learn how to love her boy since autism means being in a different country, customs different, language strange. In situations where Jonathan was banging his head against the wall his mother was not supposed to hug him, speak to him or even look at him, she had to learn to sing softly.[52] This is a lesson in a "language of love." There is a grammar to this language (the explicit or implicit rules) and a vocabulary (the ways of expression), as well as symbolic depth and a horizon of meanings. Human persons want to be loved in different ways—some people want to keep a certain distance, others prefer closeness, some like refined talk, others don't. It can be considered a sign of 'magnanimity' to effortlessly switch languages in interacting with people. Love is a force that makes us accept something which is independent from us; love leads us away from ourselves towards something alien which we appropriate and make our own by way of relationships and commitments. Sheila Barton had to learn a foreign language to be able to raise her son. This identity-shaping love gave her the strength to journey through Jonathan's challenging upbringing.

Love can be compared with leaving indelible marks; Jesuit priest Greg Boyle who works with former gang members in Los Angeles describes the results of deep personal commitments as "tattoos on the heart." He works with people who find themselves displaced within a society, who have not found a place outside of a gang. Boyle experiences the joy of people who enjoy loving him and who enjoy being loved; this is the source for the inner strength to hold on to what is good even in times of adversity. One of his main concerns and insights is the recognition of "kinship." The experience of "being part of the same whole." Lived solidarity may be risky, but it creates trust and a sense of this kinship. Students, volunteering in Sri Lanka after the 2004 Tsunami, realized the importance of signs of kinship, as expressed in a student's reflection: "(…) it is also about breaking the boundaries between people and being ordinary rather than not. They were very appreciative because they said all

---

52   S. Barton, Living with Jonathan. Lessons in Love, Life and Autism. London: Watkins
      Publishing 2011.

the strangers are drinking bottled water, so are we animals drinking this water?"[53] The missionary experience is not so much about "teaching," as becoming part of a learning community, it is not so much about sharing a mission as sharing a life.

Love is a dilatory good, we said at the beginning of this chapter. Love calls for "Magis," is based on the desire for "More," and expands our horizons. "Meister Eckhart says 'God is greater than God.' The hope is that our sense of God will grow as expansive as our God is. Each tiny conception gets obliterated as we discover more and more the God who is always greater."[54]

---

53   Tom Vickers, Lena Dominelli, Students' Involvement in International Humanitarian Aid: Learning from Student Responses to the 2004 Tsunami in Sri Lanka. *British Journal of Social Work* 45 (2015) 1905–1922, at 1913.

54   G. Boyle, Tattoos on the Heart. New York: Free Press 2010, 26.

Epilogue

The missionary experience requires inner stability, stable inner spaces in the face of displacement. Displacement can damage a person's inner resources or can disconnect a person from her inner spaces. The above-mentioned massacre in My Lai has been characterized as an erosion of these inner resources. There are situations that call for moral resistance, existential commitments that enable epistemic resilience. Philip Zimbardo has contributed to the discussion of this loss of inner resources in his studies on situational approaches to evil: It is possible to motivate people to engage in horrible activities if they are presented with proper justifications, meaningful roles, role models, a language that changes the semantics, a logic of small steps and high exist costs.[1] These devices weaken forces of inner resistance, dry out the sources of epistemic resilience. Social and political conditions matter for epistemic resilience. It is, for instance, deplorable that certain people and certain groups of people are actually *forced* into cultivating epistemic resilience. In other words, we have to distinguish two discourses—one on the question of how to strengthen, and another on the question of how to create conditions that do not require resilience as necessity for survival.

Political conditions matter: the prison experiences of Nelson Mandela, Vaclav Havel and Dietrich Bonhoeffer bear witness to this; adverse political circumstances forced them into tapping resources of epistemic resilience. Moral resistance is necessary if we are confronted with social pathologies which are pathological deformations of life worlds undermining the possibility of human flourishing; such pathologies operate, according to Christoph Zurn, "by means of second-order disorders, that is, by means of constitutive disconnects between first-order contents and second-order reflexive comprehension of those contents, where those disconnects are pervasive and socially caused."[2] This analysis views a social pathology in terms of "ideology", i.e., as false beliefs on a first-order level connected with the social inability on a second-order level to identify (let alone satisfy) the need for reflexivity. A social pathology prevents a person from understanding the mechanisms that caused the condition; a person experiences something and is unable to categorize it because of conditions that shape *both* experience and reflection. This is particularly bad

---

1 Ph. Zimbardo, A Situationist Perspective on the Psychology of Evil. In: A.G. Miller, ed., The Social Psychology of Good and Evil. New York 2004, 21–50, 28.

2 Chr. F. Zurn, Social Pathologies as Second-Order Disorders. In: D. Petherbridge, ed., Axel Honneth: Critical Essays. Leiden: Brill 2011, 345–370, 345f.

since this mechanism will even erode sources of judgment and resources of epistemic resilience.

We have seen the example of North Korean citizen Shin Dong-hyuk who was born inside a camp, without any sense of alternatives, context, or possibilities. He lived in circumstances that did not allow him to cultivate a rich inner life. Political and social circumstances matter. Politics can destroy the inner life of a person. Joseph Kim, another North Korean citizen, describes the tragedy of hunger and famine in his home country and the changes in his father's self respect; Joseph and his sister Boong Sook were confronted with the destruction of his father's soul: "Boong Sook and I didn't know what was wrong with our father. We could recognize the signs of starvation, but then there was his yellowed skin and the terrible pain—not the usual symptoms of hunger. To us, something had entered his body and was slowly eating him from the inside, hollowing out his belly. Something far worse than disease (…) A loss of dignity. Hot shame (…) I imagine my father's state of mind that night as he approached our house empty-handed, humiliated by his own flesh and blood. He believed he was going to watch Bong Sook and me die in front of him. This was his deepest fear."[3] Dignity and self respect are interlinked, shame can be an indicator about the perceived relationship between "is" and "ought," between the inner and the outer. Politics can change the conditions of the inner.

But it can also be the other way round: The inner matters for politics and the social. John Rawls developed the idea of a well-ordered society based on the acceptance of principles of justice and developing a public conception of justice.[4] Rawls postulates persons "capable of a sense of justice."[5] In other words, a shared sense of justice is the basis for a just society; he assumes "that each person beyond a certain age and possessed of the requisite intellectual capacity develops a sense of justice under normal social circumstances. We acquire a skill in judging things to be just and unjust, and in supporting these judgments by reasons."[6] A sense of justice can develop under non-pathological conditions. Here we enter the sphere of the inner life, the life of beliefs and convictions, emotions and attitudes, memories and hopes. People have to have not only a sense of justice but also a desire to act in accordance with its principles. "A sense of justice is an effective desire to apply and to act from

---

3   J. Kim (with St. Talty), Under the same Sky. From Starvation in North Korea to Salvation in America. Boston: Houghton Mifflin Harcourt 2015, 93.

4   J. Rawls, A Theory of Justice. Revised Edition. Cambridge, Mass: Belknap Press 1999, 4 and 397.

5   Ibd., 17.

6   Ibd., 41.

the principles of justice and so from the point of view of justice,"[7] and "the members of a well-ordered society desire more than anything to act justly and fulfilling this desire is part of their good."[8] We are in the middle of a language using the concept of "desire," a powerful force of the inner life as described in early Christian writings as we have seen. The stability of a society is depicted as its ability to uphold the concept of justice even under adverse circumstances; this is the language of epistemic resilience.

In times of crises, resilience is not a luxury, but a must. In times of scarce external resources, internal resources have to be stronger.[9] This challenge is particularly relevant in the face of global climate change and the future of the planet. In his encyclical *Laudato Si* (LS), addressed to "every person living on this planet," Pope Francis reminds readers of the earth as our common home and of the climate as a common good which cannot be protected by market forces (LS 23:190). There is a global challenge and this challenge is first and foremost a moral challenge—there is the moral challenge of recognizing our faith commitments: "It is good for humanity and the world at large when we believers better recognize the ecological commitments which stem from our convictions," (LS 64). "Believers themselves must constantly feel challenged to live in a way consonant with their faith and not to contradict it by their actions," (LS 200). This is a matter of ordering the inner so that one's way of life corresponds to one's beliefs. There is also the moral challenge of fundamentally changing one's inner culture through conversion.

The ecological challenges that we face need epistemic resilience, a strong culture of the inner, firmness of an inner order. *Laudato Si* encourages us to ask tough questions, the questions that are not comfortable and convenient and, more so, make us look for uncomfortable answers: replacing consumption with sacrifice (LS 9), being prepared "to make sacrifices" (LS 200). This is a matter of a genuine conversion which is a way of entering a new way of thinking ("meta-noia" as dynamics to move beyond established thinking habits). A change in behavior must be based on a change of heart.[10] And "change of heart" ("heart" meaning the core of the person or the person in all her dimensions) is what we call "conversion." Efforts made for the planet may not find a deep enough motivation without a deep conversion: "the ecological crisis is

---

7   Ibd., 497.

8   Ibd., 498.

9   I. Robertson, C.L. Cooper, Resilience. *Stress and Health* 29 (2013) 175–176.

10   This is an important thought in the Catholic Social Tradition: "The world will never be the dwelling place of peace, till peace has found a home in the heart of each and every man" (*Pacem in Terris* 165); see also *Caritas in Veritate* 9 and 16.

also a summons to profound interior conversion," (LS 217).[11] Without this deep conversion, efforts may not have the patience, passion and persistence to bring about real and sustainable change (and change towards sustainability). The ecological crisis according to *Laudato Si* does not demand changes in terms of "fixing problems," but changes in terms of "converting hearts." And this conversion is a conversion towards a common-good orientation overcoming different forms of individualism which have become so deeply rooted in modernity.[12] It will not do to find technological solutions without moral change; it will not do to reduce the burdens of the planet to intentions enabling us to continue with our way of life; it will not do to introduce external changes without spiritual transformation.

Paradoxically, it is the capacity to be displaced with its emphasis on inner strength, inner spaces and resources, and epistemic resilience that will be decisive in the question of the ultimate displacement of humanity. If we do not act quickly we may be displaced on our own planet, homeless, without spaces to act on the basis of well-deliberated choices. Inner homelessness can translate quickly into loss of home; a lack of care for our common home is a lack of proper commitment, proper love. Ultimately, it is the inner that decides about the flourishing or collapse of societies. John Rawls' famous reminder that "purity of heart, if one could attain it, would be to see clearly and to act with grace and self-command from this point of view,"[13] is a way of expressing a goal in life which John Cassian expressed as "purity of heart." Purity of heart is a matter of inner struggle, divine grace, social settings, and political conditions. It points to a quality of the inner life that Jesus connected with the promise: "Blessed are the pure in heart, for they will see God," (Mt 5:8).

---

11   The concern with too shallow an engagement with these issues has already been expressed in Arne Naess' concept of "deep ecology"—Arne Naess, The shallow and the deep, long-range ecology movement. *Inquiry* 16,1–4 (1973) 95–100.
12   See LS 219 where the encyclical quotes Guardini on this very point.
13   J. Rawls, A Theory of Justice, 514.

Bibliography

Abuhilal, F., The Discourse of Palestinian Diaspora in Edward Said's *Out of Place: A Memoir*: A Post-orientalism Analysis. *Journal of Postcolonial Cultures and Societies* 4,3 (2013) 30–50.

Adger, W.N. et al., Social-ecological resilience to coastal disasters. *Science* 309 (2005) 1036–1039.

Adger, W.N., Social and ecological resilience: are they related? *Progress in Human Geography* 24,3 (2000) 347–364.

Akula, V., A Fistful of Rice. Boston, Mass: Harvard Business Review Press 2011.

Allain-Chapman, J., Resilient Pastors. The Role of Adversity in Healing and Growth. London: Society For Promoting Christian Knowledge SPCK 2012.

Antonovsky, A., Health, stress and coping: New Perspectives on mental and physical well-being. San Francisco: Jossey-Bass Social and Behavioral Science Series 1979.

Apfel, R.J., B. Simon, Bennett, Mitigating discontents with children in war: an ongoing psychoanalytic inquiry. In A.C. Robben, M.M. Suárez-Orozco (eds.), Cultures under Siege: Collective Violence and Trauma. Cambridge 2000, 102–130.

Arendt, H., We Refugees. In: Marc Robinson, ed., Altogether Elsewhere. Writers on Exile. Boston: Faber and Faber 1994, 110–119.

Armstrong, P., Being 'Out of Place': Edward W. Said and the Contradictions of Cultural Differences. *Modern Language Quarterly* 64,1 (2003) 97–121.

Assmann, A., Der lange Schatten der Vergangenheit. Munich: Beck 2006.

Augustine, Confessions. Ed. J. O'Donnell. Oxford: Oxford University Press 1992.

Auster, P., The Invention of Solitude. New York: Penguin 1988.

Austin, J., Philosophical Papers. Ed. J.O. Urmson, G.J. Warnock. Oxford: Clarendon 1961.

Ayyash, M.M., Edward Said: Writing in Exile. *Comparative Studies of South Asia, Africa and the Middle East* 30,1 (2010) 107–118.

Bakewell, S., How to Live: Or A Life of Montaigne in One Question and Twenty Attempts at an Answer. London: Chatto and Windus 2011.

Baker, G., Wittgenstein's Method. Oxford: Blackwell 2004.

Baldwin, M., M. Landau, Exploring Nostalgia's Influence on Psychological Growth. Self and Identity (2013) 1–16.

Bandura, Albert: Self-efficacy: Toward a Unifying Theory of Behavioral Change. *Psychological Review* 84,2 (1977) 191–215.

Barbour, J.D., Edward Said and the Space of Exile. *Literature & Theology* 12,3 (2007) 293–301.

Barton, S., Living with Jonathan. Lessons in Love, Life and Autism. London: Watkins Publishing 2011.

Beck, M., Expecting Adam. New York: Three Rivers Press 2011.

Benedict XVI, Spe Salvi, 2007.

Benedict XVI, Deus Caritas Est, 2005.

Benenson, P., The Forgotten Prisoners. *The Observer* 28 May 1961.

Berger, Z. et al., Resilience of Israeli body handlers: Implications of repressive coping style. *Traumatology* 13 (2007) 64–74.

Bergoglio, Jorge, LA ACUSACION DE SI MISMO. In: *Boletín de Espiritualidad* 87 (Mayo–Junio 1984) 1–18.

Bergoglio, Jorge, Sobre la acusación de sí mismo. Buenos Aires: Editorial Claretiana 2005.

Betancourt, I., Even Silence Has and End, My six years of captivity in the Colombian Jungle. London: Penguin 2011.

Bethge, E., Costly Grace. An Illustrated Biography of Dietrich Bonhoeffer. San Francisco: Harper and Row 1979.

Bickers, R.A., R. Seton, eds., Missionary Encounters. Sources and Issues. Surrey, UK: Curzon Press 1996.

Bieri, P., Eine Art zu leben. Über die Vielfalt menschlicher Würde. Munich: Hanser 2013.

Bloch, E., Über den Begriff der Weisheit. In: Philosophische Aufsätze zur objektiven Phantasie. Werke 10. Frankfurt/Main: Suhrkamp 1969.

Blum, L., Friendship, Altruism and Morality. New York: Routledge 1980.

Boethius, The Consolation of Philosophy. London: Victor Watts 1969.

Bollnow, O.F., Neue Geborgenheit. Das Problem einer Überwindung des Existentialismus. Stuttgart: Kohlhammer ²1960.

Bollnow, O.F., Die erzieherische Bedeutung der Geborgenheit im Hause. *Viertel-jahresschrift für Heilpädagogik und ihre Nachbargebiete* 45,2 (1976) 149–158.

Bonanno, G.A., Loss, trauma, and human resilience: Have we underestimated the human capacity to thrive after extremely aversive events? *American Psychologist* 59,1 [2004] 20–28.

Bonhoeffer, D., Letters and Papers from Prison, Enlarged Edition, London: SCM Press 1971.

Boss, P., Ambiguous Loss. Cambridge, Massachusetts: Harvard University Press 1999.

Boss, P., Loss, Trauma, and Resilience. New York: W.W. Norton 2006, 83–87.

Boyle, G., Tattoos on the Heart. New York: Free Press 2010.

Boym, S., Nostalgia and Its Discontents. *The Hedgehog Review* 9,2 (2007) 7–18.

Brenkman, J., The Concrete Utopia of Poetry: Blake's 'A Poison Tree'. In: Ch. Hošek, P. Parker, Lyric Poetry. Beyond Criticism. Ithaca, New York: Cornell UP 1985, 182–193.

Bruneau, M. et al., A Framework to Quantitatively Assess and Enhance the Seismic Resilience of Communities. *Earthquake Spectra* 19,4 (2003) 733–753.

Buergenthal, Th., A lucky Child: a memoir of surviving Auschwitz as a Young Boy. New York: Little Brown and Company 2009.

Burggraeve, R., Violence and the Vulnerable Face of Others. *Journal of Social Philosophy* 30,1 (1999) 29–45.

Burrell, D., Aristotle and 'Future Contingencies'. *Philosophical Studies* 13 (1964) 37–52.

Butler, J., Five Sermons. New York: Bobbs Merrill 1950.

Campkin, B., Placing 'Matter Out of Place': Purity and Danger as Evidence for Architecture and Urbanism. *Architectural Theory Review* 18,1 (2013) 46–61.

Carey, P., Augustine's Invention of the Inner Self. Oxford: Oxford University Press 2000.

Carmichael, A., Fragments That Remain. Compiled by Bee Trehane. Fort Washington, PA: CLC Publications 2013.

Carpenter, S.R. et al., From metaphor to measurement: resilience of what to what? *Ecosystems* 4 (2001) 765–781.

Carrigan, A., Salvador Witness. The Life and Calling of Jean Donovan. Maryknoll, NY: Orbi 2005.

Carver, Ch.S., Resilience and Thriving: Issues, Models, and Linkages. *Journal of Social Issues* 54,2 (1998) 245–266.

Caulfield, C., Only A Beginning. The Passionists in China, 1921–1931. Union City, NJ: Passionist Press 1990.

Chamberlain, D.S., Philosophy of Music in the Consolation of Boethius. *Speculum* 45,1 (1970) 90–97.

Chmiel, M., The Book of Mev. Bloomington: Xlibris Corp 2005.

Cianni, J.L., La philosophie comme remède au chomage. Paris: Albin Michel 2007.

Clarke, K.M., F. Cardman, Spiritual Resilience in People Who Live Well with Lifelong Disability. *Journal of Religion, Disability and Health* 6 (2002) 23–36.

Clerkin, A., B. Clerkin, eds., A Road Less Travelled. Tales of the Irish Missionaries. Portland, OR: Four Courts Press 2011.

Coff, P., The Inner Journey: Reflections on the Awakening of Mind and Heart in Buddhism and Christianity. *Buddhist-Christian Studies* 11 (1991) 173–195.

Cohen, G., Rescuing Justice and Equality. Cambridge, Mass.: Harvard University Press 2008.

Colten, C.E. et al., Community Resilience: Lessons from New Orleans and Hurricana Katrina. CARRIE Research Report 3. Oak Ridge, Tennessee: Community and Regional Resilience Initiative 2008.

Conant, J., C. Diamond, On Reading the Tractatus Resolutely. In: M. Kölbel, B. Weiss (eds.), The Lasting Significance of Wittgenstein's Philosophy. London: Routledge, 2004, 46–99.

Conant, J., The Method of the Tractatus. In: E. Reck (ed.), From Frege to Wittgenstein: Perspectives in Early Analytic Philosophy, Oxford: Oxford University Press 2002, 374–462.

Conger, R.D. et al., Couple Resilience to Economic Pressure. *Journal of Personality and Social Psychology* 76,1 (1999) 54–71.

Conger, R.D., K.J. Conger, Resilience in Midwestern Families. *Journal of Marriage and Family* 64,2 (2002) 361–373.

Cook, M.L., The African Experience of Jesus. *Theological Studies* 70 (2009) 668–692.

Cooper, C.L. et al., Building Resilience for Success. Basingstoke, UK: Palgrave Macmillan 2014.

Countryman, L.W., Forgiven and Forgiving. Harrisburg, Pennsylvania: Morehouse Publishing 1998.

Curley, T.F., The Consolation of Philosophy as Work of Literature. *The American Journal of Philology* 108,2 (1987) 343–367.

Cyrulnik, B., Parler d'amour au bord du gouffre. Paris: Editions Odile Jacob 2004

Cyrulnik, B., Resilience. London: Penguin 2009.

Cyrulnik, B., Talking of Love. London: Penugin 2009.

Cziszek, W., He Leadeth Me. Garden City, New York: Doubleday 1973.

Danto, A., Narration and knowledge. New York: Columbia University 1985.

Darwall, St., The Second-Person Standpoint: Morality, Respect and Accountability. Cambridge, Mass: Harvard UP 2006.

Davis, F., Yearning for yesterday: A sociology of nostalgia. New York: Free Press 1979.

Davis, W.A., Inwardness and Existence. Milwaukee, Michigan: University of Wisconsin Press 1989.

De Francesco, V., Letters to Naples. A Neapolitan writes home about his work in Melbourne 1919–1928. Ballan, Australia: Connor Court 2010.

de Hennezel, M., *La chaleur du coeur empêche nos corps te rouiller*, Paris: Robert Laffont 2008.

del Rey, M., In and Out The Andes. New York: Charles Scribner's Sons 1955.

Delor, F., M. Hubert, Revisiting the concept of 'vulnerability'. *Social Science and Medicine* 50 (2000) 1557–1570.

Delp, A., Prison Writings. Maryknoll. New York: Orbis 2004.

Demenocal, P.B. and E.R. Cook, Perspectives on Diamond's Collapse: How Societies Choose to Fail or Succeed. *Current Anthropology* 46 (Supplement, 2005) S91–S99.

Deneulin, S. with M. Bano, Religion in Development: Rewriting the secular script. London: Zed Books 2009.

Diamond, C., Ethics, Imagination and the Method of the Tractatus, In: A. Crary and R. Read (eds) The New Wittgenstein, London: Routledge 2000, 149–173.

Diamond, C., Throwing Away the Ladder. *Philosophy* 63, 243 (1988) 5–27.

Diamond, J., Collapse: How Societies Choose to Fail or Survive. New York: Viking Press 2005.

Dickens, C., American Notes for General Circulation. New York: Charles Scribner's Son 1910.

Dorotheos of Gaza, Discourses and Sayings (Cistercian Studies). Ed. Eric Wheeler. Cistercian Publications 1977.

Douglas, M., Purity and Danger. New York: Routledge ARK Edition 1984.

Duffield, M., Challenging environments: Danger, resilience and the aid industry. *Security Dialogue* 43,5 (2012) 475–492.

Edgerton, R., Sick Societies. Challenging the Myth of Primitive Harmony. New York: The Free Press 1992.

Edmonds, B.R., God is not here. A Soldier's Struggle with Torture, Trauma, and the Moral Injuries of War. New York: Pegasus Books 2015.

Ellsberg, R., All Saints. New York: Crossroads 1999 (3rd printing).

Eriksson, C.B. et al., Social support, organizational support, and religious support in relation to burnout in expatriate humanitarian aid workers. Mental Health, Religion & Culture 12,7 (2009) 671–686 (Special Issue: Psychological Functioning of International Missionaries).

Eriksson, C.B. et al., Predeployment Mental Health and Trauma Exposure of Expatriate Humanitarian aid Workers: Risk and Resilience Factors. *Traumatology* April 16, 2012.

Evagrius Ponticus, The Prakticos. Chapters on Prayer. Cistercian Studies. 1972.

Faber, S., The Privilege of Pain: The Exile as Ethical Model in Max Aub, Francisco Ayala, and Edward Said. *Journal of the Interdisciplinary Crossroads* 972 (2006) 15–37.

Fardon, R., Margaret Mary Dougles 1921–2007. *Proceedings from the British Academy* 166 (2010) 135–158.

Farley, M., Personal Commitments. Maryknoll, New York: Orbis 2013.

Figes, O., Just Send Me Word. London: Allen Lane 2012.

Fischer, G., Warum ist mein Schmerz anhaltend und meine Wunde unheilbar? In: H. Hinterhuber et al. (eds.), Der Mensch in seiner Klage. Anmerkungen aus Theologie und Psychiatrie. Innsbruck: Tyrolia 2006, 150–159.

Fischer, J.M., Contribution to Martha Nussbaum's The Therapy of Desire. *Philosophy and Phenomenological Research* 59,3 (1999) 787–792.

Fischer, N., Einleitung, In: Aurelius Augustinus, Suche nach dem wahren Leben. Hamburg: Meiner. 2006, pp. XIII–XCI.

Fisher, S., Homesickness, cognition and health. London: Erlbaum 1989.

Flach, F., Resilience. How to bounce back when the going gets tough! New York: Hatherleigh Press 1998.

Flasch, K., Wert der Innerlichkeit. In: H. Joas, K. Wiegandt (eds.), Die kulturellen Werte Europas. Frankfurt/Main: Fischer 2005, 219–236.

Folke, C., Resilience: The Emergence of a perspective for social–ecological system analyzes. *Global Environmental Change* 16 (2006) 253–267.

Formosa, P., The Role of Vulnerability in Kantian Ethics. In: C. Mackenzie et al (eds.), Vulnerability. Oxford: Oxford University Press 2014, 88–109.

Frankfurt, H., The Importance of what we care about. Cambridge: Cambridge University Press 1998, 159–176.

Frankfurt, H., The Reasons of Love. Princeton: Princeton University Press 2004, 10–17.

Frankl, V., Psychotherapy and Existentialism. New York: Washington Square Press 1967.

Frankl, V., The Doctor and the Soul. New York: Alfred Knopf 1968, 105–116.

Frankl, V., The Will to Meaning. Cleveland, Ohio: The World Publishing Company 1969.

Frey, B. et al., The Corporate Governance of Benedictine Abbeys. *Journal of Management Studies* 16,1 (2010) 90–115.

Fromm, E., The Art of Loving. New York: Harper Collins 2006 (reprint).

Fuchs, A., Towards an Ethics of Remembering: The Walser-Bubis Debate and the Other of Discourse. *The German Quarterly* 75, 3 (2002) 235–246.

Fullilove, M.T., Psychiatric Implications of Displacement: Contributions From the Psychology of Place. *Annual Journal of Psychiatry* 153,12 (1996) 1516–1523.

Gandhi, M., An Autobiography or The Story of My Experiments with Truth. Ahmedabad: Navajivan Publishing House 1966 (1927).

Garmezy, N., A.S. Masten, Stress, competence, and resilience. *Behavior Therapy* 17 (1986) 500–521.

Garmezy, N., Stress, competence, and development. *American Journal of Orthopsychiatry* 57,2 (1987) 159–174.

Garmezy, N., Stress-resistant children: The search for protective factors. In: J.E.: Stevenson (ed.), recent research in developmental psychopathology. Oxford 1985, 213–233.

Genova, L., Still Alice. Lincoln, Nebraska: iUniverse 2007.

Geremia, P., Dreams and Bloodstains. The Diary of a Missioner in the Philippines. Quezon City: Claretian Publications 1987.

Glover, J., Humanity. A moral history of the Twentieth Century. London: Pimlico 2001.

Goodin, R., Protecting the Vulnerable. Chicago: University of Chicago Press 1985.

Goodin, R., On Settling. Princeton: Princeton UP 2012.

Goodman, N., Ways of Worldmaking. Indianapolis: Hackett 1978.

Greeff, A.P., B. Human, Resilience in families in which a parent has died. *American Journal of Family Therapy* 32 (2004) 27–42.

Gritti, A., Building aid workers' resilience: why a gendered approach is needed. *Gender & Development* 23,3 (2015) 449–462.

Gunderson, L.H., C.S. Holling (eds.), Panarchy: understanding transformations in human and natural systems. Washington, DC: Island Press 2002.

Gunderson, L.H., L. Pritchard (eds.), Resilience and the behavior of large-scale systems. Washington, DC: Island Press 2002.

Gundert, H., ed., Vier Jahre in Asante: Tagebücher der Missionare Ramseyer und Kühne. Basel: Missionskomptoir 1875.

Hack-Polay, D., When Home Isn't Home. A Study of Homesickness and Coping Strategies among Migrant Workers and Expatriates. *International Journal of Psychological Studies* 4,3 (2012) 62–72.

Haglund, M.E. et al., Psychobiological mechanisms of resilience. *Development and Psychopathology* 19 (2007) 899–920.

Halbwachs, M., On Collective Memory. Edited, translated, and with an Introduction by L.A. Coser. Chicago: University of Chicago Press 1992.

Harden, B., Escape from Camp 14. London: Pan Books 2013.

Havel, V., Letters to Olga. Transl. P. Wilson. New York: Alfred Knopf 1988.

Hawley, D.R., L. DeHaan, Toward a definition of family resilience: Integrating life-span and family perspectives. *Family Process* 35 (1996) 283–296.

Heim, J., ed., What They Taught Us. How Maryknoll Missioners Were Evangelized by the Poor. Maryknoll, NY: Orbis 2009.

Henderson, N., M. Milstein, Resiliency in Schools. Making It Happen for Students and Educators. Thousand Oaks, California: Corwin 2002.

Hetherington, E.M., E.A. Blechman, Stress, coping and resiliency in children and families. Mahwah, NJ: Lawrence Erlbaum 1996.

Higgins, G.O.C, Resilient adults: Overcoming a cruel past, San Francisco: Jossey-Bass 1994.

Hoggett, P., M. Mayo and C. Miller, The dilemmas of development work. Ethical challenges in regeneration. Bristol: Policy Press 2009.

Holling, C.S., Resilience and stability of ecological systems. *Annual Review of Ecology and Systematics* 4 (1973) 1–23.

Hutta, J.S., Geographies of Geborgenheit: beyond feelings of safety and the fear of crime. *Environment and Planning D: Society and Space* 27 (2009) 251–273.

Inauen, E. et al., Benedictine Tradition and Good Governance. In: L. Bruni, B. Sena (eds.), The Charismatic Principle in Social Life. London: Routledge 2012.

Inauen, E. et al., Monastic Governance: Forgotten Prospects for Public Institutions. *The American Review of Public Administration* 40,6 (2010) 631–653.

Inauen, E., B.S. Frey, Benediktinerabteien aus ökonomischer Sicht. On the extraordinary stability of an exceptional institution. Working Paper No. 388. Institute for Empirical Research in Economics. University of Zurich. Zürich 2008.

Jackson, F.C., What Mary Didn't Know. In: *Journal of Philosophy* 83 (1986) 291–295.

Jackson, F.C., Epiphenomenal Qualia. In: *Philosophical Quarterly* 32 (1982) 127–136.

James, W., The Varieties of Religious Experience. New York: MacMillan 1970.

Jaspers, K., Tragedy Is Not Enough. Transl. H.A.T. Reiche et al. Boston: Beacon Press 1952.

John Cassian, The Conferences. Translated and annotated by Boniface Ramsey. New York, NY / Mahwah, NJ: Newman Press 1997.

John Cassian, The Twelve Books of John Cassian on the Institutes of the Coenobia. Translation and Notes by Edgar C.S. Gibson. A Select Library of Nicene and Post-Nicene Fathers of the Christian Church. Second Series, Vol. 11. New York 1894.

Johnson, R.D., Economics of Good and Evil: The Quest for Economic Meaning from Gilgamesh to Wall Street. *Faith and Economics* 59 (2012) 86–90.

Kassow, S.D., Who Will Write Our History? Rediscovering a hidden archive from the Warsaw Ghetto. London: Penguin 2009.

Kay, M., Knowing One's Place in Contemporary Irish and Polish Poetry. London: continuum 2012.

Keyes, C.L.M., Risk and Resilience in Human Development: An Introduction. *Research in Human Development* 1,4 (2004) 223–227.

Khoshaba, D.M., S.R. Maddi, Early experiences in hardiness development. *Consulting Psychology Journal* 51 (1999) 106–116.

Kim, J. (with St. Talty), Under the same Sky. From Starvation in North Korea to Salvation in America. Boston: Houghton Mifflin Harcourt 2015.

Kim, J.W. et al., Influence of temperament and character on resilience. *Comprehensive Psychiatry* 54 (2013) 1105–1110.

Kitano, M.K., R.B. Lewis, Resilience and coping: Implications for gifted children and youth at risk. *Roeper Review* 27 [2005] 200–205.

Kleina, R.J.T. et al., Resilience to natural hazards: How useful is this concept? *Environmental Hazards* 5 [2003] 35–45.

Kluger, R., Still Alive. A Holocaust Girlhood Remembered. New York: Feminist Press at the City University of New York. 4th Printing 2009.

Kluger, R., weiter leben—Eine Jugend. Goettingen: Wallstein 1992.

Korff, V.P. et al., The impact of humanitarian context conditions and individual characteristics on aid worker retention. Disasters 39,3 (2015) 522–545.

Korczak, J., Ghetto diary. New Haven, Connecticut: Yale University Press 2003.

Krauss, N., Man Walks Into a Room. New York: Nan Talese 2003.

Lamond, A.J. et al., Measurement and predictors of resilience among community-dwelling older women. *Journal of Psychiatric Research* 43 (2009) 148–154.

Langmead, C., Robber of the Cruel Streets. The Prayerful Life of George Muller. Farnham: Crusade for World Revival 2006.

Layne, C.M. et al., Risk, Vulnerability, Resistance and Resilience. In: C.M. Layne, Handbook of PTSD Science and Practice. New York: Guilford 2007, 497–520.

Lerer, S., Boethius and Dialogue. Literary Method in The Consolation of Philosophy. Princeton: Princeton University Press 1985.

Lernoux, P., Hearts on Fire. The Story of the Maryknoll Sisters. Maryknoll, NY: 2012 (Centenary Edition).

Levinas, E., Totalility and Infinity. Dordrecht: Kluwer 1991.

Levine, J., Not Buying It. New York: Free Press 2006.

Lewis, C.S., A Grief Observed. London: Faber and Faber 1966 [1961].

Lewis, C.S., The Great Divorce. New York: Harper Collins 2015.

Lifton, R., The Protean Self: Human Resilience in an Age of Fragmentation. New York: Basic Books 1994.

Lindhout, A., S. Corbett, A House in the Sky. A Memoir of a Kidnapping That Changed Everything. London: Penguin 2013.

Long, C.R. and J.R. Averill, Solitude: An Exploration of Benefits of Being Alone. *Journal for the Theory of Social Behaviour* 33,1 (2003) 21–44.

Lunn, J., The Role of Religion, Spirituality and Faith in Development: A critical theory approach. Third World Quarterly, 30,5 (2009) 937–951.

Luthar, S.S. et al., Conceptual Issues in Studies of Resilience. *Annals of the New York Academy of Sciences* 1094 (2006) 105–115.

Luthar, S.S. et al., The construct of resilience: A critical evaluation and guidelines for future work. *Child Development*, 71 (2000) 543–562.

Lutz, R. (Ed.), Erschöpfte Familien. Wiesbaden: VS Springer 2012.

Mandela, N., In His Own Words. New York: Little, Brown and Company 2003.

Mandela, N., Long Walk to Freedom. London: Little, Brown and Company 1994.

Maneyna, S.B., The concept of resilience revisited. *Disasters* 30,4 (2006) 434–450.

Marcel, G., Desire and hope. In: N. Lawrence and D. O'Connor (eds.), Readings in Existential Phenomenology. Upper Saddle River, New Jersey: Prentice-Hall Inc. 1967.

Marcel, G., Homo viator: Introduction to a metaphysics of hope. New York, New York: Harper Torchbooks 1962.

Margalit, A., The Ethics of Memory. Harvard: Harvard University Press 2002.

Masten, A., Resilience in individual development: Successful adaptation despite risk and adversity. In: M. Wang, E. Gordon (eds.), Educational resilience in inner-city America: Challenges and prospects. Hillsdale, New Jersey: Erlbaum 1996, 3–25.

Masten, A.S., Ordinary magic: Lessons from research on resilience in human development. *Education Canada*, 49,3 (2009), 28–32.

Masten, A.S., J. Obradovic, Competence and resilience in development. *Annals of the New York Academy of Sciences* 1094 (2006) 13–27.

Masten A.S., J.L. Powell, A Resilience Framework for Research, Policy and Practice. In: S.S. Luthar (Ed.), Resilience and vulnerability: Adaptiation in the context of childhood adversities. New York, NY: Cambridge University Press 2003, 1–25.

Masten, A.S., Resilience in developing systems: Progress and promise as the fourth wave arises. *Development and Psychopathology* 19 (2007) 921–930.

Mathewes, Ch.T., Augustinian Anthropology: Interior intimo meo. *The Journal of Religious Ethics* 27,2 (1999) 195–221.

May, R., Power and Innocence. A Search for the Sources of Violence. New York, NY: Norton 1998.

McCubbin, M.A., H.I. McCubbin, Families coping with illness. In: C.B. Danielson et al. (eds.), Families, Health, and Illness: Perspectives on Coping and Intervention. St. Louis, Mi 1993, 21–63.

McGinn, B., The God Beyond God. Theology and Mysticism in the Thought of Meister Eckhart. *The Journal of Religion* 61,1 (1981) 1–19.

McKay, L., Resilience. Building Resilient Managers in Humanitarian Organizations: Strengthening Key Organizational Structures and Personal Skills that Promote Resilience in Challenging Environments, London: People in Aid 2011.

Meister, Eckhart, Selected Writings. Selected and translated by Oliver Davis. London: Penguin 1994.

Menke, Chr., Die Gegenwart der Tragödie. Frankfurt/Main: Suhrkamp 2005.

Mogel, H., Geborgenheit. Psychologie eines Lebensgefühls. Heidelberg: Springer 1995.

Montaiuti,, C., The Effect of Meaning-Making on Resilience Among Aid Workers. A Phenomenological Analysis. PhD Dissertation. Minneapolis, Mn: Walden University. March 2013.

Morgan, S., My Place. London: Virago Press 2012.

Morris, T., The Despairing Developer: Diary of an Aid Worker in the Middle East. London: I.B. Tauris 1991.

Müller, B., Der Weg des Weinens. Die Tradition des 'Penthos' in den Apophthegmata Patrum. Göttingen: Vandenhoeck und Ruprecht 2000.

Murdoch, I., Essentalists and Mystics. Philosophical Writings. Ed. P. Conradi. New York: Penguin 1999.

Naess, Arne, The shallow and the deep, long-range ecology movement. *Inquiry* 16,1–4 (1973) 95–100.

Nagel, Th., The Absurd. *The Journal of Philosophy* 68,20 (1971) 716–727.

Natella, St. et al., *Intangible Infrastructure: Building on the foundation.* Credit Suisse Research Institute 2008.

Newman, J.H., An Essay in Aid of a Grammar of Assent. Notre Dame, IN: University of Notre Dame Press 1979.

Newton, N., On Viewing Pain as a Secondary Quality. *Nous* 23,5 (1989) 569–598.

Niebuhr R., The Purpose of the Church and Its Ministry. New York: Harper & Row 1956.

Nkosi, L., Encounter with New York. In: M. Robinson, ed., Altogether Elsewhere. Boston: Faber and Faber 1994, 289–298.

Noone, J.M., The Same Fate as the Poor. Maryknoll, NY: Orbis 1995.

Nozick, R., The Examined Life. New York: Simon and Schuster 1989.

Nozick, R., The Holocaust. In: R. Nozick., Examined Life. New York: Simon & Schuster 1989, 236–242.

Nussbaum, M., Love and the Individual: Romantic Rightness and Platonic Aspiration. In: M. Nussbaum, Love's Knowledge: Essays on Philosophy and Literature. Oxford 1990, 314–334.

Nussbaum, M., Non scientific deliberation. The vulnerability of the good human life. In: M. Nussbaum, The Fragility of Goodness. Luck and Ethics in Greek Tragedy and Philosophy. Cambridge: Cambridge University Press 2001, 290–372.

Nussbaum, M., Therapeutic Arguments. In: M. Nussbaum, The therapy of desire. Theory and Practice in Hellenistic Ethics. Princeton: Princeton University Press 1994, 13–47.

Nussbaum, The Therapy of Desire, Princeton: Princeton University Press 2009.

Oberg, K., Culture shock: adjustment to new cultural environments. *Practical Anthropologist* 7 (1960) 177–182.

O'Connor, F., The Displaced Person. In: Flannery O'Connor, The Complete Stories. New York: Farrar, Straus and Giroux 1971, 194–235.

O'Dougherty, Wright M., A.S. Masten, Resilience Processes in Development. In: O'Dougherty/Wright (eds.), Handbook of Resilience in Childhood. New York: Springer 2006, 17–37.

Olmsted, W.R., Philosophical Inquiry and Religious Transformation in Boethius, The Consolation of Philosophy and Augustine's 'Confessions. *The Journal of Religion* 69,1 (1989) 14–35.

Olson, L., A Cruel Paradise. Journals of an International Relief Worker. Toronto: Insomniac Press 1999.

O'Reilly, Th., An Acre Sown. St Patrick's Missionary Society in Brazil. Wicklow: Kiltegan Fathers 2001.

Paasi, A., Deconstructing Regions: Notes on the Scales of Spatial Life. *Environment and Planning* 23,2 (1991) 239–256.

Paton, J.G., Missionary to the New Hebrides. An autobiography edited by his brother. New York: Fleming H. Revell 1889.

Patterson, J.M., Integrating Family Resilience and Family Stress Theory. *Journal of Marriage and the Family* 64,2 (2002) 349–360.

Pauli, J., Einleitung. In: Dorotheus von Gaza, Doctrinae Diversae. Die geistliche Lehre. Fontes Christiani 37/1. Freiburg/Breisgau: Herder 2000, 7–81.

Peters, R., Reflections on the origin and aim of nostalgia. Journal of Analytical Psychology 30 (1985) 135–148.

Pigni, A., Building resilience and preventing burnout among aid workers in Palestine: a personal account of mindfulness based staff care. *Intervention* 12,2 (2014) 231–239.

Pitcher, G., The Awfulness of Pain. *The Journal of Philosophy* 67,14 (1970) 481–492;

Polk, L.V., Toward a middle-range theory of resilience. *Advances in Nursing Science* 19 (1997) 1–13.

Pope Francis, The Way of Humility: Corruption and Sin; on Self-Accusation. San Francisco, CA: Ignatius 2014.

Power, F.C. & Fallon, S.M., Teaching and Transformation: Liberal Arts and the Homeless." In D. Groody & G Guttierez, eds., The Preferential Option for The Poor Beyond Theology: An Interdisciplinary Reader. Notre Dame IN: University of Notre Dame Press 2013.

Price, H., Belief 'In' and Belief 'That'. *Religious Studies* 1,1 (1965) 5–27.

Quash, B., Abiding. The Archbishop of Canterbury's Lent Book 2013. London: Bloomsbury 2012.

Raelin, J., "I Don't Have Time to Think!' versus the Art of Reflective Practice. *Reflections* 4,1 (2002) 66–79.

Rafroidi, P., The sense of place in Seamus Heaney's poetry. In: Jacqueline Genet, ed., Studies on Seamus Heaney. Caen: Presses universitaires de Caen 1987.

Rawlence, B., City of Thorns. Nine Lives in the World's Largest Refugee Camp. New York: Picador 2015.

Rawls, J., A Theory of Justice. Revised Edition. Cambridge, Mass: Belknap Press 1999.

Reifenberg, S., Santiago's Children. What I learned about Life at an Orphanage in Chile. Austin, Tx: University of Texas Press 2008.

Renes, M., Sally Morgan: Aboriginal Identity Retrieved and Performed within and without *My Place*. *Estudios Ingleses de la Universidad Complutense* 18 (2010) 77–90.

Renner, F., Der fünfarmige Leuchter. Beiträge zum Werden und Wirken der Benediktinerkongregation von St. Ottilien. Volume IV. St. Ottilien: EOS 1993.

Richardson, G.E., The metatheory of resilience and resiliency. *Journal of Social and Clinical Psychology* 58 (2002) 307–321.

Ripley, A., The unthinkable: who survives when disaster strikes—and why. London: Harmony 2008

Robertson, I., C.L. Cooper, Resilience. *Stress and Health* 29 (2013) 175–176.

Rorty, A.O., The Historicity of Psychological Attitudes: Love is Not Love Which Alters Not When It Alteration Finds. In: N.K. Badhwar, Friendship: A Philosophical Reader. Ithaca, NY: Cornell University Press 1993, 73–88.

Russell, J.S., Resilience. *Journal of the Philosophy of Sport* 42,2 (2015) 159–182.

Rutter, M., Resilience as a Dynamic Concept. *Development and Psychopathology* 24 (2012) 335–344.

Said, E., Reflections on Exile. In: Marc Robinson, ed., Altogether Elsewhere. Writers on Exile. Boston: Faber and Faber 1994, 137–149.

Said, E., Representations of the Intellectual: The 1993 Reith Lectures. New York: Vintage 1996.

Said, E., Out of Place. A Memoir. New York: Alfred Knopf 1999.

Said, E., Freud and the Non-European. London: Verso 2003.

Schapera, I., ed., Livingstone's Private Journals 1851–1853. Berkeley, Ca: University of California Press 1960.

Schipper, E.W., The Wisdom of Tragedy. *The Journal of Aesthetics and Art Criticism* 24,4 (1966) 533–537.

Schneider, Hilton, E.E., assisted by Angela K. Hilton, Displaced Person. A Girl's Life in Russia, Germany, and America. Baton Rouge: Louisiana State University 2004.

Schrems, S.H., Uncommon Women, Unmarked Trails. The Courageous Journey Of Catholic Missionary Sisters in Frontier Montana. Norman, Oklahoma: Horse Creek Publications 2003.

Schwartzberg, S.S., R. Janoff-Bulman, Grief and the Search for Meaning: Exploring the Assumptive Worlds of Bereaved College Students. *Journal of Social and Clinical Psychology* 10,3 (1991) 270–288.

Schweitzer, A., Zwischen Wasser und Urwald: Erlebnisse und Beobachtungen eines Arztes im Urwalde Äquatorialafrikas. Bern: P. Haupt 1922.

Sedláček, Tomas, Economics of Good and Evil. The Quest for Economic Meaning From Gilgamesh to Wall Street. Oxford: Oxford University Press 2011.

Sedmak, C., Armutsbekämpfung. Wien: Böhlau 2013.

Sedmak, C., Innerlichkeit und Kraft. Studie in epistemischer Resilienz. Freiburg: Herder 2013.

Sedmak, C., Intangible Infrastructures and Identity. In: E. Kapferer et al. (eds)., Strenghtening Intangible Infrastructures. Newcastle upon Tyne: Cambridge Scholars Publishing 2013, 3–22.

Sedmak, C., Utility and Identity: A Catholic Social Teaching Perspective on the *Economics of Good and Evil. Studies in Christian Ethics* 28,4 (November 2015) 461–477.

Sedmak, C., "My Place"? Catholic Social Teaching and the Politics of *Geborgenheit*. In: Johannes Drerup, Gunter Graf, Christoph Schickhardt, Gottfried Schweiger, eds., Justice, Education and the Politics of Childhood. Dordrecht: Springer 2016, 235–250.

Sedmak, C., Spiritual infrastructure: Memory and moral resources. *Israel Affairs* 16,4 (2010) 510–533.

Seery, M.D., Resilience: A Silver Lining to Experiencing Adverse Life Events? *Current Directions in Psychological Science* 20,6 (2011) 390–394.

Shelton, A., Pioneering in Tibet. A Personal Record of Life and Experience in Mission Fields. New York: Fleming H. Revell Company 1921.

Seigel, J., The Idea of the Self. Thought and Experience in Western Europe since the Seventeenth Century. Cambridge: Cambridge University Press 2005, 7–17.

Seih, Y.T. et al., The benefits of psychological displacement in diary writing when using different pronouns. *British Journal of Health Psychology* 13 (2008) 39–41.

Selinger, S., The Forgotten Factor: The uneasy relationship between religion and development. *Social Compass* 51,4 (2004) 523–543.

Shaikh, A., C. Kauppi, Deconstructing Resilience: Myriad Conceptualizations and Interpretations. *International Journal of Arts and Sciences* 3, 15 (2010) 155–176.

Sheffi, Y., The Resilient Enterprise. Cambridge, MA: The MIT Press 2005.

Smith, A., An autobiography, the story of the Lord's dealings with Mrs. Amanda Smith, the colored evangelist: containing an account of her life work of faith, and her travels in America, England, Ireland, Scotland, India, and Africa, as an independent missionary / with an introduction by Bishop Thoburn. Chicago, IL: Christian Witness Co. 1893.

Smith, S., Poetry and Displacement. Liverpool: Liverpool University Press 2007.

Soelle, D., F. Stefensky, Wider den Luxus der Hoffnungslosigkeit. Freiburg/Br: Herder 1995.

Solomon, R., About Love: Reinventing Romance for Our Times. New York: Simon & Schuster 1988.

Sonoda, H., A Preliminary Study of Sally Morgan's *My Place*. *The Otemon Journal of Australian Studies* 35 (2009) 157–170.

Sorabji, R., Self. Ancient and Modern Insights about Individuality, Life and Death. Oxford: Oxford University Press 2005.

Stafford, W., The Way It is. Minneapolis, Mn: Graywolf Press 1998.

Stein, E., The Interiority of the Soul. *Logos* 8,2 (2005) 183–193.

Stein, E., Endliches und ewiges Sein. Versuch eines Aufstiegs zum Sinn des Seins. Freiburg/Br: Herder 1950 (Edith Steins Werke. Edited H.L. Gelber, R. Leuven. Band II).

Steiner, G., Ten (Possible) Reasons for the Sadness of Thought. *Salmagundi* 146/147 (2005) 3–32.

Steiner, G., The Death of Tragedy. London 1961.

Steiner, P., ed., Dark and stormy days at Kumassi, 1900; or, Missionary experience in Ashanti, according to the diary of Rev. Frits Ramseyer. Translated into English by Miss Meyer. With a pref. by Thomas Nichol. London: S.W. Partridge 1901.

Storr, A., Solitude. London: Harper Collins 1997 (Orig: The School of Genius. London 1988).

Stuhlmiller, C.M., Occupational Meanings and Coping Practices of Rescue Workers in an Earthquake Disaster. *Western Journal of Nursing Research* 16,3 (1994) 268–287.

Stump, E., Second-Person Accounts and the Problem of Evil. In: E. Yandell (ed.), *Faith and Narrative*. New York: Oxford University Press 2001, 86–103.

Stump, E., The Problem of Evil: Analytic Philosophy and Narrative. In: O. Crisp., Michael C. Rea (eds.), Analytic Theology: New Essays in the Philosophy of Theology. New York: Oxford University Press 2009, 251–264.

Stump, E., Wandering in Darkness: Narrative and the Problem of Suffering. Oxford: Oxford University Press 2010.

Swinton, J., Raging with Compassion: Pastoral Responses to the Problem of Evil. Grand Rapids, MI: Eerdmans 2007.

Taylor, C., Sources of the Self. The Making of modern Identity. Cambridge, Mass: Harvard University Press 1994.

Taylor, G., Love. *Proceedings of the Aristotelian Society* 76 (1976) 147–64.

Taylor, J.V., Christian Presence amid African Religion. Nairobi: Acton 2001.

Tebutt, J., A Long Walk Home. London: Faber&Faber 2013.

ten Boom, C., The Hiding Place, London: Hodder & Stoughton 2004.

Ter Haar, G., ed., Religions and Development: Ways of transforming the world. Hurst and Co., London 2011.

Terzani, T., La Fine è il mio inizio. Un padre racconta al figlio il grande viaggio della vita. Milan: Longanesi 2006.

Terzani, T., Un Altro Giro Di Giostra. Milan: Longanesi 2004.

The Corrie Family (ed.), Let Me Stand Alone. The Journal of Rachel Corrie. New York: W.W. Norton & Company 2008.

The Philokalia. The Complete Text compiled by St. Nicodemos of the Holy Mountain and St. Macarios of Corinth. Vol. I. Transl. and edited by G.E.H. Palmer, Ph. Sherrard, K. Ware. London: Faber and Faber 1983.

The Sayings of the Desert Fathers. Transl. B. Ward. Revised Edition. Kalamazoo, MI: Cistercian Publications 1984.

Thomas, R., From stress to sense of coherence: psychological experiences of humanitarian workers in complex humanitarian emergencies. PhD Dissertation. Oxford: University of Oxford 2008.

Titus, C.S., Resilience and the virtue of fortitude: Aquinas in dialogue with the psychosocial sciences, Washington, DC: *Catholic* University of America Press 2006.

Tkacz, M.W., Augustine's Invention of the Inner Self: The Legacy of a Christian Platonist (review), in: *Journal of the History of Philosophy* 39,4 (2001) 584–585.

Turner, V., The Ritual Process. Structure and Anti-Structure. New York: Aldine Transaction 1969.

Udoh, E.B., Guest Christology: An Interpretative View of the Christological Problem in Africa. Frankfurt/Main: Peter Lang 1988.

Utsey, S.O. et al., Cultural, socio-familial and psychological resources that inhibit psychological distress in African Americans exposed to stressful life events and race related stress. *Journal of Counseling Psychology* 55,1 (2008) 49–62.

Valentine, L., L.L. Feinauer, Resilience factors associated with female survivors of childhood sexual abuse. *The American Journal of Family Therapy* 21 (1993) 216–224.

Van der geest, S., The social life of faeces: System in the dirt. In: R. van Ginkel & A. Strating (eds) Wildness and sensation: An anthropology of sinister and sensuous realms. Amsterdam: Het Spinhuis 2007, 381–397.

Van Deth, J.W., E. Scarbrough, The Concept of Values. In: Van Deth / Scarbrough (eds.), The Impact of Values. Oxford: Oxford University Press 1998, 21–47.

van Gennep, A., The Rites of Passage. Chicago: University of Chicago Press 1960.

Văn Thuân, F., The Road to Hope. A Gospel from Prison. Boston, Mass: Pauline Books & Media 2001.

Văn Thuân, F., Testimony of Hope. Boston, Mass: Pauline Books & Media 2000.

Văn Thuân, F., Prayers of Hope. Boston, Mass: Pauline Books & Media 2002.

Van Tilburg, M.A., A.J. Vingerhoets, G.L. Van Heck, Homesickness: a review of the literature. *Psychological Medicine* 26 (1996) 899–912.

Vanier, J., Drawn into the Mystery of Jesus through the Gospel of John. Mahwah, NJ: Paulist Press 2004.

Velleman, J.D., Love as Moral Emotion. *Ethics* 109 (1999) 338–374.

Verplanken, B., When bittersweet turns sour: Adverse effects of nostalgia on habitual worriers. *European Journal of Social Psychology* 42 (2012) 285–289.

Vickers, T., L. Dominelli, Students' Involvement in International Humanitarian Aid: Learning from Student Responses to the 2004 Tsunami in Sri Lanka. *British Journal of Social Work* 45 (2015) 1905–1922.

Vollman, W., Poor People. New York: Harper Collins 2007.

Wallraff, G., Aus der schönen neuen Welt. Expeditionen ins Landesinnere. Cologne: Kiepenheuer&Witsch 2009.

Walsh, F., A Family Resilience Framework: Innovative Practice Applications. *Family Relations* 51,2 (2002) 130–137.

Walsh, F., Strengthening family resilience. New York: Guilford 1998.

Walsh, F., The Concept of family resilience. *Family Process* 35 (1996) 261–281.

Weber, M., Wissenschaft als Beruf. In: Ausgewählte Schriften 1894–1922. Hg. D Kaesler. Stuttgart: Reclam 2002.

Weberman, D., The Nonfixity of the Historical Past. *The Review of Metaphysics* 50 (1997) 749–768.

Weil, S., The Love of God and Affliction. In: The Simone Weil Reader. Ed. George A. Panichas. New York: David McKay 1977, 439–443.

Wenzel, S., The Sin of Sloth: Acedia in Medieval Thought and Literature. Chapel Hill, NC: The University of North Carolina Press 1960.

Werner, E., How kids become resilient: Observations and Cautions. *Resiliency in Action* 1,1 (1996) 18–28.

Werner, E., R. Smith, Vulnerable but Invincible: A Longitudinal Study of Resilient Children and Youth. New York: Adams Bannister Cox Pubs 1989.

Werner, E., The children of Kauai: Resiliency and recovery in adolescence and adulthood. *Journal of Adolescent Health* 13 (1992) 262–268.

Werner, E., Overcoming the odds: High risk children from birth to adulthood. Ithaca, NY: Cornell University 1992.

Werner, E., R.S. Smith, Journeys from childhood to midlife. Risk resilience and recovery. Ithaca, NY: Cornell University Press 2001.

Werner, E., Vulnerable, but invincible. New York: Adams Bannister Cox Pubs 1998.

Wiesel, E., Hope, Despair and Memory. In: I. Abrams (ed.), Peace 1981–1990. Singapore: World Scientific Publishing 1997.

Wildschut, T. et al., Nostalgia: Content, Triggers, Functions. *Journal of Personality and Social Psychology* 91,5 (2006) 975–993.

Wilkinson, T., The Rise and Fall of Ancient Egypt. London: Bloomsbury 2010.

Williams, R., Interiority and Epiphany. In: R. Williams, On Christian Theology. Oxford: Blackwell 2000, 239–264.

Williams, R., Theological Integrity. In: Idem, On Christian Theology. Oxford: Blackwell 2000, 3–15.

Williams, R., On Theological Integrity. *Cross Currents* 45 (1995) 312–325.

Windle, G., What is resilience? A review and concept analysis. *Reviews in Clinical Gerontology* 21 (2011) 152–169.

Winnicott, D., The Capacity to be alone. In: D. Winnicott, The Maturational Process and the Facilitating Environment. London 1969.

Winter, M.T., The Singer and the Song. Maryknoll. NY: Orbis 1999.

Wittgenstein, L., Philosophical Investigations. Oxford: Blackwell 1967.

Wohlers, J.F.H., Memories of the life of J.F.H. Wohlers, missionary at Ruapuke, New Zealand: an autobiography / translated from the German by John Houghton. Dunedin: Otago Daily Times & Witness Newspapers Co. 1895.

Wolin, S., S. Wolin, The Resilient Self: How Survivors of Troubled Families Rise Above Adversity. New York: Villard 1993.

Worland, S.L., Displaced or Misplaced or Just Displaced: Christian Displaced Karen Identity after Sixty Years of War in Burma. PhD Dissertation. Queensland, Australia: University of Queensland 2010.

Wurmbrand, R., Tortured for Christ. London: Hodder&Stoughton 2004.

Yalom, I., The Gift of Therapy. New York: Harper Collins 2002.

Yik-yi Chu, C., The Diaries of the Maryknoll Sisters in Hong Kong 1921–1966. Basingstoke: Palgrave Macmillan 2007.

Zavaleta, Reyles, R., The ability to go about without shame. A proposal for internationally comparable indicators of shame and humiliation. OPHI Working Paper Series. Oxford: OPHI 2007.

Zimbardo, Ph., A Situationist Perspective on the Psychology of Evil. In: A.G. Miller (ed.), The Social Psychology of Good and Evil. New York 2004, 21–50.

Zimmermann, M.A., R. Arunkumar, Resiliency Research: Implications for Schools and Policy. Social Policy Report. *Society for Research in Child Development* 8,4 (1994) 1–20.

Zimmermann, R., Philosophie nach Auschwitz. Reinbeck: Rowohlt 2005.

Zurn, Chr. F., Social Pathologies as Second-Order Disorders. In: D. Petherbridge (ed.), Axel Honneth: Critical Essays. Leiden: Brill 2011, 345–370.

Index

Printed in the United States
By Bookmasters